THE 30 MOST
INFLUENTIAL PEOPLE
WORLD WAR
OF
II
A RANKING

ALAN AXELROD

PERMUTED
PRESS

A PERMUTED PRESS BOOK

ISBN: 978-1-68261-610-9
ISBN (eBook): 978-1-68261-611-6

The 30 Most Influential People of World War II
© 2018 by Alan Axelrod
All Rights Reserved

Cover art by Christian Bentulan

Permuted Press, LLC
New York • Nashville
permutedpress.com

Published in the United States of America

For Anita and Ian

CONTENTS

INTRODUCTION: JOINING THE ARGUMENT

Rare was the patch on our planet that was spared involvement in World War II at least at some time between 1939 and 1945, but the principal combatant states were Germany, Italy, and Japan—the Axis powers—and France, Great Britain, the United States, the Soviet Union, and China—the Allies. The butcher's bill this conflict left was unprecedented in extent and remains unequaled. Most authorities attribute fifty to eighty million deaths directly to the war, the vast majority of these civilians. The peak number of troops mobilized by all combatant nations was 72,928,000, and millions more civilians were committed to partisan, guerrilla, and resistance activity and to war-related industrial production—some voluntarily, others as slave laborers.

World War II devastated Europe and Asia, leaving a world-shaping legacy in its turbulent wake. One geopolitical result of the war was the extension of the power of the Soviet Union to many nations of eastern Europe. Communism also triumphed in China and established footholds in parts of Korea and Vietnam. Indeed, the world experienced a profound shift in power and influence away from the old states of western Europe and toward the United States and the Soviet Union, which, through some five decades following the war, were the only global superpowers, each armed with another momentous product of the war: nuclear (and, later, thermonuclear) weapons.

World War II is best understood as an extension of the earlier global cataclysm that was World War I (1914-1918), which left many territorial issues unresolved even as it created a host of new cultural, geopolitical, and economic incentives for war. Most immediately, the earlier conflict left the soil of Germany fertile for the growth of Adolf Hitler and Nazism; it left people in Italy so discontent that they supported the rise of Benito Mussolini and Fascism; and it created a militaristic outlook in Japan. World War I created the conditions in which the Bolshevik Revolution transformed Russia into the Soviet Union and set up the mighty polarity of Fascist and Nazi right versus Communist left—with both sides posing a challenge to the Western democracies.

While the economic, territorial, and even ideological causes of the war are relatively easy for those of us living in the twenty-first century to grasp, we need to understand that all of these dimensions reached far beyond politics to encompass racial mythologies held by Hitler and the Nazis as well as by the Japanese militarists (and to a far lesser degree, by the Italian fascists), in which the aggressors saw themselves as a master "race" naturally and inexorably opposed to a number of lesser "races" (often defined as subhuman). These lesser races were properly subject to conquest, including economic exploitation for labor and other resources and even genocidal extermination— the latter most infamously exemplified in Nazi anti-Semitism, which gave rise to the genocidal Holocaust in Europe and Japan's brutal, even genocidal, treatment of conquered peoples and defeated armies.

All of this said, we are left with yet one more dimension to the war's origins, course, and outcome. That is the human dimension, the people who were most significant in instigating, fighting, shaping, and influencing the war as well as determining its outcome.

In 1840, the Victorian philosopher and historian Thomas Carlyle wrote in his *On Heroes, Hero-Worship and the Heroic in History* that "The history of the world is but the biography of great men." It is not likely that any historian today believes this so-called great man theory is a sufficient explanation of history. But also insufficient are explanations of history that leave out the "great men"—in this book we call them the "most influential people." The materialist theory of history put forth by Karl Marx, that history is essentially the story of capitalists appropriated the "surplus labor" of the proletariat, is a *necessary* view, but it is not a *sufficient* view.

Joseph Stalin reportedly once observed that "A single death is a tragedy; a million deaths, a statistic." In ethical and moral terms, all people, of course, are significant. In causing and influencing any given event, however, some people are more significant than others. They are the people we call *influential.* A proper who's who of influential people in World War II would run to at least several hundreds of thousands of words. This book devotes something just over ninety-thousand words to the "30 Most Influential People" in the conflict. The criteria for inclusion is my sense of consensus on who had the greatest impact on the war—how and why it began, how it was fought, how the masses caught up in it were moved and persuaded, how and why it ended, and, finally, what the war came to mean.

I am under no illusion that this book will settle any arguments. In fact, I believe the people who will be most interested in reading this book are people most inclined to argue about causes, motives, outcomes, and major players. Writing for these readers, I will be pleased if I can make their arguments more informed, more interesting, and perhaps more productively heated. If I can also interest others to join the argument, I will have achieved a genuine success. I admit that the title of this book suggests a conclusion. In fact, I hope what I have written will be a beginning—of new arguments, new considerations, and a curiosity to find everything and everyone I have left out.

World War II Timeline

- January 30, 1933
Nazi Party leader Adolf Hitler is appointed Germany's chancellor, second-highest office in the country.

- March 23, 1933
Following the burning of the Reichstag, Hitler forces passage of the Enabling Act, giving him dictatorial power over Germany.

- March 7, 1936
Hitler unilaterally militarizes the Rhineland, Germany's western borderland, which was demilitarized by the Treaty of Versailles (1919) and the Locarno Pact (1925).

- March 13, 1938
Germany annexes Austria in the *Anschluss* ("joining"), politically unifying Austria and Germany. Austria thereby becomes the first country Hitler seizes.

- September 30, 1938
In a bid to prevent war by "appeasing" Hitler, British Prime Minister Neville Chamberlain signs the Munich Pact with him, Italian Prime Minister Benito Mussolini, and French Premier Édouard Daladier, allowing Germany to annex the German-speaking Sudetenland, of Czechoslovakia.

- March 15, 1939
Hitler violates the Munich Pact by occupying Bohemia and Moravia, adding these to the Sudetenland, thereby effectively seizing all of Czechoslovakia. The European democracies decline to go to war in defense of the Czechs.

- August 23, 1939
  The foreign ministers of Russia and Germany, Vyacheslav Molotov and Joachim von Ribbentrop, sign the Molotov-Ribbentrop Pact, a non-aggression treaty between Russia and Germany.

- September 1, 1939
  World War II begins with the German invasion of Poland.

- September 3, 1939
  In response to the invasion of Poland, Britain and France declare war on Germany.

- April 9, 1940
  Germany invades Norway and Denmark.

- May 10, 1940
  Germany begins the Battle of France with a "Blitzkrieg" invasion of Belgium, the Netherlands, Luxembourg, and France.

- June 10, 1940
  Italy's "Duce," Benito Mussolini, declares war on France and Britain.

- June 22, 1940
  The Battle of France ends with French capitulation to Germany. The nation is divided into the German-occupied north (including Paris) and a puppet state in the south, popularly called Vichy France, which is under the ostensible leadership of Philippe Pétain.

- July 10, 1940
  Germany launches its first air raid against Great Britain, commencing the Battle of Britain—in which the Royal Air Force will ultimately triumph against the German Luftwaffe.

- September 13, 1940
  Italian forces invade British-controlled Egypt with the objective of capturing the Suez Canal.

- September 27, 1940
  Germany, Italy, and Japan sign the Tripartite Pact, creating the "Axis" alliance.

- June 22, 1941
  Germany launches Operation Barbarossa, the invasion of the Soviet Union. The largest operation of World War II, it drives Joseph Stalin to join the Allied nations in opposition to Hitler.

- December 7, 1941
  Japan attacks Pearl Harbor, Hawaii Territory, causing great damage to the U.S. Pacific Fleet.

- December 8, 1941
  U.S. President Franklin D. Roosevelt responds to the Pearl Harbor attack by asking Congress for a declaration of war against Japan.

- December 11, 1941
  The Axis Powers—Germany, Italy, and Japan—declare war on the United States.

- February 15, 1942
  Japan captures Singapore from the British, thereby depriving Britain of its remaining military foothold in the East.

- February 19, 1942
  President Roosevelt signs Executive Order 9066, ordering the internment of Japanese-Americans living on or near the West Coast; more than 100,000 are confined to "internment" camps.

- May 12, 1942
  Japan completes the capture and occupation of the Philippines.

- May 26, 1942
  Japan captures Burma from the British.

- June 7, 1942
  In the Battle of Midway, the U.S. Navy defeats the Japanese fleet. The turning point of war in the Pacific, the American victory puts Japan on the defensive.

- November 16, 1942
  Operation Torch, the successful Anglo-American occupation of Morocco and Algeria, begins the Allied conquest of Axis-held North Africa.

- February 2, 1943
  In a catastrophic defeat, the German Sixth Army surrenders to the Soviet Red Army at the epic Battle of Stalingrad. This is the turning point against Germany on Europe's Eastern Front.

- May 13, 1943
  After three years of seesaw battle in North Africa, Axis troops surrender to Allied forces in Tunisia.

- August 17, 1943
  Operation Husky successfully concludes the Anglo-American invasion and occupation of Sicily, the Allies' first toehold in Europe.

- September 8, 1943
  Breaking with the Axis, Italy surrenders to the Allies.

- November 28-December 1, 1943
  The "Big Three"—President Franklin D. Roosevelt, British Prime Minister Winston Churchill, and Soviet Premier Joseph Stalin—meet in Tehran, Iran, to plan the Allied invasion of German-occupied France, which will open combat on the Western Front as the Soviets continue to fight on the Eastern Front.

- June 6, 1944
  On this day—"D-Day"—American, British, and Canadian troops cross the English Channel and land on the beaches of Normandy, France. The greatest amphibious military operation in history, the invasion begins the liberation of France and, ultimately, all of Europe.

- October 26, 1944
  The U.S. Navy decisively defeats the Japanese fleet at the Battle of Leyte Gulf near the Philippines. It is the first step in the liberation of the Philippines.

- December 16, 1944-January 16, 1945
  Having suffered one defeat after another on both the Eastern and Western Fronts, as well as in Italy, an all-but-beaten German military rallies to launch a stunning offensive in the Ardennes region of Belgium and Luxembourg. The resulting Battle of the Bulge is the biggest and bloodiest battle of the Western Front in World War II. After absorbing heavy losses, U.S. and British forces launch a counteroffensive that breaks the back of the German military.

- February 4-11, 1945
  President Roosevelt, Prime Minister Churchill, and Premier Stalin meet in Yalta, Crimea, and agree on fighting the war to total victory, accepting nothing less than the unconditional surrender of Germany. Stalin agrees to join in the war against Japan, following Germany's surrender.

- March 26, 1945
  After a horrific month-long battle with dug-in Japanese forces, U.S. marines and soldiers capture Iwo Jima. Of somewhat dubious strategic value, the costly capture of the island, symbolized by AP photographer Joe Rosenthal's iconic image of marines raising the Stars and Stripes over Mt. Suribachi, is a great moral triumph, assuring the American public that victory in the war would soon come.

- April 12, 1945
  President Franklin D. Roosevelt dies suddenly of a cerebral hemorrhage; his vice president, Harry S. Truman, becomes president.

- April 28, 1945
  Italian Partisans kill Benito Mussolini, his mistress Clara Petacci, as well as certain members of the deposed Fascist government.

- April 30, 1945
  Adolf Hitler and his wife of a single day, Eva Braun, commit double suicide in a bunker beneath the garden of the Chancellery, Berlin.

- May 7, 1945
  Germany surrenders to the Allies in Reims, France, ending World War II in Europe. The Soviets insist on a separate surrender ceremony on May 8.

- August 6, 1945
  The Manhattan Project culminates in the U.S. dropping of an atomic bomb on the Japanese city of Hiroshima.

- August 9, 1945
  The United States drops a second atomic bomb on Japan, this time against Nagasaki.

- August 14-15, 1945
  Reeling from the two atomic attacks, the Japanese government notifies the Allies on August 14 that it has accepted the Potsdam Declaration of July 26, demanding the nation's unconditional surrender. The next day, a recorded message from Emperor Hirohito is broadcast to the people of Japan, ordering them to "endure the unendurable" by laying down their arms.

- September 2, 1945
  In a ceremony presided over by U.S. General of the Army Douglas MacArthur, Japanese representatives sign an "Instrument of Surrender" aboard the USS *Missouri* in Tokyo Bay, ending World War II.

#1
ADOLF HITLER

Founder of Nazism, dictator of Gemany, architect of genocide, and initiator of World War II

Adolf Hitler reviews a parade of Storm Troopers (SA) at the Nuremberg Nazi Party rally of September 1935. (credit: *Charles Russell Collection, National Archives and Records Administration*)

The man who initiated World War II—the deadliest war in history, a war built on genocide and ended with two nuclear detonations, a war that resulted in fifty to eighty million deaths—struck most who casually met him, and historians and biographers who later wrote about him, as quite unimpressive. He seemed, in short, ordinary, an example of what the great German-born American political theorist Hannah Arendt called the "banality of evil" that characterized his Third Reich. Hitler's utter unlikeliness as a latter-day Atilla, a man too ordinary to get very far, makes his political and military career that much more obscene and incomprehensible.

He was born on April 20, 1889, in Braunau am Inn, Austria, but was raised mainly in Linz, the son of a minor customs official. Alois Hitler, his father, was of illegitimate birth and used his mother's maiden name, Schickelgruber, until 1876, when he took the name Hitler. (During World War II, the Allied mass media frequently made derisive use of the comical-sounding *Schickelgruber* in place of the name *Hitler*.)

Alois Hitler was, by all accounts, an obtuse and brutal father, who criticized what he considered his son's dreamy and effeminate nature. Young Adolf Hitler was indeed an indifferent student, who left secondary school in 1905 without obtaining a graduation certificate. His early ambition was to become an artist, and his drawings and watercolors, while competent, were passionless and unoriginal, lifeless landscapes and architectural renderings. His work twice failed to gain him admission to the Academy of Fine Arts in Vienna, and his being thwarted in this way wounded him. Nevertheless, after the death of his mother, who, in vivid contrast to his father, had doted on him and whom he both idolized and idealized, Hitler went to Vienna, hoping, even without an academy education, to make a name for himself as an artist. He managed from 1907 to 1913 to eke out a living by painting advertisements, postcards, and the like, but his existence was marked by drift, its only hint of direction provided by a growing racial hatred focused primarily on "the Jews." Drawing on a long-standing central European heritage of anti-Semitism and on his own understanding of German-Nordic mythology, heightened by a passion for the music of Richard Wagner, Hitler formulated a world view in which Jews figured as a political, economic, and even genetic threat to the pure Germanic—or "Aryan"—race.

In 1913, Hitler moved from Vienna to Munich, apparently to avoid conscription into the Austro-Hungarian army. Despite this effort, he was recalled to Austria in February 1914 for a pre-induction examination, only to be rejected as unfit, his years of financial struggle, sometimes including sustained periods of homelessness, having rendered him frail. Nevertheless, the outbreak of World War I in July 1914 rejuvenated the young Hitler, who rushed to enlist not in the Austrian service, which had rejected him, but in the 16th Bavarian Reserve Infantry (List) Regiment.

Service in the war transformed the drifter into a passionate, rigid, and militaristic German nationalist. He never advanced beyond the rank of corporal, but his service in combat was distinguished. He volunteered for the particularly hazardous duty of front-lines runner (messenger) and was decorated four times, even receiving, on August 4, 1918, the Iron Cross 1st Class, a decoration rarely given to enlisted soldiers. Hitler was seriously wounded in October 1916, and he was gassed at the end of the war.

Although he did not advance into the officer corps, Hitler decided to remain with his regiment after the armistice, through April 1920. In the postwar German army, he served as a uniformed political agent and as an undercover agent. At the army's direction, he joined the German Workers' Party in Munich in September 1919. He was supposed to be a government spy, but his political ambitions soon eclipsed his official assignment. Beginning in April 1920, he went to work full time in the propaganda section of the German Workers' Party.

The aftermath of World War I was a desperate and heady time for German society and politics. The Treaty of Versailles, which ended World War I, was harshly punitive against Germany, bringing to the nation both economic ruin and collective humiliation. The chaos and hard times of postwar Germany seemed to make the country ripe for a communist revolution. It never came to pass, but violence was nonetheless in the air and on the streets. For the first time in his life, war had fired up Adolf Hitler. Now, after Germany's defeat, the general dejection and despair around him, the growing sentiment that the German people had been betrayed into surrender by the politicians who were now running the Weimar Republic, fired him up a second time. By August 1920, Hitler was instrumental in transforming the German Workers' Party into the *Nazionalsozialistische Deutsche Arbeiterpartei,* or Nazi Party (NSDAP). He forged an alliance with a former army staff officer and Freikorps (rightwing citizen militia) activist, Ernst Röhm, which gained him sufficient support to be elected president of the nascent party in July 1921.

Hitler proved to be a dynamic political agitator and an accomplished street-corner orator. He identified Germany's problem as the Treaty of Versailles and Germany's enemies as the Allied nations that had forced the treaty on Germany, the German democratic leaders that had accepted the treaty, the Communists, and, most of all, the Jews (whom he casually conflated with the Communists). By the late fall of 1923, Hitler decided that his Nazi Party was sufficiently influential to lead a full-scale *coup d'etat*, at least in Bavaria, the heart of the so-called *Völkisch* movement, a combination of German nationalism and populism energized by hatred of the Weimar republican government. On November 8-9, 1923, Hitler led the Munich Beer Hall Putsch. His plan was to seize Munich and make the city a base from which to launch the overthrow of the Bavarian government. Once Bavaria fell to him, Hitler was confident that all of Germany would follow, and the hated Weimar Republic would be replaced by a genuine German nation. Wholly premature, the uprising was quickly contained and crushed. A small number of government troops (the *Reichswehr*) and Bavarian state police put down more than two thousand Nazis and others. Sixteen of those involved in the uprising were killed and several dozen injured. Hitler was arrested, tried for treason, and convicted. Unwilling to make a martyr of him, however, the court handed down a light sentence of five years' confinement in Landsberg Prison, a facility in which political prisoners were commonly sequestered.

Hitler's accommodations were more like those of a hostel than a jail. His room had a feather bed, a chair, and a comfortable desk for writing, as well as a window with a pleasant view. What is more, Hitler was free to see visitors, including members of the Nazi Party. As for his fellow inmates, most of them were like-minded political offenders. If the sentence was intended to take Hitler out of circulation, it did that—but only more or less. What no one had contemplated was that Hitler would use his time in Landsberg to write his political memoir/manifesto, *Mein Kampf* (*My Struggle*), a crude but highly effective work, in which he expressed the political philosophy of Nazism and proclaimed his eternal opposition to Jews, Communists, liberals, and exploitive capitalists the world over. In *Mein Kampf*, Hitler sought to bring about the rebirth of German racial purity and sought to reawaken a national will to power and greatness. In *Mein Kampf,* Hitler envisioned a Germany risen, phoenix-like, to become the dominant power in the world, a Germany that would successfully claim *Lebensraum*—"living space"—in central Europe and in Russia.

Adolf Hitler was released from prison on December 20, 1924, having served a little more than a year of his five-year sentence, during which he completed the first volume of *Mein Kampf,* having dictated most of it to his deputy, Rudolf Hess. The first volume was published in 1925, and a second volume, completed after his release, was published in 1926. The book was a bestseller, selling 280,000 copies by 1932. When Hitler was named chancellor of Germany in 1933, a million copies of *Mein Kampf* flew off the shelves. Adolf Hitler would embark upon his dictatorship a wealthy author.

Released from prison, he immediately set about the task of reviving the Nazi Party, which had slid into near-dormancy during his absence. He set about consolidating his grip on the Nazi movement and increasing the party membership. It was during this period that he was joined by many of the others who would lead Germany into a policy of atrocity and world war. Among the early Nazis were World War I air ace Hermann Göring, propaganda master Joseph Goebbels, political terrorist Heinrich Himmler, and anti-Semitic journalist Julius Streicher. With the onset of a worldwide economic depression in 1929, the political climate ripened further for the growth of the Nazi Party, and Hitler forged an alliance with the Nationalist Party headed by industrialist Alfred Hugenberg. In the elections of May 1928, the Nazis won just twelve Reichstag seats, two fewer than they had gained in December 1924 elections. In the elections of September 1930, following the onset of the Great Depression, the Nazis increased the number from twelve to 107.

To promote and ensure the rise of his party, Hitler and fellow World War I veteran Ernst Röhm created the *Sturmabeteilung* (SA, Storm Troopers), also called Brownshirts, the party's thug-like paramilitary arm. Its purpose was to provide security at Nazi rallies—and to beat down the opposition in the streets of Germany. Hitler and his SA campaigned throughout Germany for the next two years. In 1932, with the economic situation still desperate, Hitler ran against World War I hero Paul Von Hindenburg for the presidency of the German republic. Although Hitler came in second, his party polled

37 percent of the vote and gained a total of 230 Reichstag seats, making it the largest single party represented in the legislature.

Without doubt, Hindenburg detested Hitler, but he knew he could not ignore him. The magnitude of his electoral showing demanded that he create with him a coalition government, and on January 30, 1933, he appointed Hitler *Reichskanzler* (Reich Chancellor), effectively the prime minister of Germany. At last, Hitler was in a position of great *legitimate* power, and his dynamism rapidly overtook and overshadowed the eighty-six-year-old Hindenburg. On February 27, 1933, fire destroyed the Reichstag. It was an arson to which a Dutch communist named Marinus van der Lubbe confessed, but many historians believe it was the work of the Nazis themselves. Hitler seized on it as a pretext for legally abolishing the Communist Party and rounding up for imprisonment its principal leaders. This action was followed on March 23, 1933, by passage of the Enabling Act, which granted him four years of unalloyed dictatorial powers as Hindenburg receded into the status of figurehead.

Pursuant to the Enabling Act, Hitler set about disbanding all German political parties, save the Nazis. He purged Jews from all government institutions and brought every government office under the direct control of the party. Then he turned to the ranks of his own party. On June 30, 1934, during the Night of the Long Knives, he directed the round-up and, ultimately, the murder of Ernst Röhm and hundreds of other SA members and Nazis who (he believed) posed a threat to his absolute domination of the party. In August 1934, Hindenburg died, leaving Hitler not merely to assume the functions of the presidency, but to replace the very title of *president* and the republican concept it represented with that of *Führer*, Supreme Leader. He was now the head of a regime he called the Third Reich.

In short order, Hitler replaced the SA with the *Schutzstaffel* (SS, Protection Squadron), also known as the Blackshirts, under the leadership of Himmler, who was subordinate to no one but Hitler alone. The SS and the new secret police, the Gestapo, were created by Hermann Göring but quickly assigned to the command of Himmler, who also began setting up a network of concentration camps. At first, the camps mainly housed political enemies, but soon, under Hitler and Himmler, the system developed into a vast complex of concentration and death camps, which would become the places of confinement and murder of some of the six million Jews in The Holocaust. Racial and religious persecution, political and ethnic purging, and, ultimately, genocide were key aspects of Hitler's vision for Germany, and at his behest, in 1935, Nazi-affiliated German jurists created the Nuremberg Laws, which deprived Jews of citizenship and authorized the policy of persecution that eventuated in the Final Solution.

❖

Throughout his rise and the process of consolidating his power, Hitler combined outright terror and police-state tactics with a highly sophisticated program of propaganda orchestrated by minister of propaganda Joseph Goebbels. Hitler also presided over a remarkable economic recovery by forging an alliance with German industrial and financial interests and ramping up production to rearm the nation in defiance of the Treaty of Versailles. Hitler created a *Luftwaffe* (air force) under Göring; remilitarized, in 1936, the Rhineland (which had been demilitarized by the Treaty of Versailles); and built up the army as well as the navy far in excess of what the treaty permitted. He gambled that the western democracies, Britain and France, permanently war weary and pacifistic, would do nothing substantive to oppose his abrogation of the Versailles terms.

His gamble paid off.

During the period of his earliest climb to power within the fledgling Nazi Party and through his rise in German government, Hitler turned an admiring eye toward Benito Mussolini, since 1922 the fascist dictator of Italy. In 1936, he concluded with Italy and with militaristic Japan the Anti-Comintern Pact, which foreshadowed the 1939 "Pact of Steel" between Hitler and Mussolini and the 1940 Axis (Tri-Partite) Pact among Germany, Italy, and Japan. Having met no resistance from the democracies after remilitarizing the Rhineland, Hitler took the next step in his aggressive expansion of Germany in March 1938 when he invaded and annexed Austria in the Anschluss. After this, he browbeat Great Britain's prime minister, Neville Chamberlain, to acquiesce in Germany's annexation of the Czech Sudetenland—the German-speaking portion of Czechoslovakia—which was followed a short time later by his takeover of virtually the entire Czech nation, which had been created by the Treaty of Versailles.

Chamberlain persuaded his French counterparts that allowing Hitler to gobble up Czechoslovakia, a nation both Britain and France were bound by treaty to defend, would "appease" German expansionism. As it turned out, appeasement only whetted the Führer's appetite for more. With an eye on Poland, he shocked the world by concluding the German-Soviet Non-Aggression Pact (Ribbentrop-Molotov Pact) with his ideological antithesis, Soviet dictator Joseph Stalin, on August 23, 1939. The very next month, on September 1, taking as his pretext a staged Polish "attack" on a border outpost (orchestrated by propaganda minister Goebbels), Hitler invaded Poland and thus started World War II.

The Invasion of Poland and the Battle of France that followed put Hitler in control of most of the European continent. Of the Western democracies, only Great Britain held out against him, and at this point, Hitler, always eager to assert what he considered his military genius, blundered. First, he issued orders that allowed the British Expeditionary Force (BEF) to escape France and total destruction via a shipborne evacuation from Dunkirk. Next, instead of preparing for an invasion of Great Britain, Hitler misdirected the Luftwaffe to raid British cities instead of British Royal Air Force (RAF) bases. This spared the RAF, which, during July-October 1940, prevailed against the Luftwaffe in the Battle of Britain. Denied air supremacy in the skies over the British Isles, Hitler was forced to abandon Operation Sealion, his planned invasion of Great Britain.

Nevertheless, during the rest of 1940 and into 1941, Hitler's armies came to control territory from North Africa to the Arctic and from France to central Europe. In April 1941, Hitler's armies invaded the Balkans, occupying Yugoslavia and Greece, and on June 22, 1941, Hitler summarily abrogated his non-aggression pact with Stalin by launching Operation Barbarossa, the Invasion of the Soviet Union. As they had in Poland and France, Blitzkrieg tactics made for rapid and devastating gains in Russia. These were accompanied by atrocities on a massive scale, including those pursuant to both the Final Solution and the obliteration of Soviet government through Hitler's infamous *Kommissarbefehl,* or "Commissar Order," whereby local Soviet political leaders, along with Jews, were massacred wherever they were encountered.

At length, the Russian winter and the resilience of the Russian people and the Red Army, dogged and heroic, slowed and then stopped Hitler's forces, first at the Battle of Moscow in December 1941 and then, during the winter of 1942-1943, at the Battle of Stalingrad. It was at Stalingrad that the tide of war on the Eastern Front turned—catastrophically—against the Germans.

In the meantime, the Japanese attack on Pearl Harbor on December 7, 1941, brought America into World War II. This was a contingency for which Hitler had never really planned, although, with characteristic arrogance, he did not hesitate to declare war against the United States on December 11, 1941. It would take some time for U.S. military forces to make an impact on Germany, but by 1943, the turning point was reached not only on the Russian Front, but elsewhere. Germany had lost North Africa, and Mussolini had fallen to the Allied invasion of Italy. American and British bombers were pummeling German cities by day and by night. The situation reached its crisis for Germany with the Allies' Normandy Invasion, which began on "D-Day," June 6, 1944. Now Hitler and his Third Reich were menaced from the east, south, and west.

The Allied invasion of France drove Hitler to make increasingly desperate and irrational demands of his military, and a significant cadre within the German officer corps turned against the Führer. In the best known of no fewer than seventeen attempts on Hitler's life, Colonel Klaus von Stauffenberg, a highly decorated officer who had suffered grievous wounds, masterminded a plot to assassinate Hitler at his Eastern Front military headquarters, *Wolfsschanze* (Wolf's Lair), east of Rastenburg (now Ketrzyn, Poland). On July 20, 1944, Stauffenberg planted a briefcase with a bomb in the conference room. Although it detonated as scheduled, Hitler survived the blast with non-life-threatening wounds. The *coup d'etat* that had been planned to follow the assassination collapsed, and the July 20 plot moved Hitler to conduct a general purge, in which some five thousand officers and others were arrested, many of them executed.

The war, in any real military sense, had been lost, but from December 16, 1944, to January 1945, Hitler committed his last reserves to a final surprise counteroffensive, the Battle of the Ardennes, which included the Battle of the Bulge. His hope was to divide the advancing Allied forces and retake what was now a key Allied port and supply depot at Antwerp. The Ardennes offensive caught the Allies completely by surprise and precipitated a harrowing struggle, which nevertheless ended in a crushing defeat that broke the back of both the Wehrmacht and the Waffen-SS. With the last credible German resistance destroyed, the Allies advanced on the German heartland.

As the Soviet Red Army began the Battle of Berlin, Hitler retreated to the *Fürherbunker*, a hardened underground command shelter beneath the garden of the Chancellery and the streets of the German capital. From these grim quarters, he attempted to direct a suicidal defense of Berlin—to the last German man, woman, and child. His intention, it seemed clear, was to see Germany destroyed with him.

On April 29, 1945, as the Battle of Berlin drew rapidly to an end, Hitler married his long-time mistress, Eva Braun, who occupied the bunker with him. In his last will and testament, he appointed Admiral Karl Dönitz to succeed him as head of state, and, on April 30, Hitler and his bride committed suicide: Braun by taking cyanide, Hitler, apparently, by a combination of cyanide and gunshot. Dönitz hastily concluded the surrender of Germany on May 8, 1945. With this, the would-be empire Adolf Hitler had called the Thousand-Year Reich came to an end.

#2

WINSTON CHURCHILL

His insistent warnings about the rise of Hitler were largely ignored by the British people, but when Nazi Germany overran all of Europe, he led Britons to take a stand, ultimately saving not only their island nation, but civilization itself

Winston Churchill delivers a speech at Uxbridge, Middlesex, on June 27, 1945, during the general election campaign. Despite victory over Germany and impending victory over Japan, he lost his bid for reelection to Labor Party candidate Clement Attlee. (credit: *Imperial War Museum*)

From the beginning, Winston Churchill's greatest urge was to be at the center of the action. As prime minister of the United Kingdom during most of World War II, that is precisely where he was—with the fate of his nation, of democracy, and of Western civilization riding on his wisdom and resolve.

Winston Spencer Churchill was born on November 30, 1874, in a bedroom of Blenheim Palace, the family's magnificent seat in Woodstock, Oxfordshire. His father, the prominent Tory politician Lord Randolph Churchill, was descended from John Churchill, first duke of Marlborough, hero of the War of the Spanish Succession (1701-1714). Named for the Battle of Blenheim (August 13, 1704), Britain's greatest victory in the war, Blenheim Palace was Parliament's gift to Marlborough, the triumphal commander. The descendants of the first duke—the second through the sixth dukes of Marlborough—fell far short of the heroic prototype. They were profligate men, who wasted the family fortune and reputation. The seventh duke, Winston Churchill's grandfather, managed to restore the family's reputation but was unable to replenish its material fortune. He and his successor, Winston's uncle, the eighth Duke of Marlborough, sold off property as well as many of the furnishings of Blenheim, including a collection of Old Master paintings. The ninth duke, Winston's cousin, known as Sunny, married a very wealthy American, one of the Vanderbilt daughters, but was soon divorced from both his bride and her cash. He died on the verge of bankruptcy.

Finally, Lord Randolph Churchill, Winston's father, married yet another American heiress, the extraordinarily beautiful Jennie Jerome, daughter of a New York financier and stockbroker, who was part owner of the *New York Times* and a string of racehorses. Lord Randolph was a Tory politician who nevertheless appealed to the working classes. A member of Parliament, he attained the post of secretary of state for India, followed by chancellor of the exchequer, the equivalent of U.S. secretary of the treasury. An unwise and premature bid to become prime minister backfired, and Lord Randolph Churchill ended up without a political career. Worse, he dissolved into the effects of late-stage syphilis and died, on January 24, 1895, at the age of forty-six, when Winston was a young man of twenty-one. "All my dreams of comradeship with him," Churchill later wrote, "entering Parliament at his side and in his support, were ended. There remained for me only to pursue his aims and vindicate his memory."

Churchill enrolled as a cadet in Sandhurst, Britain's Royal Military College, during his father's final months. He had ended up there because he was academically unprepared to gain admission to any better educational institution. Churchill boys traditionally prepped at Eton, but Lord and Lady Churchill had settled on Harrow for Winston as a lesser but acceptable alternative. Even here, the boy floundered in what were considered the "important" subjects. He failed French, the classical languages, and mathematics. Only in history and recitation did he excel. He was put in a remedial class, where he learned to write, to write masterfully, as it turned out, getting into his very "bones" (Churchill later wrote) "the essential structure of the ordinary British sentence—which is a noble thing." Along with a love for the English language came a love of England and the English.

If graduating from Harrow would not get one into Oxford or Cambridge, it would get one into training as an army officer. His performance on the Sandhurst entrance exam did not qualify him for admission to the infantry, artillery, or engineers, but he could find a place in the cavalry, which was considered the branch best suited to the slow-witted. He entered Sandhurst ranked 95th out of an incoming class of 104 cadets. By the time he completed his training, he had ascended to 20th out of his graduating class of 130. He joined the 4th Hussars, an elite cavalry regiment, in February 1895.

He was slated for service in India, which entitled him to a long period of leave before embarking on what would be a nine-year term of service away from home. Instead of remaining with his family, however, Subaltern Churchill sailed to Cuba, intending on covering for a newspaper the revolution then under way against the island's Spanish rulers. By the end of November 1895, Winston Churchill was attached to a Spanish unit fighting the Cuban insurgency. When he came under fire, he found the experience "exhilarating." That was one great lesson he took away from his experience in Cuba. The other was more profound: it was the revelation of the power possessed by an absolutely determined people. Churchill quickly learned to admire the Cuban insurgents. Not only were they supremely skilled in unconventional warfare and guerrilla tactics—the use of which Churchill would champion during World War II in such units as the Special Operations Executive (SOE) in Europe and the Chindits in Burma—they thrived on adversity, drawing their strength from all Spain's efforts to crush them. It was a lesson in the compelling force of skillful defiance.

After making a name for himself as a war correspondent in Cuba, Churchill rejoined his regiment. At home on leave in the spring of 1897, he got news of fighting on India's Northwest Frontier; he boarded the first available ship for Bombay (Mumbai) and joined the Malakand Field Force as, once again, a newspaper correspondent. On September 16, 1897, his brigade fell under attack by Pashtun tribal forces, suffering heavy casualties and narrowly avoiding total annihilation in the mountainous passes of the Northwest borderland. Churchill barely escaped with life—but escape he did, and he took with him the material for his first book, *The Story of the Malakand Field Force.* Published in 1898, it made him famous.

He set off next for North Africa, where he was attached to Lord Kitchener's Nile Army. On September 2, 1898, three miles outside of Khartoum, Sudan, in the Battle of Omdurman, forty thousand hostile "dervishes" descended upon him—and an Anglo-Egyptian army of just twenty-six thousand. Churchill claimed to have killed six of the enemy with his Mauser pistol in this battle, a battle that, for the time being at least, quenched his thirst for military action. As soon as Kitchener's Nile Campaign had been officially concluded early in 1899, he resigned his commission, returned to England, and wrote his second book, *The River War*, an account of the expedition. Once again, he found himself a celebrity, and seizing the moment, the Conservative Party ran him for Parliament from working-class Oldham, Lancashire. He lost—though not by much—and promptly took off for South Africa, determined to earn a handsome living as a correspondent covering the Great Boer War for *The Morning Post.*

More adventures followed, including a harrowing encounter with Boer commandos on November 15, 1899, which resulted in Churchill's capture as a POW. He quickly escaped, hopped a freight train, and managed to reach the house of an English mine manager, who hid him for three days at the bottom of a mineshaft until the arrival of another freight train, bound for Mozambique, at the time a Portuguese colony. From the port town of Lorenço Marques (Maputo), Churchill boarded a ship to Durban, British South Africa, which he reached on the eve of Christmas Eve, December 23.

The capture, prison break, and successful escape, coming as they all did during what was the nadir of British fortunes in the Great Boer War, made Winston Churchill a national hero. He parlayed his fame into an appointment as assistant adjutant of the South African Light Horse, with which he fought in and around Ladysmith—actions culminating in the relief of the siege on February 28, 1900—and then participated in the victorious British advance through the Transvaal. On his return to England, a new book quickly flowed from his pen, *London to Ladysmith via Pretoria,* earning him a modest fortune. He stood again for election to Parliament in 1900, and this time won a seat, which he took in February 1901.

Churchill rapidly earned a reputation as a brilliant orator but also drew condemnation for his sudden defection, in 1904, from the Tories to the Liberals, primarily over the issue of free trade, which he favored. The Liberal Party embraced their celebrated convert, and Churchill quickly rose to the ministerial post of undersecretary of state for the colonies, and then, in 1908, to the presidency of the Board of Trade, which carried with it a seat on the Cabinet. In this same year, he married Clementine Hozier, a Mayfair peeress and woman of striking beauty and indomitable will. She would prove to be her husband's lifelong support, inspiration, and spur.

In 1911, Churchill briefly served as Home Secretary but soon left the Home Office to become first lord of the admiralty. In the midst of a growing military crisis—an arms race with the Germany of Kaiser Wilhelm II—Churchill championed and directed the rapid modernization of the Royal Navy and ensured that it remained superior to the expanding German fleet. He secured the largest naval expenditure in British history, so that the Royal Navy, far more than the army, was adequately prepared when World War I broke out in July 1914. His confidence in the navy led him, early in 1915, to plan a daring amphibious assault on the strait dividing the Balkans from Asia Minor, the Dardanelles, which was held by German-allied Turkey. Gain control of the Dardanelles, Churchill reasoned, and a supply line would be opened wide to Britain's key ally on the Eastern Front, Russia. This was Winston Churchill's first essay in grand strategy, and it was characteristically bold, yet its architect lacked the patience to pursue the tactical and logistical details necessary to execute it. The failure of the naval assault resulted in Churchill's removal as first lord of the Admiralty. The Gallipoli Campaign, which was the land component of the assault, was also connected to him by virtue of his being the instigator of the offensive. This operation failed far more catastrophically, with Allied losses amounting to 252,000, including

46,000 battle deaths over eight agonizing months. Under fire, Churchill severed all connection with the government in November 1915.

He found, however, that he could not long remain out of the war. He sought and accepted command as colonel of the 6th Royal Scots Fusiliers, personally leading them in combat on the Western Front until May 1916, when he returned to England. In July of the next year, his friend, political ally, and new prime minister, David Lloyd George, named him to the post of minister of munitions. Although the new office was not the equivalent of first lord of the admiralty—it did not carry a Cabinet seat—Churchill dedicated himself to the work with great energy and imagination, increasing munitions production so dramatically that an actual shell surplus was achieved before the war ended. He also championed the development and manufacture of what was called at the time the "land ship" but soon became known as the tank. Despite formidable technological problems encountered in its development, Churchill believed that this heavily armored all-terrain vehicle was precisely the weapon needed to break the intractable stalemate of the Western Front. Although the tank remained unperfected in World War I, it would become a major weapon in World War II, forever transforming the way ground wars were fought.

From the munitions ministry, Churchill advanced, immediately after the armistice in 1918, to secretary of state for war and air, stunning everyone by zealously slashing military expenditures, even as he called for British intervention in Russia's ongoing Bolshevik Revolution. He moved to the Colonial Office in 1921, where he wrestled with British mandates in the Middle East, affirming Britain's support for Palestine as a Jewish homeland while also recognizing the continuation of Arab rights. In 1922, when insurgent Turks threatened the Dardanelles "neutral zone" created by the treaties ending World War I, Churchill urged a firm stand, but the shell-shocked British public, fearing the outbreak of a new war, turned against him. An acute attack of appendicitis prevented his defending himself or campaigning in the elections, and as Churchill himself put it, he suddenly found himself "without an office, without a seat, without a party, and even without an appendix."

His involuntary hiatus from politics gave him time to write, and his personal history of the Great War (World War I), *The World Crisis*, earned him enough money to finance the purchase of a fine country estate, Chartwell, in Kent. In 1923, however, Churchill lost his seat in Parliament and the following year accepted nomination for a Conservative seat from the London suburb of Epping. At the time, he was still a member of the Liberal Party but, during the campaign, made the switch to the Tories and won. He remained a Conservative for the rest of his life. Seeking to form a coalition government, the new Conservative prime minister, Stanley Baldwin, appointed Churchill chancellor of the exchequer. It was a post for which Churchill was woefully unsuited. No sooner was he seated in the cabinet than he restored the gold standard in 1925, which instantly triggered deflation, followed by widespread unemployment and a miners' strike that exploded into the nationwide general strike of 1926.

The rival Labour Party ascended, and in 1930 Churchill withdrew from the Baldwin government. Throughout the 1930s, he languished outside of the inner circle of British government. As something of a voice crying in the wilderness, he began warning of the danger posed by the rise of Adolf Hitler and Nazi Germany, advocating that Britain should assume a full war footing. He urged especially a program to match Germany's growing air power, reasoning that Hitler would first attack Britain from the air in an attempt to bring the nation to its knees and soften it for invasion. Churchill became the leading opponent of the policy Baldwin's successor, Neville Chamberlain, introduced, "appeasement"—the attempt to buy off rather than resist Adolf Hitler's aggressive expansionism. In an effort to avoid a war for which he felt Britain was woefully unprepared, Prime Minister Chamberlain connived at Germany's annexation of the Sudetenland, the German-speaking region of Czechoslovakia. Churchill argued that no dictator could be appeased and that, moreover, sacrificing Czech sovereignty was not only immoral and cowardly, it was strategic folly. Czechoslovakia's central position made it the keystone of middle Europe, and its coal fields were of great value to any power. When Chamberlain returned from the Munich Conference (September 29-30, 1938), having yielded to Hitler the Sudetenland and claiming to have achieved thereby "peace for our time," Churchill bluntly labeled the act a "total and unmitigated defeat."

Events, of course, proved Winston Churchill right, and after Hitler invaded Poland on September 1, 1939, starting World War II, Chamberlain offered Churchill his former post of first lord of the admiralty. With his characteristic aggressiveness, Churchill proposed an immediate assault on

Norway to dislodge the Germans there. Like the Gallipoli campaign of World War I, the invasion proved a fiasco and had to be aborted. This time, however, it was Chamberlain, not Churchill, who took the fall. He resigned on May 10, 1940, and Churchill, on the recommendation of Chamberlain himself and at the request of King George VI, replaced him as prime minister during the very darkest period of World War II.

Churchill's very first act as prime minister was to thank Neville Chamberlain for his support, and such was the new prime minister's character in a crisis that he did not for a moment brood on the Norway disaster, but instead went about the business of saving his nation—and did so in the knowledge that, by defending England, he was defending the entire free world. He took upon himself all the responsibilities of a war leader. With Europe rapidly falling to the Germans, he turned to the United States, a neutral nation reluctant to involve itself in yet another "European" war. Churchill established an intensely personal relationship with President Franklin D. Roosevelt, whom he patiently persuaded to drift away from neutrality, first by developing the policy of lend-lease. This provided England (and, soon, other Allies, most notably the Soviet Union) with arms, materiel, aircraft, and ships not on the former cash-and-carry basis but in a moneyless exchange for strategic cooperation with the United States.

Lend-lease was a great step forward in Britain's war effort, but in 1940, the German juggernaut seemed unstoppable. In June, the British army was beaten back—and very nearly annihilated—at Dunkirk, on the North Sea coast of France. Only a nearly miraculous trans-Channel evacuation saved the mass of the army. Later in the summer, the Battle of Britain commenced as the German *Luftwaffe* did what Churchill had predicted years earlier, conducted a massive bombing campaign of London and other English cities. Britons prepared to be invaded—or, more accurately, Churchill prepared his people to resist invasion with everything they had. On June 4, 1940, in one of many great and immeasurably effective speeches delivered to Parliament, Churchill declared, "Even though large tracts of Europe and many old and famous States have fallen or may fall into the grip of the Gestapo and all the odious apparatus of Nazi rule, we shall not flag or fail. We shall go on to the end, we shall fight in France, we shall fight on the seas and oceans, we shall fight with growing confidence and growing strength in the air, we shall defend our Island, whatever the cost may be, we shall fight on the beaches, we shall fight on the landing grounds, we shall fight in the fields and in the streets, we shall fight in the hills; we shall never surrender..."

Churchill possessed the personal character and rhetorical skill to maintain his courage and to fire the courage and determination of his people. To the stunned surprise of Nazi Germany and, for that matter, the rest world, it was the British who emerged victorious in the Battle of Britain, the Royal Air Force (RAF) defeating the Luftwaffe and foiling invasion.

Churchill was a hands-on prime minister, who formed a true working partnership with the military. He demanded that British forces never permit themselves to be tied down to a defensive posture. Churchill believed that the best defense was a vigorous offense, and he boldly diverted an entire armored division—one of only two in Britain—to take the war to the armies of Hitler and Mussolini in the Middle East. At the same time, he forged an alliance with the Soviet Union, pledging to aid it after it had been invaded by Germany—this even though Churchill was an outspoken and implacable foe of communism.

With the entry of the United States into the war following the Japanese attack on Pearl Harbor on December 7, 1941, the prime minister stepped in to hammer out a three-way alliance among the United States, Soviet Union, and Great Britain. His war strategy for the Allies was controversial, and its wisdom is still debated by historians. He proposed postponing any invasion of the European mainland until what he called the "soft underbelly of Europe" had been breached by clearing North Africa and the Mediterranean of the enemy. Over the objections of top U.S. generals George C. Marshall and Dwight Eisenhower, President Franklin D. Roosevelt acceded to Churchill's plan, and it was not until the summer of 1943 that the Allies invaded Sicily and then mainland Italy, having fought the first part of the "European" war in North Africa. A year later, Churchill was instrumental in planning and supporting the principal invasion of Europe, via Normandy, on "D-Day," June 6, 1944.

Although Churchill's "soft underbelly" strategy had governed much of the war in Europe, his influence rapidly diminished once the Normandy campaign was under way. With victory in sight, Churchill now saw the Soviets as a postwar threat. It was not only that he hated communism, but that the hard lessons of two world wars had taught him to oppose *all* totalitarian regimes. He therefore advocated a drive by the Western Allies directly into Berlin, specifically to preempt the city's occupation by Soviets. Churchill foresaw the dangerous shape of a postwar "Cold War" world. With the concurrence of President Roosevelt and his successor, Harry S. Truman, Churchill's proposal was overruled by Allied commander in chief Dwight D. Eisenhower, who believed it necessary first to crush the last German resistance in southern Germany and Austria. While British and American forces turned away from the German capital, the Russians fought a tremendously costly battle to take eastern Germany, including Berlin.

For immediate tactical purposes, Ike's plan was the soundest and least costly; but Churchill typically looked beyond the tactical range to see the overall strategic consequences of an action. In this case, he looked beyond World War II itself. Later, in a speech delivered at a small college in Missouri, he would coin the phrase "iron curtain" to describe the hard pall of Soviet influence and tyranny that had descended across Eastern Europe, thanks to the inroads made as a result of the Allies' World War II strategy.

In some ways, Churchill was disappointed by the final conditions of the Allied victory in Europe. On top of this came a blow any other man would have felt as crushing. In July 1945, a general election failed to return him to office following the unconditional surrender of Germany and just before the capitulation of Japan. Ousted in 1945, Churchill was returned to office as prime minister in 1951 and was subsequently knighted in recognition of his great service to the nation and the world. In July 1953, he suffered a stroke, which left him weakened and ailing. Nevertheless, he fought back to partial recovery and continued in office until April 1955, when he was succeeded by his handpicked candidate, Anthony Eden.

Churchill spent his final decade pursuing his favorite recreation, painting, and seeing to the publication of the last of his great literary works, the four-volume *History of the English Speaking Peoples*. Published in 1956-1958, it followed his even more epical six-volume *The Second World War* (1948-1953), which earned him the Nobel Prize for literature. In 1963, two years before his death (on January 24, 1965), President John F. Kennedy and the United States Congress conferred upon Churchill honorary American citizenship—the first and, thus far, only such honor ever rendered by this country.

#3
HIROHITO

*The emperor who let Japan go to war and, in the end,
allowed the war to end rather than accept nuclear
annihilation*

Hirohito, emperor of Japan, in a photograph taken December 31, 1934.
(credit: *Library of Congress*)

By the mid-twentieth century, constitutional monarchy was a familiar concept throughout the world. Modern nations that embraced some form of representative government yet also wished to retain their traditional inherited monarchies adopted forms of government in which the king or queen was clearly a figurehead, with no appreciable governing power. In Japan, the Meiji constitution of 1889 lent support to the traditional belief that the emperor was an *arahitogami,* a divinity incarnate. Yet, by the twentieth century, Japan was a modern nation with a ministerial government and a Diet, an elected parliamentary legislature. While the emperor was head of state, the prime minister was head of the government; at the same time, the emperor's power was absolute and eternal. Thus, Hirohito, who ascended the Chrysanthemum Throne on December 25, 1926, was in an exquisitely precarious position. His authority was absolute, his constitutional status was defined as divinity incarnate, and yet he had no real executive, legislative, or judicial power. Still, the people—at least most of them—looked on him as an embodiment of divinity, the incarnation of Japan itself.

Hirohito was born on April 29, 1901, at the Aoyama Palace in Tokyo and was provided an education befitting a future emperor, at the Peers' School and at the Crown Prince's Institute. He was, in fact, inclined to study, and he grew into a thoughtful and scholarly young man, who wrote poetry and pursued an intense interest in marine biology, a subject on which he became an internationally recognized authority and the author of a number of books in the field. Although his upbringing was closely sheltered, he was also an urbane figure, who became the first Japanese crown prince to travel abroad when he toured Europe in 1921. He was named prince regent on November 29, 1921, when his father, the emperor Taishō, suffering from mental illness, stepped down from the throne. Hirohito married his distant cousin, Princess Nagako Kuni, on January 26, 1924, and, upon the death of his father, became emperor on December 25, 1926. His wife became Empress Kōjun.

At the start of Hirohito's reign, an honorific name was conferred—Shōwa, meaning "Abundant Benevolence" or "Enlightened Peace." The designation would prove supremely ironic, as Hirohito, head of the Japanese state, bore personal responsibility for his nation's aggressive actions first against China in the Sino-Japanese War (1937-1945) and then, in World War II, against other subject peoples as well as the Allied nations.

As the head of state, Hirohito may have had legal responsibility for making war, yet it is difficult to assess his actual role in the war. Indeed, most Western historians believe that Hirohito personally opposed going to war against the Allies and, in particular, against the United States. His paradoxical position as an emperor of modern Japan, in principle absolute and supreme in his authority but in practice subject to the will of ministers, advisers, and the military, gave him limited latitude in avoiding the conflict. Still, even while conceding the ambiguous position Hirohito occupied, a significant minority of historians argue that Hirohito did, in fact, actively participate in planning for the expansion of the Japanese empire beginning as early as 1931. At the very least, he never affirmatively acted to oppose the rise of right-wing militarists in the Japanese government, and his silence may, some assert, be taken as a token of his tacit approval—especially in a society in which the emperor rarely communicated beyond his courtiers and circle of advisers. Those near the emperor perpetually struggled to interpret his will.

While Hirohito *reigned* before and during World War II, he did not *rule*. Subject to the Meiji Constitution of 1889, his political and administrative prerogatives were limited, and most governing and administrative power was delegated to a variety of ministers. This notwithstanding, Hirohito was widely revered as a god on Earth, and he might well have brought moral pressure to bear in preventing the war. As it was, during the conflict, he made appearances among the troops, always astride a white horse, and exhorted them to render their supreme effort in battle. What is more, when the emperor made such exhortations, it was in the context of the soldiers' knowledge that to die for the emperor was an honor beyond question or challenge. If we are grasping for a just means of judging Hirohito, we can say little for certain except that he could do little enough to counter the will of the militarists in the government, but he did not do even what little was available to him. Beyond this, his appearances before the troops were unambiguously martial in nature.

❖

For all the pain, loss, suffering, and devastation Hirohito's Japan inflicted on the rest of the world, the agony endured by the Japanese themselves was horrific. Out of a population of more than seventy-one million (as of 1939), the nation suffered 2.1 to 2.3 million military deaths and 550,000 to 800,000 civilian deaths, for a total loss of roughly 4 percent of the population.

Hirohito was doubtless mindful of this when he finally asserted his moral authority in August 1945, after the atomic bombings of Hiroshima and Nagasaki. Even after the attacks of August 6 and August 9, in which the devastation was unparalleled and the effect upon the injured—blast injuries, radiation burns, and radiation sickness—was bewildering and horrifying, many of the hardcore militarists in the government and the army (far more than in the navy) continued to oppose surrender. Many of these believed that it was now the duty of all Japanese to die in defeat. Indeed, in its thousands of years of history, Japan had never been successfully invaded, and it had never surrendered. American authorities widely believed that the very concept of surrender was not so much anathema to the Japanese as simply non-existent in the people's minds and imaginations. Surrender was not part of the nation's culture.

All of this notwithstanding, on August 10, 1945, the official Japanese news agency, Domei, broadcasted a message declaring that the government of Japan was prepared to accept unconditional surrender, but with the understanding that the emperor would remain on the throne. The Allies' unmovable demand was for unconditional surrender, period, and U.S. President Harry S. Truman acknowledged that what Japan offered was unconditional surrender on one condition. Some of the president's advisers counseled him to reject the offer. By the time the broadcast had been made, a third atomic bomb was ready for use. Use it, they urged.

But Truman ordered that no more atomic bombs were to be dropped without his explicit directive. He told Secretary of Commerce Henry A. Wallace that he could not endure the thought of killing "all those kids," by which he meant Japanese kids. Instead, Truman decided that he could grant the Japanese their single condition—but only by modifying it with a condition of his own. Japan could retain Hirohito, who would, however, be wholly "subject to the Supreme Commander of the Allied Powers." Truman ordered that the reply be transmitted immediately. While awaiting the Japanese response, the president ordered the resumption of air raids using conventional, non-nuclear bombs, to recommence on August 13. The Japanese government communicated its acceptance of Truman's terms on

August 14, and, the very next day, on August 15, 1945, the people of Japan heard their emperor. It was a message he had recorded the day before in his palace. He risked provoking a *coup d'etat* by siding with the ministerial faction that advocated surrender, and his counselors feared that to venture to the radio studio for a live broadcast would risk assassination.

"To Our good and loyal subjects," his message began:

After pondering deeply the general trends of the world and the actual conditions obtaining to Our Empire today, We have decided to effect a settlement of the present situation by resorting to an extraordinary measure.

We have ordered Our Government to communicate to the Governments of the United States, Great Britain, China and the Soviet Union that Our Empire accepts the provisions of their Joint Declaration [the Potsdam Declaration, which demanded unconditional surrender].

To strive for the common prosperity and happiness of all nations as well as the security and well-being of Our Subjects is the solemn obligation which has been handed down by Our Imperial Ancestors, and which we lay close to heart. Indeed, We declared war on America and Britain out of Our sincere desire to ensure Japan's self-preservation and the stabilization of East Asia, it being far from Our thought either to infringe upon the sovereignty of other nations or to embark upon territorial aggrandizement. But now the war has lasted for nearly four years. Despite the best that has been done by everyone—the gallant fighting of the military and naval forces, the diligence and assiduity of Our servants of the State and the devoted service of Our one hundred million people, the war situation has developed not necessarily to Japan's advantage, while the general trends of the world have all turned against her interest. Moreover, the enemy has begun to employ a new and most cruel bomb, the power of which to damage is indeed incalculable, taking the toll of many innocent lives. Should We continue to fight, it would not only result in an ultimate collapse and obliteration of the Japanese nation, but also it would lead to the total extinction of human civilization. Such being the case, how are We to save the millions of Our subjects; or to atone Ourselves before the hallowed spirits of Our Imperial Ancestors? This is the reason why We have ordered the Acceptance of the provisions of the Joint Declaration of the Powers....

It was the first time that the Japanese people had heard Hirohito speak since he had taken his place on the Chrysanthemum Throne. However we assess Hirohito's role in bringing about the war and in the brutal, even criminal conduct of the war, whether by his acts of commission or omission, we cannot deny that he was instrumental in ending the war.

In the weeks and months that followed the surrender, Hirohito neither solicited nor received any offer of immunity from prosecution for war crimes. And there were many in the governments of the Allied nations, especially Australia and including the United States, who were eager for the emperor to be brought to trial. The Truman administration, however, strongly favored permitting Hirohito to remain on the throne unmolested, albeit subject to the authority of the Supreme Allied Commander, General Douglas MacArthur, who headed the government of military occupation. Truman argued that this would help to ensure compliance among the Japanese and would prevent a popular uprising against the occupation forces.

As for Emperor Hirohito, he seemed at this point anxious for nothing more than the welfare of the Japanese people going forward. He closely and personally cooperated with MacArthur. He allowed himself to be photographed with him—a gesture that dramatically signaled his approval. His deportment promoted the harmonious and highly effective administration of the occupation government.

Hirohito also actively advocated the introduction of genuine democracy in Japan. In a radio broadcast of January 1, 1946, he explicitly repudiated the divine status of Japan's emperors, himself included. This prepared the environment in which the people of Japan, by a free and open plebiscite, accepted a new constitution, which had been drafted chiefly by MacArthur and other United States occupation officials. From this point on, Japan became a constitutional monarchy on the Western model.

Whatever power Hirohito had before and during the war, at least in theory and by virtue of his title, he now relinquished. The old Meiji constitution had explicitly defined the emperor's authority as inherited and divine. The new constitution defined it as given by the expressed will of the people. Sovereignty was a popular gift, not a divine right. Hirohito went beyond endorsing the letter of the new law. He sought to promote throughout Japan a truly democratic spirit by making himself publicly accessible to a degree unprecedented not only in his reign but in Japanese history. He was now frequently seen and heard in public. Perhaps more astoundingly, his oldest son, Crown Prince Akihito, married a commoner, Shōda Michiko, in 1959. This ended a 1,500-year tradition of an insular imperial family. In 1971, Hirohito became the first reigning Japanese emperor to travel abroad when he made a tour of Europe. Four years later, he made a state visit to the United States. The imperial succession was preserved, however, as Akihito ascended the throne upon the death of Hirohito in 1989.

#4
ISOROKU YAMAMOTO

Architect of "infamy" at Pearl Harbor

Isoroku Yamamoto, architect of Japan's attack on Pearl Harbor, December 7, 1941.
A resounding tactical triumph, the attack was a strategic catastrophe: it brought
the United States into World War II and sealed the doom of Japan. (credit:
Japanese National Diet Library)

Other than Adolf Hitler, no single individual had a more profound effect on the outbreak and course of World War II than the Japanese admiral who planned and executed the December 7, 1941, surprise attack on the U.S. naval, army, and army air base at Pearl Harbor, Hawaii. Among the greatest tactical triumphs of the war, the Pearl Harbor operation was also the single most consequential strategic defeat. For while the attack resulted in a devastating heavy loss of life and damage to the U.S. Navy Pacific Fleet (though not as permanently extensive as initially believed), it galvanized the war will of the American people and propelled the once "neutral" United States into the century's second world war. This ensured the ultimate defeat of Japan in the Asia-Pacific theater and of Germany in the European-Atlantic theater.

Born Isoroku Takano to a samurai father in Nugata prefecture on April 4, 1884, the future admiral of the Japanese Imperial Navy was adopted by the Yamamoto family, whose members were also celebrated samurai. He subsequently took their name. After graduating from the naval academy in 1904, Yamamoto saw action at the battle of Tsushima during the Russo-Japanese War (1904-1905) and was wounded on May 26, 1905, losing two fingers from his left hand. His injury nearly resulted in his dismissal from the navy, and for the rest of his career he disguised his maimed hand with a glove.

As it had for naval experts the world over, the Japanese victory in the 1904-1905 war taught Yamamoto much about the potential of massive naval firepower as deployed from well-built, well-armored battleships. After the war with Russia, he served aboard several vessels and graduated from the Imperial Navy Torpedo School in 1908. His promise was recognized early, and he was enrolled in the prestigious Naval Staff College, the institution in which future leaders of the fleet were trained. Yamamoto graduated in 1911 and, that same year, completed the Naval Gunnery School course as well. Appointed an instructor there, he was promoted to lieutenant commander in 1915, and then graduated from the senior course of the Naval Staff College a year later.

After completing the advanced course, Yamamoto was appointed a staff officer serving with the Second Fleet and was sent to the United States for study at Harvard University from 1919 to 1921. He returned to Japan as an instructor at the Naval War College from 1921 to 1923, when he was promoted to captain and dispatched to the United States and Europe as an admiral's aide for a tour of inspection and observation. The experience from 1919 to 1923 instilled in Yamamoto an affection for the United States, together with a tremendous respect for its navy and, even more, for its industrial prowess. He came to believe that the prejudice many Japanese military leaders harbored against the Americans, whom they regarded as soft and frivolous, lacking in any warrior spirit, was dangerously misplaced. His experience in America and Europe persuaded Yamamoto that it behooved Japan to come to productive terms with the West and thereby to avoid war at all costs. Even at the time of Pearl Harbor, Yamamoto held to this belief.

In 1924, Yamamoto was made deputy commander of Kasumiga Ura Naval Air Station, an assignment that awakened in him recognition of the full potential of air power at sea. He began to conceive what it took the leaders of the U.S. Navy (and those of other Western navies) considerably longer to realize: that airpower and aircraft carriers were bound to displace the artillery of battleships and cruisers as the primary weapons of modern naval warfare.

In 1925, Yamamoto was appointed Japanese naval attaché in Washington, D.C. Serving at the embassy through 1928, he made many valuable connections with U.S. military and political figures. The experience served only to reinforce his high regard for American government and for the military implications of the nation's innovative and productive capacity. He was, however, happy to leave military diplomacy and return to Japan, where he was given command of the new aircraft carrier *Akagi* in 1928. This seagoing assignment proved short-lived, however. In 1929, he was promoted from captain to rear admiral and, a year later, was appointed chief of the Technological Division of the Imperial Navy Technological Department. From this position, Yamamoto advanced Japanese naval aviation and in 1933 was assigned to command the 1st Naval Air Division. The following year, promoted to vice admiral, he was appointed to head the Japanese delegation to the London Naval Conference of 1934-1935. The conference was intended to limit the expansion of the world's navies through 1942, and although Yamamoto was personally opposed to Japan's official position, which was a demand for naval parity with Britain and the United States, he followed his instructions in rejecting any further extension of the tonnage ratios—Japanese warship tonnage versus that of other major powers—that had been established by the Washington Naval Treaty on 1922. Although Japan ultimately declined to participate directly in the 1934-1935 conference and the treaty it produced, it did subscribe to that treaty. Yamamoto would later play a key role in Japan's abrogation of the treaty and its limits.

Upon his return to Japan from London in 1935, Yamamoto was made chief of Naval Aviation Headquarters. From this position, he championed the construction and deployment of new aircraft carriers and argued for their use as the principal offensive weapon of the navy. His advocacy defined and deepened a growing rift between more conservative naval strategists—who continued to see fleets built around battleships as the backbone of the Imperial Navy—and the younger officers, who became Yamamoto's zealous disciples in his fight for the strategic supremacy of naval aviation.

From 1936 to 1939, Yamamoto served in the Japanese cabinet as Minister of the Navy. In this post, he advocated moderation and accommodation with the Western powers. His hope was that the navy would serve as a moderating influence against the extreme militarism of a government that had increasingly come under the influence of the navy's service rival, the army. The senior officers of the Imperial Army saw themselves as the inheritors of Japanese warrior traditions and, under Hideki Tojo, were leading Japan to the precipice of war.

While Yamamoto fought a losing battle against the slide toward world war, he also accepted a position concurrent with his cabinet post as Navy minister. In 1938, he was reappointed chief of Naval Aviation Headquarters. The following year, however, he left both the cabinet and aviation headquarters to serve at sea as commander of the Combined Fleet. In 1940, he also became commander of First Fleet. Yamamoto reasoned that if he could not prevent war, he could take all steps necessary to give Japan winning advantages against the navies of both Britain and the United States. As commander of the fleets, Yamamoto embraced chief responsibility for making preparations for war against these nations. With regard to America, his approach to his mission was darkly fatalistic. He was convinced that America's industrial power and huge, well-educated population would make it almost impossible for Japan to win a war, especially a long war, against that nation. It was in the context of this fatalism that he conceived the attack on Pearl Harbor.

In the late 1930s and first two years of the 1940s, the American president, Franklin Delano Roosevelt, imposed embargoes on export of critical raw materials to Japan. He saw these actions as alternatives to war. Others, however, predicted that Japan would take them as provocations, especially after the Roosevelt administration also began actively discouraging U.S. banks from extending credit to Japan. The termination of a U.S.-Japanese trade treaty in July 1939 triggered a series of high-level conferences through 1940 intended to reverse the deterioration of relations between the two nations. But Japan's continued aggression in Asia and against China in particular moved Roosevelt to widen the embargo.

Increasingly, Japan's militarists saw war as the only way to end the American stranglehold. When FDR issued an executive order on July 26, 1941, freezing Japanese assets in the United States and bringing under strict government control all financial and trade transactions in which Japanese interests were involved, the Japanese government believed its choice had come down to capitulation or war. When the leadership chose war, Yamamoto reluctantly sought a route to victory. He believed that the major obstacle to Japan's ongoing conquest of Southeast Asia was the U.S. Pacific Fleet. He believed that a massive blow against the fleet, which was concentrated at Pearl Harbor, Hawaii Territory, would allow Japan to achieve an instant and complete triumph in the Pacific, which, he argued, was the only hope—and a slim one at that—of prevailing against the United States. He told Navy minister Koshiro Oikawa, "We should do our very best...to decide the fate of the war on the very first day." Yamamoto reasoned that the American president was aware that the United States would soon be called on to fight against Germany and so would be motivated to conclude a quick negotiated peace with Japan. In the worst case, if the blow against Pearl Harbor did not knock the United States out of the Pacific war, it would at least buy the Imperial Japanese Navy time—perhaps six months—in which it could wreak havoc in the Pacific before the U.S. Navy would be in any position to retaliate. Yet, privately, Yamamoto believed that entering into a war against the United States would not end well.

In attacking Pearl Harbor and decimating the fleet, Yamamoto believed he might force the surrender of the president through a massively demoralizing blow. He had speculated about the feasibility of attacking Pearl Harbor as early as the spring of 1940, even as he faced two daunting negatives: Number one, how possibly could a large aircraft carrier fleet escape detection as it sailed toward Hawaii? Number two, Pearl Harbor was shallow, too shallow for attack by torpedoes dropped from planes. Such torpedoes would sink too deeply and bury themselves in the harbor bottom before reaching their targets.

On November 11, 1940, Yamamoto noted that British carrier-based torpedo bombers made a highly successful attack against the Taranto naval base in southern Italy. He knew that, like Pearl Harbor, Taranto was very shallow, but the British pilots had trained to drop their torpedoes in a way that kept them from bottoming out. Yamamoto reasoned that Japanese pilots could learn the necessary tactics as well, but he also worked with Japanese engineers, who rigged the torpedoes with wooden fins, which greatly reduced their plunge. Between the flight training and the design tweak, the shallow harbor would no longer be an obstacle to attack. As for sailing undetected, the secret, Yamamoto realized, was to observe strict radio silence except for deceptive decoy radio messages. American naval planners, he gambled, would be unable to imagine that a large ship movement could be carried out without continual radio communication. Moreover, Yamamoto decided to come at the Americans from an unexpected place. The obvious point from which to launch an attack on Hawaii was the Marshall Islands, which were controlled by Japan. Instead, the fleet would start from Kure naval base near Hiroshima and would assemble at in the Kurile Islands, then proceed toward Pearl.

Yamamoto solved his technical and strategic problems even as ongoing negotiations between the United States and Japan were breaking down. During an "Imperial Conference" of September 6, 1941, Hideki Tojo ordered what he called the "Hawaiian Operation" to proceed. War was now inevitable.

A strike force consisting of two fleet carriers, two light carriers, a carrier that had been converted from a battleship, a carrier converted from a cruiser, two battleships, two cruisers, a screen of destroyers, and eight support vessels, embarked. On December 2, the approaching strike force received a message, "Climb Mt. Niitaka"—code authorizing the attack.

At six o'clock on Sunday morning, December 7, 1941, the strike force was 230 miles north of Oahu. Six carriers turned into the wind to launch the first wave—183 planes. As soon as the aircraft were aloft, carrier crews prepared the second wave, launching 167 more planes shortly after seven o'clock. A few aircraft had to drop out, leaving a total of 350 to make the attack. The first wave homed in on Pearl Harbor by following the signal of commercial radio broadcasts from Honolulu. The thick cloud cover screened the approach of the planes, and then—as luck had it—the clouds broke wide open over Oahu, suddenly giving the pilots perfect visibility over their targets.

The primary target was the American aircraft carriers. But when the flight leader discovered that the carriers were not in port, he ordered the planes to go for the secondary target, "Battleship Row," along which the great battleships were closely lined up, bow to stern. The first torpedoes fell at 7:55 a.m. while Japanese ground-attack aircraft struck the airfields at Kaneohe, Hickam, Ewa, Bellows, and Wheeler fields. Within two hours, American air power in Hawaii was almost totally destroyed—on the ground.

The first-wave assault was over by 8:25. Fifteen minutes after this attack, high-level bombers moved in, then at 9:15 the dive bombers of the second wave struck, withdrawing by 9:45. Surprise was total, and the toll was devastating. The battleship *Arizona* was obliterated, and the *Oklahoma* capsized. The battleships *California*, *Nevada*, and *West Virginia* sank in shallow water. Three cruisers, three destroyers, and four other vessels were damaged or sunk. One hundred sixty-four aircraft were destroyed on the ground and another 128 were damaged. Casualties included 2,403 service personnel and civilians killed and 1,178 wounded. Japanese losses were negligible: twenty-nine aircraft (with fifty-five airmen) and six submarines, five of which were ultra-small "midget" subs.

The first wave aircraft began touching down on their carriers about 10 a.m. At this time, aircraft were being readied for a third-wave assault against numerous targets that had yet to be hit, including the naval shipyard and oil-storage tank farm. But Admiral Chuichi Nagumo, in direct command of the operation, decided to scrub the third wave, arguing that the American carriers and other ships that had not been in port at Pearl Harbor were now surely on the hunt and would make a massive counterattack. Declaring his mission accomplished, Nagumo was anxious to avoid incurring heavy losses against the strike force. By one o'clock, the ships were turning back toward Japan.

It was a fatal error. Had the third wave been launched to destroy repair facilities and fuel installations, Pearl Harbor would have been knocked out of the war for a long time, perhaps permanently. The fact was that Pearl Harbor returned to service quickly, and while the losses to Pacific Fleet were indeed heavy, those battleships that had been damaged but not sunk were repaired fairly quickly. Moreover, all but two that had been sunk in the shallow harbor water were eventually refloated, so that six of the eight battleships attacked at Pearl Harbor returned to service before the end of the war, as did all but one of the other major vessels sunk or damaged. Worse for Yamamoto and Japan, the American nation was far from demoralized by the treacherous "sneak attack." America was enraged, its people instantly galvanized into destroying Japan. As Yamamoto reportedly remarked to subordinates, "I feel all we have done is to awake a sleeping giant and fill him with a terrible resolve."

Realizing that the attack on Pearl Harbor had failed to win the war in a single day, Yamamoto set about launching vigorous follow-up campaigns that captured the East Indies during January–March 1942 and that achieved significant success in the Indian Ocean during April 2–9, 1942. Only by unrelenting aggression, he believed, could Japan yet achieve victory.

In June 1942, Yamamoto launched an operation intended to lure what remained of the U.S. Pacific Fleet to a showdown battle around Midway Island. He anticipated administering there the death blow the fleet had escaped at Pearl Harbor. Under Admiral Chester W. Nimitz, however, the three aircraft carriers and assorted combat vessels turned the tables on the superior Japanese force. The Battle of Midway (June 4-7, 1942) cost the U.S. Pacific Fleet heavily, but it was utterly catastrophic for Yamamoto. After Midway, the Imperial Navy lost the initiative and never again mounted an offensive attack.

Yamamoto's confidence was shattered. He was also a marked man. As the "mastermind" of Pearl Harbor, he was targeted by the Americans for personal vengeance and, on April 18, 1943, acting on an intercepted Japanese radio message revealing that Yamamoto was flying on a tour of Japanese bases on Shortland Island, U.S. fighter aircraft were dispatched to shoot down the bomber transporting him.

Isoroku Yamamoto was killed near Bougainville, and his death was yet another blow against an Imperial Japanese Navy that was already back on its heels. The rest of the Pacific War was a long Japanese retreat, costly to both sides.

#5
HIDEKI TOJO

The man Americans loved to hate

Hideki Tojo stands trial as a war criminal, which sentenced him to death on November 12, 1948. (credit: *National Archives and Records Administration*)

Prime minister of Japan's extensively militarized World War II government, Hideki Tojo also served as the nation's generalissimo during the Second Sino-Japanese War, which began in 1937 and was absorbed into the larger conflict. During the period of the world conflict, it is safe to say that the only man the people of the Allied nations reviled as much as much as Adolf Hitler was Hideki Tojo. Yet, unlike Hitler, who was a genuine political leader, Tojo was a new kind of tyrant, a hyper-empowered bureaucrat. He rose to the top of the military regime that dominated the Japanese empire not because he was a popular leader of his countrymen—indeed, they hardly knew him and rarely saw him in public—but because he was the consummate modern bureaucrat. He had an almost superhuman reputation for getting things done, and, among government insiders, he earned the sobriquet Kamisori ("Razor") because he sliced through red tape, distractions, obstacles, and people to seize the nub of any issue and instantly act upon it. That he apparently had neither emotion nor empathy was widely regarded as the very highest qualification of character for the job at hand.

Tojo was born on December 30, 1884, into a venerable military family, celebrated for having produced over the centuries many samurai. His parents lived in Iwate prefecture, a district that had seen intense fighting during the Boshin War, a civil war fought during 1868-1869, which ended the regime of the Tokugawa shogunate and restored imperial rule to Japan. Thus, Hideki Tojo was, from the very beginning of his life, steeped in a military tradition wedded to imperial nationalism. His father, Eikyo Tojo, was a lieutenant general in the Imperial Army and had rendered distinguished service during the Russo-Japanese War (1904-1905). Hideki was expected to graduate from the military academy and to pursue a career in the army.

He met both expectations. After graduating in 1905, Tojo entered the army and held regimental staff assignments from 1905 to 1909. In 1915, he graduated from the Army Staff College and, during 1919-1921, served in Switzerland and then in Berlin as assistant military attaché, attaining the rank of major. On his return to Japan, Tojo was appointed to the War College as an instructor.

Although his rise was rapid, all his accomplishments had been achieved in peacetime rather than on the field of battle. He emerged not as a glorious warrior, but as an industrious, perceptive, and highly efficient staff officer—in short, as a military bureaucrat. His diplomatic service drew him into the inner circles of the government and positioned him to make important contributions to the military's efforts to seize control of national policy and administration. Promoted to lieutenant colonel in 1924, Tojo became chief of the Army Ministry's important Mobilization Plans Bureau, where he had a hand in directing Japan's preparations for war.

After a promotion to colonel in 1929, Tojo was given a regimental command and then assumed the position of chief of the Army General Staff's Organization and Mobilization Section. He served in this capacity from 1931 to 1933, when he was promoted to major general and named deputy commandant of the Military Academy. It was at this point that he became known as *Kamisori*—the Razor.

Tojo was very politically active within the military, joining the so-called Control Group, a clique of army officers who believed the military should have more control over Japanese government. The group further held that Japan could solve both its economic and population problems at the expense of other countries in Asia, most notably China. The group's idea resembled what Adolf Hitler, in Germany, called *Lebensraum*—living space, acquisition of territory into which the nation could and should rightly expand. As Tojo and the other members of the Control Group saw things, it was imperative for Japan to undertake the conquest of parts of China and other areas of southeast Asia. This would not only allow further settlement, it would provide access to sources of raw materials needed for Japanese industry.

The notion of regional expansion was only half of the Control Group's vision. Its other leading doctrine was the assumed opposition of the Western nations—paramount among which was the United States. With considerable justification, the Control Group believed that Western chauvinism and racism dictated opposition to virtually anything Japan might undertake to establish itself in the world. Accordingly, these mostly young officers believed Japan would have to assume an unconditionally aggressive posture of self-defense—or, more accurately, of preemptive defense, which amounted to offensive aggression.

Fully ensconced within the Control Group, Tojo was promoted to major general in 1933 and, two years later, was assigned as the chief of the military police for the Kwangtung Army—the army of conquest and occupation in

China. He prosecuted his command with an iron fist, cracking down on the local population with strict enforcement of Japanese law. His unsparing administration earned the admiration of his superiors, and in 1937, at the outbreak of the Sino-Japanese War, he was appointed chief of staff of the Kwangtung Army. Now at last he had an opportunity to prove himself as a wartime combat leader, a role in which he quickly distinguished himself not only as a strategist and a tactician, but as a samurai willing to treat the Chinese as a thoroughly conquered people. He showed no mercy, ordering his forces to lay waste to many of the cities and villages they invaded.

It should be noted that Tojo waged his brutal war almost exclusively from behind a desk. Only once did he participate in combat on the field—in August 1937, when he personally directed operations against the Chinese in Chahar, in the vicinity of Zhangjiakou. The culminating showdown battle of the Sino-Japanese War, however, was the campaign to take Shanghai. Although large, the Chinese army was ill-trained, ill-equipped, and led by corrupt commanders. Nevertheless, Chinese forces resisted the Japanese assault on Shanghai for four months, from August to November 1937, but Tojo's persistence and willingness to both take and spend lives resulted in the fall of China's most prosperous city, the trading nexus with the West. In the process, Japanese soldiers devastated what was at the time the capital of China, Nanking. In December 1937, Tojo's armies carried out what has been called the Rape of Nanking, a genocidal assault on the city and its surrounding area. By the time the campaign ended, some 100,000 Chinese civilians were made prisoners of war and subsequently raped, tortured, and killed.

In May 1938, Tojo was called back to Tokyo to serve in the government of Prime Minister Fumimaro Konoye. He took an uncompromisingly aggressive stance among the civilian ministers and bureaucrats, declaring as an absolute certainty that Japan would have to go to war against both China and the Soviet Union to reach its goals of economic and territorial expansion. He was adamant that Japan's chronically anemic economy could be improved only if the military became ever stronger.

In December 1938, Tojo left the civilian ministerial government and returned to the military proper as inspector general of army aviation. This proved a key move, since building a formidable air force—both under the army and the navy—would become a prime weapon for fighting a war of aggression. Having made inroads into the civilian government, pushing it further toward military control, Tojo now turned his attention to honing the military for a war that he was working hard to force the government to demand.

In July 1941, Tojo achieved appointment to the position from which he could do a very great deal to determine the destiny of the nation. He became minister of war. Although Japan was still fighting China, he oversaw another invasion, this one into Korea. When the United States government protested these blatant aggressions, Tojo pointed out to his government that all he had predicted about Western opposition was coming to pass. His vision was further vindicated by the embargo on the export to Japan of U.S. goods, especially raw materials (including much-need oil and steel), that President Franklin D. Roosevelt put in place. Under the embargo, Japan's domestic economic woes increased, and Tojo was quick to point out that the nation's pain was being created by the United States of America.

By 1941, the Japanese government had reached a tipping point. The leadership was divided between those advocating a retreat from confrontation with the West, most notably the United States, and those who clamored for launching a quick, highly aggressive war that would forever end Western opposition to Japan's realization of its imperial destiny. The moderates in the government wanted to immediately withdraw troops from China and open negotiations with the American government. At this, Tojo rose in righteous opposition—opposition driven by Japan's samurai traditions. He rapidly drew up new plans for an even more aggressive war against China, and he also promoted the Tripartite, or Axis, Pact. Concluded in Berlin on September 27, 1940, among Germany, Italy, and Japan, the pact was one of the foundational documents of World War II, serving as the primary treaty creating the alliance of the three major "Axis" powers. The pact came early in the war, a time of triumph for Germany, which had already invaded and conquered Poland, occupied France and created the puppet Vichy government in the unoccupied portion of the country, and appeared well positioned to invade and defeat Great Britain.

Hitler's hope for the Tripartite Pact was that it would provide the leverage he needed to coax Britain into coming to terms with Germany and withdrawing from the war. Moreover, Hitler hoped that the pact would dissuade the ostensibly neutral—but by now clearly British-leaning—United

States from intervening in Europe and prompt it instead to turn its attention to the Pacific, where Japanese aggression presented a more immediate threat to American security. By formally bringing Tokyo into the Berlin-Rome Axis, the pact would threaten the Soviet Union with a two-front war—once Germany had invaded that country. Finally, if the United States and the Soviet Union were distracted or threatened on the Asian-Pacific front, Great Britain would see itself as truly standing alone, and this would bring the British, at last, to the bargaining table.

Such was Hitler's grand plan. As Tojo saw it, a Japanese alliance with Germany and Italy would *discourage* the United States from antagonizing Japan any further. Tojo reasoned that America would not want to fight a two-front war any more than Russia did. A Japanese alliance with two European powers, Tojo believed, would intimidate Roosevelt and bring him to the conference table.

In the end, the Axis Pact achieved neither the outcomes Hitler nor Tojo wanted and envisioned. Indeed, its creation served only to reinforce and intensify pro-British U.S. policy—and it failed to bring Japan into a war against the Soviet Union. Still, the pact gave Japan license (as far as Germany and Italy were concerned) to expand into and dominate East Asia, and it crystallized the "*Lebensraum*" concept Hitler and Tojo shared:

> The governments of Germany, Italy, and Japan, considering it as a condition precedent of any lasting peace that all nations of the world be given each its own proper place, have decided to stand by and co-operate with one another in regard to their efforts in greater East Asia and regions of Europe respectively wherein it is their prime purpose to establish and maintain a new order of things calculated to promote the mutual prosperity and welfare of the peoples concerned.

❖

In October 1941, Fumimaro Konoye resigned as prime minister, creating a vacancy. Promoted to general in 1941, Tojo was quickly named as prime minister. Even members of the government who objected on principle to such blatant military domination of the government approved Tojo's selection as a way of staving off an outright military coup. He established a hard line in international and military affairs, pushing Japan closer and closer to war even as he steadily expanded the scope of that imminent war. Tojo was not only the functional head of Japan's civilian government—thereby effectively militarizing it—he also remained chief of the departments of war, education, commerce, and industry. Among his first acts as prime minister, "The Razor" cut the cords that connected him to any previous promises the Japanese may have made to the United States or other Western governments. Moreover, he declared Japan no longer under any obligation to negotiate with the United States. Japanese policy, he said, was now a "clean slate."

Tojo was very powerful at this point. The military was in control of the government, and he was the top administrator of that government. Yet it would be a mistake to see him as a dictator in the way that Mussolini and Hitler were dictators. Lofty though it was, Tojo's position was subordinate to the Supreme Command, a body consisting of both civilian and military leaders. Nominally, he was also, of course, subject to the will of the emperor, Hirohito (1901-1989); yet the Japanese monarch was a strange combination of semi-divinity and hollow figurehead. The people of the nations that were about to go to war with Japan—especially the United States—tended to see Hirohito as a mere puppet of the military. They saw Tojo, however, as the precise equivalent of Hitler and Mussolini.

On December 7, 1941, even as Japanese diplomats were in Washington, D.C., still meeting with American leaders in an ostensible effort to avert war, Japanese naval air forces launched a devastating surprise attack on the U.S. naval and army base at Pearl Harbor, Hawaii. In a single stroke, the U.S. Pacific Fleet was badly damaged: four battleships sunk, four more damaged, three cruisers damaged, three destroyers damaged, two other ships sunk, and three other ships damaged. One hundred eighty-eight navy and army aircraft were destroyed, almost all of them on the ground, and another 159 were damaged. Two thousand three hundred thirty-five sailors and soldiers were killed and another 1,143 wounded. For Japan, it was one of the great tactical victories of the war—yet it was also Japan's most catastrophic strategic defeat, for it propelled the United States to declare war against Japan.

President Franklin D. Roosevelt asked Congress for a war declaration on December 8. Tojo made a speech of his own at that time, broadcasting a radio message to the Japanese people, warning them that "to annihilate this enemy and to establish a stable new order in east Asia, the nation must necessarily anticipate a long war."

From the end of 1941 to 1944, Tojo often governed in the manner of a dictator, although his wide-ranging dictatorial powers in foreign and domestic affairs were always subject to the word of the Supreme Command. For most of the war, Prime Minister Tojo continued to serve as chief of the Army General Staff. In this position, he directed military operations with ruthless but hardly consummate skill. He never managed to develop a long-term strategy, and by 1944, it was increasingly clear that, under Tojo, Japan was losing the war. After the fall of Saipan to Allied forces on July 12, 1944, a coalition of Japanese statesmen exerted their influence to force Tojo's removal as military head. Shaken by his country's rapidly deteriorating military situation, Tojo did not protest but bowed to the coalition without a struggle.

On September 11, 1945, nine days after the surrender of Japan, U.S. soldiers bearing an arrest warrant surrounded Hideki Tojo's house. He responded not in the manner of a samurai, by committing *seppuku* with a ceremonial sword, but resorted to a far more modern method of suicide. He shot himself. The target he chose, however, was his own chest, not his head, and he missed his heart by a wide margin. Taken into custody, he was given medical treatment and, after he was out of danger, was committed to Sugamo Prison. When he was fully recovered from his self-inflicted wound, Tojo was bound over for trial by a newly created International Military Tribunal for the Far East. Made up of justices from the key Allies, the tribunal found Tojo guilty of a wide range of war crimes. Among these were the deaths of between three and fourteen million prisoners of war and civilians by massacre, execution, starvation, forced labor, and medical experimentation. Upon his conviction, Tojo quietly accepted the "entire responsibility for the war in general." Sentenced to death, he was hanged on December 23, 1948.

#6
BENITO MUSSOLINI

Apostle of Fascism in Italy and prototype for Hitler

Benito Mussolini with Adolf Hitler, June 1940. The photograph was seized by the U.S. government from the photo album of Eva Braun, Hitler's mistress, bride, and partner in suicide. (credit: *National Archives and Records Administration*)

Ideologically, World War II pitted against democratic governments—whose economies were based on free-market capitalism—a form of radical authoritarian nationalism, in which all power flowed from a dictatorial state that suppressed all political opposition, controlled industry and commerce, and engaged in ruthless conquest. While Adolf Hitler and Nazism are most often cited as the chief form of authoritarian nationalism in World War II, the essential model of that government and governing philosophy was fascism, and no figure is more closely associated with it than Benito Mussolini.

Because of Hitler's early admiration of Mussolini and his wartime alliance with him, the two dictators are forever linked in modern history. Yet Adolf Hitler and Benito Mussolini emerged from very different backgrounds. Whereas Hitler was the son of a minor Austrian government functionary—a civil servant—Benito Amilcare Andrea Mussolini, who was born on July 29, 1883, was the son of a blacksmith who lived in Dovia di Predappio, a village in the northern Italian province of Forli in the Romagna. At the time, this region was known as the "Red" Romagna because leftwing socialist sentiment was especially pervasive there. Alessandro Mussolini, his father, was an avid socialist, who chose his son's name to honor his heroes: the leftist Mexican nationalist revolutionary Benito Juárez and two prominent Italian socialists, Amilcare Cipriani and Andrea Costa. In contrast to his anti-Church father, Mussolini's mother, Rosa Maltoni, the local schoolmistress, was a conventionally observant Italian Roman Catholic. Alessandro often treated Benito and his two younger siblings brutally, whereas Rosa doted on him. Nevertheless, Benito took after his father. "My father was a blacksmith," Mussolini wrote in his 1928 *Autobiography,* "a heavy man with strong, large, fleshy hands. Alessandro the neighbors called him. Heart and mind were always filled and pulsing with socialistic theories. His intense sympathies mingled with doctrines and causes. He discussed them in the evening with his friends and his eyes filled with light."

Benito grew into a singularly spirited, even wild youth, who embraced his father's revolutionary beliefs. Yet he embellished these with the romantic, quasi-mystical tendencies of his mother, who encouraged her son's innate narcissism by praising him effusively and telling him that he was clearly destined for great things. He earned a local reputation as a violent bully. In church, he pinched other boys hard enough to make them cry. A childhood friend recalled that he was always ready and eager to start a fight and that he "sought quarrels for their own sake." In 1925, Mussolini's mistress and early political mentor, Margherita Sarfatti, wrote *The Life of Benito Mussolini*, in which she reported that five-year-old Benito positively terrorized the children in his mother's school. He targeted in particular a pretty seven-year-old girl, whom he frequently ambushed on her way from school, pulling her hair, forcing his kisses on her, then riding her as if she were a horse. When he'd had enough, he summarily ordered her home. At age nine, when he was packed off to a boarding school run by the Salesian fathers, Mussolini stabbed a fellow student with a knife and was expelled. Later, at another boarding school, he was suspended—again, for stabbing a classmate.

But he was no simple-minded brute. From adolescence on, Mussolini was a voracious reader, who consumed the works of such political philosophers as Louis Auguste Blanqui, Friedrich Wilhelm Nietszche, Niccolò Machiavelli, and the nineteenth-century French philosopher Georges Sorel (whose embrace of myth and defense of violence are often seen as direct precursors of fascism). When the time came to choose a career, he enrolled in the Salesian college of Faenza and then the teachers college, from which he obtained a teaching certificate. At age eighteen, Mussolini obtained a post as a provincial schoolteacher. He also traveled, living for several years in Switzerland and the Austrian Trentino. With this broadened experience behind him, he gave up teaching for socialist journalism, becoming editor of the Milan Socialist Party newspaper *Avanti!* in 1912. At this stage in his development, the socialist Mussolini was a pacifist, who wrote article after article arguing against Italy's entry into World War I only to suddenly abandon the socialist party line and passionately urge Italy's entry into the war on the side of the Allies. This was among the most momentous decisions of his life, and yet the almost casual shifting of intellectual gears would become a Mussolini trademark. Fascism was, in fact, so freighted with contradictions and irrationalities that, after Mussolini assumed power and commissioned a specially selected committee of scholars to write a comprehensive and definitive encyclopedia of this political philosophy, the scholars found it quite impossible to complete.

As for Mussolini's sudden embrace of Italian entry into the Great War, the Socialist Party responded by firing the young man as editor of *Avanti!* and finally expelling him from the party itself. Undaunted, he founded in Milan two newspapers of his own, *Il popolo d'Italia* (*The Italian People*) and *Fasci Rivoluzionari d'Azione Internazionalista* (*Revolutionary Fascists for International Action*). In the latter vehicle, he developed and broadcast the message of what became the fascist movement. First, however, Mussolini enlisted in the Italian army as a private in 1915, serving until he was wounded in the buttocks by trench mortar shrapnel early in 1917. Like Hitler, the highest rank he attained was corporal.

After recovering from his wounds, Mussolini resumed publication of his newspaper, and, on March 23, 1919, both encouraged and inspired by the flamboyant poet, novelist, patriot, and adventurer Gabriele d'Annunzio, he and other war veterans founded in Milan a revolutionary nationalistic group they called the Fasci di Combattimento—the Fasci of Combat, a name derived from the Italian word *fascio*, "bundle" or "bunch," which suggested unity, and the symbol of the *fasces*, a bundle of rods bound together around an ax with the blade protruding, the ancient Roman emblem of power.

The Fasci di Combattimento drew energy from outrage over the puny rump portion of the spoils of the Great War that the Treaty of Versailles awarded to Italy. The treaty gave the nation the Trentino and Trieste, but not, as had been promised by Britain and France when Italy agreed to enter the war, Fiume as well as the rest of Istria, Dalmatia, and the Dodecanese Islands. Nor was there the promised international recognition of an Italian "zone of influence" in Albania. As for Jubaland in Africa, which Britain had pledged in the secret Treaty of London to cede to Italy, no action was taken. Thanks to the incompetence of its military leadership, Italy had suffered horrific casualties in the war and, it seemed, had received little in return.

Mussolini blamed the Italian government of Prime Minister Vittorio Orlando, whom he denounced as a traitor. He also denounced the Italian Socialist Party for its continued policy of internationalism, and when the party invited to Italy hungry children from Vienna—capital city of the former Austro-Hungarian Empire, Italy's foe—Mussolini fulminated. Italian children were also hungry, he cried. Why not raise money to feed *them?*

Beyond the Orlando government and the Italian Socialist Party, Mussolini attacked the other Allies—and most of the rest of the world, for that matter—for having turned against Italy. He condemned the newly established League of Nations, which he had supported in the newspapers he edited, as part of an international plot to crush Italy's bid for empire. Mussolini demanded that Italy annex Fiume and Dalmatia with or without international consent. He also wanted Italy to send military aid to the peoples of India, Egypt, and Ireland, who were rebelling against the English, whom he condemned as perfidious Anglo-Saxons. Hitler, early in his rise, had developed the theory of the "big lie": repeat the biggest of untruths loudly and often enough, and the masses will believe them. Well before Hitler, Mussolini, the journalist agitator, learned that even the boldest reversals and self-contradictions could be made palatable if they were sufficiently extreme and stated with sufficient vehemence. Extremism, Mussolini discovered, appealed to people.

In outrage over betrayal by the Treaty of Versailles, Mussolini found the most fertile soil in which to develop the Fasci di Combattimento into a mass political movement and a new political party. Yet the Fasci di Combattimento were slow to kindle much popular enthusiasm. In the turbulence of postwar Italy, the new party looked like nothing more than a miscellaneous gathering of anarchists, communists, syndicalists, republicans, nationalists, Catholics, and liberals. Only one faction among the new Fasci drew early attention beyond the party itself. These were the "Futurists," led by the artist Filippo Tommaso Marinetti. He had coined the word "Futurism" in a 1909 manifesto written and titled in French *Le Futurisme*. He now called on Italians to create a new art, an art that embodied the beauty of speed and that glorified the violence of war. Art, Marinetti wrote, was the very essence of violence, cruelty, and injustice. By the time he and some of his followers joined the Fasci di Combattimento, Marinetti aimed not merely to reinvent art, but life itself. In the population of the modern, technological world he saw the opportunity to create a new technological race of human beings, their powers vastly multiplied and magnified by their machines.

Aside from Marinetti's declarations, early fascism espoused pretty standard revolutionary stuff. The Fasci shared an anticlerical point of view, they opposed the Church, and they wanted the government to nationalize and confiscate Church property not used directly in worship. They wanted to see an end to the monarchy, but they did not favor a dictatorship or any other form of arbitrary, absolute, central power. The judiciary was to be independent of any other branch of government. The Fasci further demanded an end to any sort of government censorship, whether on moral, religious, or political grounds. They demanded suffrage for all Italians over the age of eighteen, without regard to property ownership. Women were to be given the vote as well as men. The first meeting of the Fasci as a political party also called for reform of the Chamber of Deputies, the lower house of the Italian parliament. A system of proportional representation was to be demanded, and the qualifying age for election as a deputy was to be lowered from thirty-one to twenty-five. The upper house of parliament, the Senate, was to be abolished, and newly elected deputies were to form a National Assembly to draw up a new constitution for Italy. For the present, it was agreed that the constitution would guarantee an eight-hour workday.

It dawned on Mussolini that the program of the Fasci di Combattimento was fairly indistinguishable from that of Italian socialism. Then came April 15, 1919, and Mussolini saw a way to transform the nascent party into something new and unique.

Among the assorted groups whose members gravitated to the Fasci di Combattimento were loosely constituted gangs of discharged Italian soldiers known as the *arditi*, the "intrepid ones." The *arditi* of postwar Italy were roughly similar to the *Freikorps* of postwar Germany, although far less organized. (The German Freikorps was a collection of private armies recruited by former senior officers in the demobilized German army to defend Germany's borders against what was believed to be an impending invasion by the Soviet Red Army. After this menace apparently passed, the Freikorps took it upon itself to oppose all homegrown attempts at revolution in Germany by beating up—and sometimes killing—left-wing radicals and demonstrators.)

Ferruccio Vecchi, a member of the Fasci di Combattimento, was an *arditi* leader. On April 15, with Marinetti, he led the *arditi* in an attack on the offices of the socialist newspaper—Mussolini's former employer—*Avanti!* They destroyed a printing press, a linotype machine, and the paper's subscription list. Then the violence spread to the street, and a full-scale riot erupted. Although Mussolini did not participate in this, he exploited the riot to begin recruiting his own personal force of *arditi* and, using funds from *Il Popolo d'Italia*, purchased cheap military-surplus arms and ammunition with which to equip his men. He transformed his editorial offices into an armory. At this point, Mussolini also added a new enemy to oppose. It was not just the government that needed to be overthrown, it was the menace of international Communism spawned by the Russian Revolutions of 1917 and spread by the Moscow-based Comintern, the international communist movement.

Now Fascism quickly evolved from its origins in leftwing socialism to become a radical rightwing, anti-Communist nationalism. Mussolini captured the public's imagination and support with a nationalist message opposing Communism and infused with gauzy visions of restoring to modern Italy its ancient imperial Roman grandeur and global authority. Mussolini's new fascist message proved popular not only with the common man, but with avant-garde artists like Marinetti and literary figures, most notably d'Annunzio. The anti-Communist message resonated powerfully with large landowners in the lower Po valley, leading industrialists, and senior army officers. Money began pouring into the party, and Mussolini funded the transition of the *arditi* into a large private army of thugs known as the Blackshirts. These men—who would serve Hitler as a model for his *Sturmabteilung* (Storm Troopers, or SA)—waged a street-level civil war against all comers: Socialists, Communists, Catholics, and Liberals.

By 1922, Mussolini sensed that he had a decisive fraction of the Italian people behind him, including the support of the rich and powerful and key cultural influencers. On October 28-29, he organized a fascist "March on Rome," in which some 30,000 Blackshirts and others assembled on the plain of the Po River and then advanced, en masse, into Rome. It was a bloodless demonstration that nevertheless so intimidated King Victor Emmanuel III that the monarch formed a coalition government with what was now called the National Fascist Party. As the party's leader, Mussolini obtained from the king the kind of power enjoyed by the dictators of ancient Rome. He was given dictatorial authority set for a period of one year. His brief was to achieve nothing less than the transformation of Italy's ailing economic structure into a healthy, modern economy.

Backed by prominent industrialists and bankers, Mussolini slashed government expenses for public services, reduced taxes on industry to encourage production, and both centralized and consolidated government bureaucracy. The result was indeed remarkable, as the Italian economy suddenly took on new life. People said of Mussolini that he "made the trains run on time." More to point, he made the trains run, period.

During his initial dictatorial year, Mussolini replaced the king's guard with his own Blackshirts and a secret police force called the Orva. These organizations were invaluable in suppressing all opposition. At the same time, he greatly increased Italy's international prestige when he responded to the murder of some Italian officials at the hands of bandits on the Greek-Albanian border by demanding a huge indemnity from the Greek government, then bombarding and seizing the Greek island of Corfu. He also negotiated an agreement with Yugoslavia to obtain Italian possession of long-contested Fiume.

In the beginning, Mussolini took care to avoid attacking labor, even though he did not hesitate to brutally suppress strikes that threatened to cripple the nation's industry. The reinvigoration of the economy pleased the wealthy but also trickled down to the common man. Feeling that he had the support of the people, Mussolini took the bold step in 1924 of publicly renouncing his dictatorial powers and calling for new elections. It was not the act of altruistic democracy that it seemed. Mussolini had prepared for the gesture by engineering passage of legislation that guaranteed the Fascist Party a two-thirds parliamentary majority regardless of the outcome of the popular vote. His power, ostensibly relinquished, was, in fact, guaranteed.

Among the handful of Socialists elected in 1924 despite Fascist domination was Giacomo Matteotti, who made a series of withering speeches in opposition to Mussolini and his party. Matteotti exposed Fascist political outrages that ranged from acts of intimidation and violence, to misuse of public funds, to political assassination. Shortly after these speeches, however, Matteotti's own murdered body was discovered. This touched off a protracted parliamentary crisis, and, emboldened, the opposition press attacked Mussolini and his followers. Mussolini responded by dropping all pretense of democracy. He wielded his absolute power absolutely, imposing on Italy a single-party dictatorship by outlawing all other political parties. He augmented this with a policy of strict censorship. Mussolini dispatched his Blackshirts to terrorize would-be opponents, and one liberal editor was even beaten to death.

Mussolini also found his moment to move openly against labor, solidifying his power base among Italian capitalists by abolishing free trade unions. At the same time, he coopted the Catholic church by negotiating with the Vatican the Lateran Treaty of 1929, by which Vatican City was established as an independent state under the absolute temporal sovereignty of the pope.

The Lateran Treaty of 1929 was the last step in the elevation of Benito Mussolini to absolute dictator of Italy. He was now universally hailed as *Il Duce*, "the Leader," and he turned from domestic policy to the prosecution of an aggressively expansionist foreign policy during the balance of the 1930s.

Seizing as pretext a clash over a disputed zone on the Italian Somaliland border, he invaded Ethiopia during 1935-1936 without a declaration of war, unleashing aerial bombardment and poison gas on the civilian population. On May 9, 1936, Italy annexed the African nation. When the nation's emperor, Haile Selassie I, laid his country's case before the League of

Nations, that post-World War I precursor of the United Nations proved incapable of materially opposing Italy's actions. The impotence of the League convinced both Mussolini and his admirer Adolf Hitler that the European democracies lacked the will to interfere with the acts of a truly strong and ruthless leader.

During the 1930s, Mussolini also assisted Generalissimo Francisco Franco in the Spanish Civil War, helping him to establish a fascist government in Spain. Between 1936 and 1939, Mussolini further developed a fateful alliance with Adolf Hitler's Germany. In 1937, Italy joined Japan in the Anti-Comintern Pact with Germany. Two years later, after Italy annexed Albania, came the "Pact of Steel," by which Germany acknowledged Italy's hegemony over both Ethiopia and Albania and extolled the "close relationship of friendship and homogeneity...between Nationalist Socialist Germany and Fascist Italy." In contrast to most military alliances, which are activated only in the event that one of the signatories is attacked, the "Pact of Steel" was to become active "If, contrary to the wishes and hopes of the High Contracting parties, it should happen that one of them became in warlike complications with another Power or Powers." Furthermore, the treaty called for ongoing "collaboration in the military field, and in the field of war economy." It was, in effect, a contract creating an unprecedented offensive military partnership.

Yet, even as Mussolini sent his armies to occupy Albania, he stayed out of World War II, which Germany had begun on September 1, 1939, by invading Poland. By June 1940, however, after the fall of France seemed inevitable, Mussolini was persuaded that Germany was invincible. This prompted him to sign the Tripartite Pact of September 27, 1940. It united Germany, Italy, and Japan in an ostensibly defensive military alliance—an "Axis"—that was, in fact, a three-way partnership in a war-making enterprise.

Yet the war never went well for Mussolini's Italy. Conquering the relatively primitive Ethiopian army was one thing, but against more sophisticated powers, the Italian military suffered one disaster after another in Greece and North Africa. By the middle of World War II, with the United States now in the fight, the fortunes of Italy were in sharp, irreversible decline, and the popular tide was rapidly turning against *Il Duce*. The leaders of his own party began to desert him, and on July 25, 1943, King Victor Emmanuel III formally dismissed Mussolini as premier, ordering his arrest. The Grand Council of Fascism voted a motion of no confidence, and Mussolini was summarily replaced by Marshal Pietro Badoglio, who, following the king's command, effected Mussolini's arrest.

At this point, Adolf Hitler intervened by sending a daring rescue mission under SS Captain Otto Skorzeny, who, in an aerial mission consisting of gliders and a light *Storch* (Stork) observation aircraft, liberated Mussolini from Campo Imperatore in Italy's Gran Sasso massif in the Apennines on September 12. Skorzeny presented himself to Mussolini by announcing, "Duce, the Führer has sent me to set you free!"

"I knew that my friend would not forsake me!" Mussolini replied.

Il Duce was flown to Germany and then, at the behest of Hitler, returned to northern Italy as the puppet leader of the Italian Social Republic—also called the Republic of Salò—a much-reduced portion of the Italian peninsula. By the spring of 1945, Allied forces had retaken most of the Salò republic and were rapidly closing in on Mussolini himself. In April, Mussolini and his mistress, Clara (Claretta) Petacci, set out for Switzerland with the object of flying from there to Franco's Spain—a fascist country, but one that had remained neutral throughout the war. On April 27, Mussolini, Petacci, and fifteen others (officials of the Salò government) were intercepted by communist partisans near the village of Dongo on Lake Como. From here, they were brought to Mezzegra. Despite earlier agreements between the Italian partisans and the Allies that, if captured, Mussolini would be turned over for trial as a war criminal, a partisan known to history only as Colonnello Valerio ordered the execution of Mussolini and the other Italian Social Republic officials with him. Clara Petacci was given the opportunity to flee, but she chose to stand with her lover. She was executed, by firing squad, with her paramour and the others.

On April 29, 1945, all of the bodies were transported by van to Milan, where they were dumped on the ground at the Piazzale Loreto. The corpses were unceremoniously hung from their heels, suspended, half naked, from the overhanging outdoor roof of an Esso filling station. There, a crowd of Milanese stoned, battered, and spat upon them until they were unrecognizable.

#7
JOSEPH STALIN

The Western Allies' strangest bedfellow

Joseph Stalin, official photograph as Secretary General of the Communist Party of the Soviet Union, 1942. (credit: *Library of Congress*)

Collaborator with Vladimir Lenin in the creation of the Soviet state, Stalin maneuvered to succeed him as leader of the Communist Party and Russian government. Stalin managed to honor the cult of personality that had grown up around Lenin while simultaneously fostering an even larger and more passionate cult about himself. In the years between the world wars, Stalin became the icon of the international communist revolutionary movement and was, in fact, universally hailed by both communists and liberals in democratic nations for his opposition to the growing fascist and Nazi movements.

By the 1930s, the Western world was becoming polarized between the ideology of communism, represented by Stalin, and that of fascism and Nazism, represented chiefly by Mussolini and Hitler. So powerful was the identification of each of these dictators with their respective ideologies that world leaders, politicians, and others who opposed fascism and Nazism embraced Stalin. In doing this, they turned a blind eye to the reality that whatever political leaders in the so-called Age of Great Dictators might label themselves—fascists, Nazis, or communists—they were, first and last, all brutal tyrants. While the lawless violence wielded by Hitler and Mussolini (and, in Spain after the Spanish Civil War, Francisco Franco) was condemned by leaders of the free world as well as political leftists, the very same violence and persecution was minimized or even denied when perpetrated by Stalin. The fact is that nobody knows just how many Russians were killed at Stalin's behest during the period of his power, 1924 to 1953, but estimates—excluding battle deaths in World War II itself—range from a low of 8.5 million to a high of more than sixty million, with a median figure of about thirty million. These numbers include millions who perished in the great famines brought on by the forced collectivization of Russian farms—a cataclysmic failure that depressed food production far below the levels required to sustain life. They also encompass the millions executed or exiled (a fate that often as not resulted in death) during Stalin's Great Purge of 1934-1939.

Throughout most of the interwar years, Stalin and his government so thoroughly managed the information emerging from Russia, creating a magnificent domestic and international propaganda machine, that Stalin was widely revered as "Uncle Joe," the avuncular, kind, and wise leader-guide of the Russian people. Hence the profound shock created in August of 1939 when Stalin and Hitler, through their foreign ministers Vycheslav Molotov and Joachim von Ribbentrop, concluded a Non-Aggression Pact between Nazi Germany and Communist Russia. Here, at last, was proof that totalitarianism, as a mode of governing, trumps all ideology, even those that are diametrically opposed.

If Stalin and Hitler were strange bedfellows, Hitler's betrayal of Stalin with Operation Barbarossa, the German invasion of the Soviet Union beginning on June 22, 1941, instantly rehabilitated Uncle Joe in the West by thrusting him into the arms of the British and, soon, the Americans in an alliance against Hitler. The Allied propaganda machine worked overtime to portray Joseph Stalin as a hero in defense of civilization.

Born Josef Vissarionovich Djugashvili on December 21, 1879, in Gori, a hill town in tsarist Georgia, Stalin endured a brutal childhood at the hands of his alcoholic and abusive father, an impoverished shoemaker. After his father's death in a brawl, eleven-year-old Josef was indulged by his doting mother, who groomed him for the Orthodox priesthood. By the time he entered the Tiflis Theological Seminary at age fourteen, however, the youth's rebelliousness had earned him the nickname Koba, after a legendary Georgian bandit and rebel. He quickly bridled under the harsh corporal discipline of the seminary and, by 1898, became involved in radical anti-tsarist political activity. In 1899, he abruptly left the seminary to become a full-time revolutionary organizer. Within three more years, he was a member of the Georgian branch of the Social Democratic party, touring the Caucasus, stirring up laborers, and organizing strikes. Like his German contemporary, Adolf Hitler, young Koba came from a squalid and brutal family background and showed remarkably little early promise. Unlike Hitler, the aspiring Georgian revolutionary possessed neither personal magnetism nor appreciable rhetorical skills. What he did have in abundance was fearlessness, ruthlessness, and a positive genius for organization.

In 1903, the Social Democrats split into two groups, Vladimir I. Lenin's radical Bolshevik ("majority") faction and the more moderate faction Lenin dubbed the Mensheviks, meaning the "minority." He had chosen both labels specifically because the Mensheviks actually outnumbered the Bolsheviks. Lenin put more value on what people called things than on the things themselves. For him, perception was reality—and that was a lesson Stalin would learn well as he fell in with the radicals and grew close to Lenin. For the next decade, from 1903 until he was exiled to Siberia in 1913, Stalin worked to expand the party's power, organizing cell after cell across the nation and financing the party's work by planning and executing daring robberies. His activities caused him to be arrested many times, but he always managed to escape. In 1912, Lenin elevated him to the Bolshevik Central Committee, the party's inner circle. Though taciturn and even downright inarticulate, Stalin became the first editor of *Pravda* (*Truth*), the Bolsheviks' official propaganda organ in the guise of a newspaper. As for Josef Vissarionovich Djugashvili, he also took a new name for himself. It was *Stalin*—literally, "Man of Steel."

In 1913, Stalin's talent for escaping capture and punishment at last failed him, and he was sentenced by the tsar to Siberian exile. He endured this through four fateful years, returning to Russia only after the overthrow of Tsar Nicholas II in March 1917. In the wake of the failure of the first Bolshevik attempt to seize power during the summer of 1917—and in the absence of Leon Trotsky, who had been arrested, and Lenin, who had gone into hiding—Stalin worked alone to reorganize the party, thereby playing a major role in its successful acquisition of power during the November Revolution. With Lenin's return from self-imposed exile, Stalin was given a succession of commissar posts, all the while working quietly to consolidate greater power for himself.

By 1922, considerable friction was developing between Lenin and Stalin, especially concerning the nature of the Soviet state, the creation of which the two men were leading. Lenin wanted to create a nation to be renamed the Union of Soviet Republics of Europe and Asia, to reflect his vision of expansion across the two continents. Stalin, whose outlook was more forcefully totalitarian, was concerned that this name would foster a drive for independence among non-Russians. He argued for making the ethnic minorities "autonomous republics" within what he proposed calling the Russian Soviet Federative Socialist Republic. This brought Lenin's condemnation of Stalin for "Great Russian chauvinism." In response, Stalin accused Lenin of manifesting "national liberalism." As the men came to loggerheads, a compromise was hammered out by which the new communist country would be renamed the Union of Soviet Socialist Republics (USSR).

The USSR was formally created in December 1922—but this did not resolve the growing friction between Stalin and Lenin, who spent what would prove to be the last two years of Lenin's life writing or dictating notes that criticized Stalin. These became the founder's last political testament, and when he died in 1924, Stalin's opponents read them publicly.

Stalin responded with a show of humility that included an offer to resign as Communist Party General Secretary even as he made a great demonstration of reverence for the departed Lenin. The combination of humility and piety resulted in the public perception that he had been the Communist leader's handpicked successor. With his position solidified, Stalin ruthlessly set about to eliminate—one way or another—all who opposed him.

Stalin quickly demonstrated his ability and willingness to manipulate ideology in order to ensure his personal supremacy. He began by announcing a retreat from Lenin's ideal of world communist revolution by advocating what he called "socialism in one country." He also proposed an economic program far less radical than what others who had been close to Lenin envisioned. Leon Trotsky, Lev Kamenev, and Grigory Zinoviev, all party leftists, responded by going on the offensive against Stalin and his moderate policies. It was to no avail. By 1928, Stalin had consolidated the party's right wing in opposition to the left and thereby managed to oust the leftist leadership. Having accomplished this, he performed an abrupt about-face and summarily adopted radical leftist economic programs, including the wholesale collectivization of agriculture and greatly accelerated industrialization. This maneuver allowed him to attack those he saw as his rivals in the party's right wing, led by Nikolai Bukharin. Thus, within a year, opposition on the left *and* on the right was crushed, leaving Stalin absolute dictator of the Soviet Union.

Stalin's whipsaw maneuvers came at a terrible cost. The effort to force the rapid transformation of the Soviet Union from a primarily agricultural nation into a modern industrial power required the sacrifice of human life on an unprecedented scale. This prospect gave him no pause. Late in 1928, he summarily expropriated the lands of the middle-class farmers (called "kulaks"), "deporting" (exiling them to Siberia) or executing those who offered resistance. Stalin's bureaucracy promulgated a series of "five-year plans," by which collectivization and industrialization were to be simultaneously achieved. His administration adhered rigorously to the plans, raising capital to finance industrialization by exporting grain and other produce—despite an increasingly devastating famine that swept the Soviet Union in 1932. Millions who resisted were executed, and millions more starved to death.

A comprehensive but far from definitive 1988 estimate put the number of deaths that directly resulted from the forced collectivization of 1928-1933 at twenty-five million.

During the period of the first five-year plan, opposition to Stalin mounted, and there was a short-lived peasant revolt, which the dictator easily crushed. When the Seventeenth Party Congress showed support for Sergei Kirov, a moderate and a potential rival, Stalin engineered his assassination in December 1934. Having disposed of Kirov, he then used his murder as a pretext for arresting most of the party's highest-ranking officials as counter-revolutionary conspirators. Through 1939, Stalin conducted a long series of public "show trials" in which party officials and many in the senior officer corps of the Red Army were convicted of outrageous crimes or acts of treason. The results of the "Great Purge" were devastating. By 1939, ninety-eight of the 139 central committee members elected in 1934 had been executed, and 1,108 of the 1,966 delegates to the Seventeenth Congress arrested. Even worse, under KGB (secret police) chief Lavrenti Beria, agents arrested, shot, exiled, or imprisoned millions of individuals in the general population. By the eve of World War II, Stalin had destroyed all serious opposition and had terrorized his nation into submission even as he built it into an industrial giant and created about himself an unassailable cult of personal worship. What he failed to appreciate, however, was that the Great Purge had taken a heavy toll on the senior officer ranks of the Red Army, stripping it of leaders who would be sorely missed in the world war to come.

As Adolf Hitler came to dominate more and more of Europe in the late 1930s, Stalin lost any desire to oppose this ideological antithesis of communism. In what he clearly saw as the conflict to come, Stalin made overtures to the leaders of the Western democratic powers but was rebuffed. So, at last, he turned instead to Hitler himself, concluding a Nazi-Soviet non-aggression pact on August 23, 1939. Via a secret portion of the agreement, Hitler and Stalin agreed that Germany would invade Poland but leave the eastern part of that country available for Russian invasion and annexation. When Germany invaded Poland beginning on September 1, 1939, Stalin moved to increase Soviet influence in the West by invading Finland on November 30,

1939. A brief but very costly war (The Winter War, November 30, 1939-March 13, 1940) secured Finland's surrender.

All looked promising for the Soviet Union in a world at war for the second time in the twentieth century. Then, on June 22, 1941, Hitler summarily abrogated the non-aggression pact with Operation Barbarossa, a surprise invasion of the Soviet Union.

Early resistance to the invasion was poorly coordinated, in large part because Stalin's purges had stripped the Red Army of thousands in its senior officer corps and because the invasion stunned Stalin into a kind of mental paralysis. Yet, after an initial period of panic and disorganization, he more than rose to the occasion, taking personal command of the Red Army and organizing an increasingly effective counterforce. Stalin acted swiftly to move vital war industries east, into Siberia and Central Asia, just ahead of the advancing German juggernaut. He rallied the Soviet people by appealing to patriotism and even disbanded the Communist International and officially rehabilitated the Orthodox Church—moves intended to reconnect the people with the traditions of Russia. Despite the damage he himself had inflicted upon his officer corps, Stalin identified dependable—even brilliant—commanders in Marshals Georgi Zhukov and Ivan Konev, supporting them in extremely costly but ultimately successful campaigns against the invaders.

Stalin himself took an active hand in planning strategy and campaigns, revealing a distinct military talent. Indeed, by the middle of the war, Stalin had earned substantial international prestige as a military leader and was in a strong negotiating position at the major Allied wartime conferences conducted in Tehran, Yalta, and Potsdam. By the end of the war, many Russians—and others—were once again willing to overlook the enormities of Stalin's regime, the foolhardiness and moral repugnance of his short-lived alliance with Hitler, and his early stumbles in the conduct of the war. He was now almost universally hailed as the savior of his nation when Germany surrendered on May 8, 1945.

Having triumphed over Hitler, Stalin did not hesitate to institute a new regime of terror and repression at home, imposing more taxes on peasants and announcing fresh discoveries of anti-communist sabotage and conspiracy.

Hard on the heels of victory in World War II, the dictator aggressively expanded the Soviet sphere of influence into neighboring regions, setting up puppet regimes and client states among the nations of the Balkans and eastern Europe, creating what Winston Churchill called an "Iron Curtain" separating the communist realm from the rest of the world, and touching off more than four decades of so-called Cold War between Soviet-aligned nations and the West, especially the United States.

In 1953, Stalin declared that he had discovered a plot among the Kremlin's cadre of physicians, and the Soviet people trembled on the brink of what seemed a certain and imminent round of new blood purges. Doubtless, the people's dread would have been amply justified had the dictator not died on March 5, 1953, of a massive cerebral hemorrhage before he could implement his program.

Under Stalin the Soviet Union had borne the heaviest burden in the European theater of World War II. Without question, his leadership and the resources of the Red Army were indispensable to the Allied victory in that conflict. On the other hand, his prodigal bloodletting during the 1930s, his early embrace of Adolf Hitler, and his strategic errors during the early phase of the German invasion of Russia cost his nation very dearly. A cruel and incredibly complex leader, he was engulfed in political paranoia that caused him to purge key political as well as military leaders. These actions made Russia vulnerable to attack and invasion. There can be no denying, however, that he also built the Soviet Union into an industrial power and a military superpower, whose only rival after World War II was the United States.

#8

FRANKLIN DELANO ROOSEVELT

*America's war president and democracy's answer
to the Age of Great Dictators*

Franklin Delano Roosevelt, whom polio (or possibly Guillain-Barré Syndrome)
left as paraplegic, never appeared in public in his wheelchair, making this a rare
photo. He is seen with his beloved Scottie, Falla, and Ruthie Bie, granddaughter of
the caretaker of FDR's Hyde Park, New York, home. The photograph was taken at
Top Cottage, Hyde Park, by the president's sixth cousin and confidante, Margaret
Suckley, who later served as archivist of the Roosevelt Presidential Library.
(credit: *FDR Presidential Library and Museum*)

Franklin Roosevelt was a most unlikely warrior. He had been born, on January 30, 1882, into a world of privilege and raised on a genteel estate at Hyde Park, New York. His father, already fifty-two when Franklin was born, was an austere, even remote figure. His mother, however, doted on her son to the point of suffocation. She oversaw his education, at home, by governesses and tutors, until he was fifteen. At that point, he was enrolled at Groton School in Massachusetts. It was a fortunate departure for the youngster. The school smelled of old American money, but its head-master, Endicott Peabody, was a socially conscious progressive, who taught his students that their privileged circumstances imposed on them weighty responsibilities. Peabody frequently quoted the New Testament Parable of the Faithful Servant (Luke 12:48): "For unto whomsoever much is given, of him shall be much required: and to whom men have committed much, of him they will ask the more." Wealth, the headmaster taught, carries with it a debt to society: an obligation to create a better world. Young Franklin Roosevelt was not a brilliant student, but this lesson was never lost on him.

From Groton, Roosevelt went on to Harvard, from which he gradu-ated in 1904. He passed through the institution without particularly dis-tinguishing himself, but it was during these years that he fell in love with Anna Eleanor Roosevelt, his fifth cousin once removed and the niece of President Theodore Roosevelt. Married in 1905, the couple had a fruitful union, five children (a sixth died in infancy) in eleven years. Outwardly, the marriage was decorous and apparently satisfactory yet inwardly troubled. Overbearing as a mother, Sara Delano Roosevelt was tyrannical as a mother-in-law. Continually forced to divide his allegiance between Eleanor and his mother, Franklin was often unfaithful. Nevertheless, what he and Eleanor had proved to be a profound partnership. Eleanor effectively completed the moral picture Headmaster Peabody had sketched. Like her husband, she was born to wealth, but from an early age, she practiced what Peabody preached. She was a social activist who kindled in her husband a deepening social consciousness. He attended Columbia University Law School until the spring semester of 1907, when, after passing the New York state bar examination, he joined a Wall Street firm and never returned to Columbia to complete his law degree. Moreover, while practicing corporate law was the kind of gentlemanly yet lucrative profession expected among those of his social circle, Roosevelt found it dull and empty. He volunteered to take the cases no one else in the firm wanted to touch—the low-paying matters for "small" clients and *pro bono* work for the downright indigent.

His work among poorer clients prompted Roosevelt to run for the New York State Senate on the Democratic ticket. A natural politician, he won handily, even though he ran in a heavily Republican district. As a legislator, he quickly earned a reputation as a progressive reformer and a foe of New York's infamous Tammany Hall political machine. He earned a minor national reputation with his vigorous support for the presidential candidacy of Woodrow Wilson in 1912 and, for himself, won reelection to the state senate—only to resign his seat when President Wilson offered him the sub-cabinet post of assistant secretary of the navy under Secretary of the Navy Josephus Daniels.

The post was appealing to Roosevelt for two reasons. First, as an avid amateur sailor, he loved ships and the sea; second, the appointment took him to Washington and into the fringes of national politics. Nor was it lost on him that Eleanor's uncle Theodore had begun his national political career with an appointment as assistant secretary of the navy. Much like TR, FDR distinguished himself in a post that was ordinarily more or less anonymous. Josephus Daniels was an old man, as slow-moving as he was affable. Franklin Roosevelt, in contrast, was downright dynamic. After the Great War erupted in Europe in the summer of 1914, Roosevelt revealed himself as a passionate advocate of war preparedness, including the rapid development of a large navy backed by a globally engaged foreign policy. Personally, Roosevelt favored U.S. entry into the war sooner rather than later, and in 1918, the year after President Wilson took the nation to war, he visited the Western Front.

Yet Roosevelt had no special affinity for military tactics or strategy. His talent was political, and he found that he could deal effectively with people on all levels and of every class—from admirals, to legislators, to departmental bureaucrats, to shipyard union leaders. He triumphed over corruption, collusive bidding, and price-fixing among naval contractors, and Daniels routinely used him as his ramrod to get things done. It was with a modest but growing national reputation that Roosevelt cheerfully accepted nomination as the Democratic vice-presidential candidate, running with Governor James M. Cox of Ohio. The young politician knew that, in the isolationist political atmosphere of post-World War I America, he and Cox stood no chance against Republican Warren G. Harding and his promise of a "return to normalcy." But he relished the exposure and the opportunity to campaign. Following the anticipated defeat, he returned to the practice of law, established his own firm, and accepted appointment as vice president of a financial enterprise, biding his time for the next political opportunity.

Then life took a detour. While vacationing at the Roosevelt family compound in Campobello Island, New Brunswick, Canada, in August 1921, Roosevelt contracted a disease diagnosed as polio. (Some recent medical authorities believe that it was more likely another neurological affliction, Guillain-Barré syndrome.) The illness left him a paraplegic, his legs paralyzed. The assumption was that his political life was over. His mother in particular treated him as an invalid and tried to persuade him to retire from all pursuits. Among his inner circle, only Eleanor Roosevelt encouraged him to resist despair and defeat. With her support, Roosevelt fought his way to recovery, managed to stand and walk with the aid of leg braces, and even drove himself in an automobile modified with hand controls. His public comeback was a dramatic appearance at the 1924 Democratic National Convention, where he delivered a stirring nomination speech on behalf of the presidential candidacy of Al Smith. Four years after this, Roosevelt was elected governor of New York. The victory was made sweeter by its having been won during a year that was otherwise a Republican sweep.

Roosevelt served two terms as governor, battling a majority Republican legislature to usher in many progressive reforms, including several that prefigured the New Deal he would introduce as president: a reforestation program, state-supported old-age pensions and unemployment insurance, forward-looking labor legislation, and the public development of rural electric power. As the Great Depression deepened in 1931, Roosevelt became the nation's first governor to establish an effective state relief administration. He also introduced the so-called Fireside Chat, making innovative use of the still-new medium of radio to broadcast informal addresses to America. Direct, informal, and frank communication with the people would become a hallmark of FDR's presidential leadership during the Depression and World War II. In an emerging "Age of Great Dictators," as the run-up to the war was often called, Roosevelt came to apply his eloquence, his empathy, and his unwavering optimism to counter a flood of totalitarian messages with the enduring narrative of democracy. In this way, he would enter the world stage as a formidable ideological, emotional, political, and spiritual presence.

FDR's policies as New York governor were accepted by many other states as a pattern for relief and recovery during the economic crisis. With the nation focused on him, Roosevelt received the 1932 Democratic presidential nomination, which he accepted with a speech in which he declared: "I pledge you, I pledge myself, to a new deal for the American people."

That "New Deal" was breathtaking in scope, encompassing massive federal spending for relief and public works, a plan to curb the agricultural overproduction that was depressing farm prices, a policy of conservation of environmental resources, a program to generate public electric power, a program to provide old-age pensions and unemployment insurance, and a policy to regulate the stock exchange. The American people approved, and Roosevelt defeated incumbent president Herbert Hoover by a landslide. He was inaugurated on March 4, 1933, at the very nadir of the Depression amid runaway unemployment, an epidemic of bank failures, and a general panic. He announced, in his inaugural address, that "The only thing we have to fear is fear itself," and he told the American people that he intended to obtain from Congress "the one remaining instrument to meet the crisis—broad executive power to wage a war against the emergency, as great as the power that would be given to me if we were in fact invaded by a foreign foe." The Great Depression was to be the war he fought before World War II.

He attacked the crisis with the aggressive élan of a great general. In a Napoleonic echo, the opening months of the administration were dubbed "the Hundred Days," and they saw the introduction of a dazzling array of unprecedented programs and agencies, including the Federal Emergency Relief Administration, the Civil Works Administration (CWA), the Home Owners Loan Corporation (HOLC), the Public Works Administration (PWA), and the Civilian Conservation Corps (CCC). The CCC was, in fact, a civilian army, organized along military lines and led in part by serving military officers. It employed more than 2.5 million young men in conservation work. HOLC furnished emergency assistance to mortgagors and homeowners, enabling the latter to avoid foreclosure, and the PWA created great public works projects. In addition to emergency relief, the New Deal included agencies of long-range reform. The Federal Deposit Insurance Corporation (FDIC) insured bank deposits, the Securities and Exchange Commission (SEC) inaugurated the regulation of the stock exchanges, and the Tennessee Valley Authority (TVA) built great multipurpose dams to control floods and generate cheap hydroelectric power.

The effectiveness of the New Deal in helping to end the Depression is still hotly debated. That it provided emergency relief, however, is beyond doubt, as are the ways it demonstrated President Roosevelt's vigor, aggressive approach, strategic flexibility, ability to inspire, and his compassion. The economic emergency also required him to navigate a most perilous course between preserving democracy, capitalism, and a free market economy, on the one hand, while providing needed government intervention, support, and control on the other. Buoyed by overwhelming public approval, Roosevelt pushed the envelope with the New Deal, introducing in his second term a "court reform" plan that amounted to an attempt to pack the Supreme Court with judges favorable to many of his constitutionally questionable programs. The court itself overruled it.

No sooner did controversies involving the New Deal flare up than the rise of Italy's Benito Mussolini and Germany's Adolf Hitler and the growth of a military dictatorship in Japan eclipsed them in the public mind. Fear of a new world war became widespread. Roosevelt employed an intensely personal brand of diplomacy in an effort to gather allies. He proffered diplomatic recognition to the Soviet Union at a time when much of the international community refused to do so. He developed a network of reciprocal trade agreements and, seeking to create solidarity among the governments of the Western Hemisphere, instituted a "good neighbor policy" toward the nations of Latin America. Even as these positive steps were made, war clouds darkened. In accepting the Democratic nomination to run for a second term, Roosevelt declared, "This generation of Americans has a rendezvous with destiny." The words were prophetic.

As assistant secretary of the navy during World War I, Franklin Roosevelt had shown himself to favor active engagement with the world. No isolationist, he hoped that Woodrow Wilson would hasten American entry into the war. During the 1930s, President Roosevelt reluctantly endorsed a series of congressional neutrality acts. Ostensibly designed to keep the United States out of another world war, each new set of acts was, in fact, less restrictive than its predecessor. Finally, by early 1939, the rapidly increasing aggression of Hitler's Germany compelled Congress to accept FDR's toughening international posture. On November 4, 1939, two months after World War II began in Europe with the German invasion of Poland, President Roosevelt signed into law the Neutrality Act of 1939, which permitted the sale of arms and other war materiel to those belligerents the president did not specifically exclude. These sales were to be made on a cash-and-carry basis because Congress did not want U.S. financial and business interests to hold the debt of a belligerent country. The act was amended on November 17, 1941, to permit the arming of U.S. merchant vessels and to permit those vessels to carry cargoes into belligerent ports.

Roosevelt was very much inclined to prepare the nation for war. This inclination was assiduously nurtured by British prime minister Winston Churchill. On September 11, 1939, days after Britain declared war on Germany following the Polish invasion, Roosevelt wrote to Churchill, who was then serving as first lord of the Admiralty. Alluding to their shared background in naval administration, FDR wrote, "I want you to know how glad I am that you are back again in the Admiralty.... What I want you and the Prime Minister [Neville Chamberlain] to know is that I shall at all times welcome it if you will keep me in touch personally with anything you want me to know about." After Churchill replaced Chamberlain as prime minister, he cabled Roosevelt on May 15, 1940. Air attacks, he wrote, are "making a deep impression upon the French," and the "small countries are simply smashed up, one by one, like matchwood.... We expect to be attacked here ourselves, both from the air and by parachute and air-borne troops.... If necessary, we shall continue the war alone and we are not afraid of that. But I trust you realize, Mr. President, that the voice and force of the United States may count for nothing if they are withheld too long. You may have a completely subjugated, Nazified Europe established with astonishing swiftness, and the weight may be more than we can bear." He concluded: "All I ask now is that you should proclaim non-belligerency, which would mean that you would help us with everything short of actually engaging armed forces." He asked the president to give Britain forty or fifty obsolescent World War I-era American destroyers, several hundred new aircraft, anti-aircraft defense equipment, and steel. He asked that a U.S. Navy squadron be sent to make a "prolonged" visit to an Irish port to discourage what he believed to be an impending landing in neutral Ireland by German paratroopers. He asked that FDR send warships to call at the port of British-held Singapore as a warning to the Japanese.

Roosevelt replied on May 17, 1940, largely demurring in response to these requests but also pointedly keeping the door open. FDR also pointedly ignored the reports of his own ambassador to Britain, Joseph P. Kennedy Sr., father of the future president John F. Kennedy, who predicted the imminent collapse of the UK and advised total U.S. neutrality. Addressing the graduating class of 1940 at the University of Virginia Law School on June 10, Roosevelt spoke of extending "to the opponents of force the material resources of this nation; and, at the same time, we will harness and speed up the use of those resources in order that we ourselves in the Americas may have equipment and training equal to the task of any emergency and every defense. Signs and signals call for speed—full speed ahead." The speech was broadcast, and Roosevelt knew Churchill would hear it.

By January 1940, the president had already secured from Congress 1.8 billion dollars for national defense, including nearly 1.2 billion dollars and a program to produce fifty thousand aircraft. In mid-May, he requested an additional 2.5 billion dollars to expand the army and the navy. On May 31, he presented the Accelerated U.S. Defense Plan and requested another 1.3 billion dollars to enable the army and navy to meet expansion requirements. On June 20, the Burke-Wadsworth Bill was introduced to reactivate the Selective Service System. It was passed on September 16 as the Selective Training and Service Act of 1940, creating the first peacetime draft in United States history.

On June 3, 1940, after the British Expeditionary Force (BEF) successfully avoided mass surrender by withdrawing from Dunkirk and crossing the English Channel back to its home bases, Churchill asked Roosevelt for weapons and equipment to replace those left behind in France. FDR immediately shipped huge quantities of obsolete but still serviceable rifles, machine guns, field artillery pieces, and ammunition. On September 2, 1940, Roosevelt and Churchill agreed that the U.S. Navy would transfer fifty World War I-era destroyers to the British Royal Navy in exchange for ninety-nine-year leases on British naval and air stations in Antigua, the Bahamas, Bermuda, British Guiana, Jamaica, Newfoundland, St. Lucia, and Trinidad. The exchange was followed on November 20 by the Stimson-Layton Agreement, in which U.S. Secretary of War Henry Stimson and British Minister of Supply Sir Walter Layton agreed to standardize certain British and American weapons, thereby enabling their free exchange. The agreement also pooled war-related U.S. and British intellectual property, including weapons patents. On March 11, 1941, the so-called Lend-Lease Act was signed into law, authorizing the president to give aid to any nation whose defense he deemed critical to that of the United States. Most importantly, the cash-and-carry requirement was dropped. The government could now accept payment "in kind or property, or any other direct or indirect benefit which the President deems satisfactory."

By early 1941, FDR had taken the United States to the verge of war. During August 9–12, 1941, he met with Prime Minister Churchill aboard naval vessels of the United States and Great Britain in Placentia Bay, off the coast of Newfoundland. Together, these leaders drafted the Atlantic Charter, which set forth the basic principles of an alliance—without yet actually striking an alliance.

Back in October 1939, by the Declaration of Panama, concluded between the United States and twenty-one Latin American countries, a three-hundred-mile "neutrality zone" in the waters of the Americas was declared off limits to all belligerents. The U.S. Navy now began actively patrolling these waters. Early in 1941, this "neutrality patrol" was pushed out to a distance of two thousand miles from the U.S. coast. In August 1941, U.S. naval vessels began escorting fast supply convoys partway to Britain. By mid-September, navy vessels were escorting convoys between Newfoundland's Grand Banks and Iceland. An undeclared naval war between the United States and Germany had begun on the Atlantic.

From the American point of view, Europe was the focus of the war. Yet FDR also hoped to contain Japan's aggressive, violent expansion throughout Asia. He imposed an embargo on the export of many goods to Japan, including steel, aluminum, and other war materiel. The president intended this as an alternative to going to war with Japan. The last thing he wanted was to ignite wars on two vast fronts. Yet his strict embargo emboldened Japanese militarists to plot a surprise attack against Pearl Harbor, home of the U.S. Pacific Fleet in what was then the U.S. Territory of Hawaii. The attack, which took place on December 7, 1941, prompted President Roosevelt to appear before a special joint session of Congress the next day and ask for a declaration of war against Japan. His speech, among the most famous in American history, began, "Yesterday, December 7, 1941, a date which will live in infamy, the United States of America was suddenly and deliberately attacked by naval and air forces of the Empire of Japan." With grim frankness, the president reported that the attack "caused severe damage to American naval and military forces. I regret to tell you that very many American lives have been lost. In addition, American ships have been reported torpedoed on the high seas between San Francisco and Honolulu." He also catalogued other Japanese attacks across the Pacific and Asia, but he concluded with determination and positive certitude of victory: "With confidence in our armed forces—with the unbounding determination of our people—we will gain the inevitable triumph, so help us God." It was vintage FDR and characteristic of his leadership throughout the war.

Three days after the U.S. declaration against Japan, on December 11, Germany, Japan's ally, declared war on the United States. FDR now faced the two-ocean, two-front war he had sought to avoid. As a wartime president, he relied heavily on his military advisors, but he also took a hands-on approach to directing prosecution of the war, even as he promoted the all-out mobilization of industry at home. The leftist leanings of the New Deal were suppressed and suspended as he offered corporations generous contracts and tax breaks and downgraded progressive domestic reforms for the sake of getting American industry on a full war footing. FDR emphasized competition among his advisers, key industrialists, and others. While he formed various boards and agencies to control prices, develop manpower policy, and supervise the allocation of scarce raw materials, Roosevelt refused to appoint a central production "czar" to oversee the war effort. Instead, he resorted to naked capitalism in the expectation that a highly competitive atmosphere would produce the best and most cost-effective results.

Militarily, Roosevelt took on the full weight of his constitutional responsibility as commander-in-chief. For this, he absorbed some praise and much criticism. Critics blamed him for leaving Pearl Harbor unprepared for attack while others believed it a grave mistake to refuse any peace terms short of unconditional surrender. To this day, some condemn Roosevelt for bowing to Churchill's insistence on delaying the cross-Channel invasion to carry out the North African and Italian campaigns first. Others believe that Roosevelt was right to heed Churchill's warning that the Allied forces were simply not yet prepared to invade successfully from the west. Most of all, Roosevelt would be criticized for authorizing the forced relocation of Japanese-Americans, including U.S. citizens of Japanese ancestry, and their forcible internment in "relocation" camps from February 19, 1942, to March 20, 1946.

In the end, of course, the Allies prevailed—and this was due, at least in some significant measure, to the leadership of Churchill and Roosevelt. One can argue with the decisions they made, but they did make them. President Truman once observed that the only truly "bad" presidents were those who failed to make the necessary decisions. Roosevelt never failed in this way. Thanks in large part to him, difficult alliances were held together and victory achieved. He earned reelection to a fourth term in 1944, serving less than three months before succumbing to a cerebral hemorrhage on April 12, 1945. He was only sixty-three, but the myriad burdens of the Great Depression and the biggest, most destructive war ever fought on the face of the planet aged him far beyond his years.

#9
ALBERT EINSTEIN

Created the theory and wrote the letter behind the
development of the atomic bombs that ended World War II

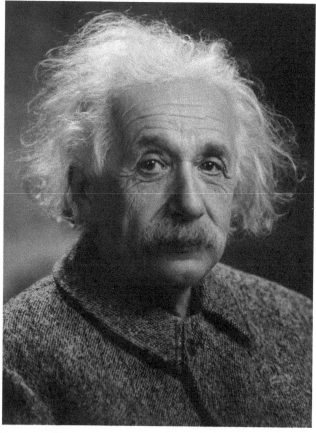

Albert Einstein, in a portrait from 1947. (credit: *Library of Congress*)

In the history of modern science, 1905 is called the *Annus Mirabilis,* the "Miraculous Year," because Albert Einstein, a twenty-six-year-old assistant patent examiner at the Swiss Patent Office in Bern, had published in a prestigious physics journal four articles that created modern physics, transformed concepts of reality itself, and in the process laid down the theoretical background from which atomic energy and atomic weaponry would be created. These papers also set Einstein on a course to becoming the most famous scientist of his time, universally recognized as the most important physicist since Isaac Newton.

Albert Einstein was born at Ulm, in Württemberg, Germany, on March 14, 1879. His father, Hermann, was a salesman and engineer, and his mother, Pauline Koch, was a homemaker. The family moved to Munich six weeks after Albert was born, and it was here that Hermann and his brother Jacob founded a company that made electrical equipment. Although the Einsteins were Jews, they were non-observant, and Albert was enrolled in a Catholic elementary school from age five to eight, when he entered the Luitpold Gymnasium, which was later renamed for Einstein. When Hermann's company failed in 1894, Einstein's parents moved to Italy to start anew, leaving Albert in Munich to finish his gymnasium studies. He rebelled against the strict rote learning regimen there and, in December 1894, feigned illness so that he could leave the school to join his parents in Pavia. While waiting to take examinations required to enroll in the Swiss Federal Polytechnic Institute in Zurich, he wrote his first scientific paper, "On the Investigation of the State of the Ether in a Magnetic Field." He was all of sixteen.

After initially failing to get into the Polytechnic Institute, Einstein enrolled in the Argovian cantonal school in Aarau, Switzerland, filled in his knowledge gaps, reapplied to the Polytechnic, and was admitted. He graduated in physics and mathematics from the Polytechnic in 1901. To avoid conscription in the German army, Einstein became a Swiss citizen, and unable to find a teaching position, he went to work instead as "technical assistant" in the Swiss Patent Office. Simultaneously, he attended the University of Zurich, from which he received his doctorate during that same Miraculous Year of 1905.

In 1908, Einstein was appointed *Privatdozent* (lecturer) at the University of Bern and the next year became Professor Extraordinary at the University of Zurich. He was appointed Professor of Theoretical Physics at the University of Prague in 1911, returning to the University of Zurich in 1912 to accept a similar position. Two years later, he became director of the prestigious Kaiser Wilhelm Physical Institute and simultaneously held a professorship in the University of Berlin. In 1914, he once again took out German citizenship and lived in Berlin until 1933, the year in which Adolf Hitler became the nation's chancellor.

The papers of 1905 included "On a Heuristic Viewpoint Concerning the Production and Transformation of Light," which formed the basis for quantum theory; "On the Motion of Small Particles Suspended in a Stationary Liquid, as Required by the Molecular Kinetic Theory of Heat," which presented the first empirical proof of atomic theory; "On the Electrodynamics of Moving Bodies," which postulated the epoch-making Special Theory of Relativity; and "Does the Inertia of a Body Depend Upon Its Energy Content?" which established the equivalence of mass and energy. He expressed this last principle in the most famous equation in the history of science: $E = mc^2$. Mass-energy equivalence meant that anything with mass has an equivalent amount of energy—and vice versa. Thus, energy (E) may be calculated as mass (m) multiplied by the speed of light squared (c^2). Conversely, anything that has energy has a corresponding mass (m) given by its energy (E) divided by the speed of light squared (c^2). Mass and energy are equivalent. From this would follow the idea that, if the force holding the atoms of matter together were liberated, the result would be a release of energy. This, in turn, led to scientific efforts to achieve nuclear fission—to "split the atom"—which led next to the creation of the world's first sustained nuclear chain reaction by a U.S. team under physicist and refugee from Mussolini's Italy Enrico Fermi on December 2, 1942, and the design and construction of the world's first nuclear weapons by other scientists of the Manhattan Project.

The papers of 1905 made Einstein famous. In 1916, he added to his renown by publishing his "Foundation of the General Theory of Relativity," arguing that gravitation is not a force, as Newton held, but a curved field in what he called the space-time continuum. Along with his 1905 papers, this created a profound impact on modern physics and elevated Einstein to scientific superstar status.

While he was revolutionizing the field of physics, Einstein became increasingly committed to social and political activism, including the cause of global peace. He used his growing international fame as a scientist as a platform for presenting his social and political views. Einstein toured the United States in the spring of 1921 to raise money for the Zionist Palestine Foundation Fund. He was treated as a celebrity in America, and he conceived an instant affection for the country. This same year, he was awarded the Nobel Prize for Physics. Yet the heyday of Einstein's theoretical innovations was over. During the later 1920s and 1930s, he devoted as much time to the cause of pacifism as he did to science.

At the start of 1933, Einstein set off again for the United States for his third two-month visiting professorship at the California Institute of Technology (Caltech). With his second wife, Elsa, he sailed back to Europe in March. During their voyage, they learned that Nazis had raided and looted their summer cottage in Germany. When the Einsteins landed at Antwerp, Belgium, on March 28, they made a beeline for the local German consulate, surrendered their passports, renounced their German citizenship, and rented a house in Belgium. They subsequently stayed in England for a time, and when an effort on their behalf to obtain British citizenship failed, they left again for the United States, where Einstein accepted a position as resident scholar at Princeton University's Institute for Advanced Study—a place already well known as a haven for scientists in flight from Nazi Germany, many of them, like Einstein, Jews. In 1935, Einstein applied for U.S. citizenship and became a citizen in 1940. He would live in Princeton for the rest of his life.

In 1939, the great Danish physicist Niels Bohr told Einstein that the German physicist Lise Meitner had succeeded in creating nuclear fission, splitting the nucleus of the uranium atom, which resulted in the conversion of its mass into energy—as Einstein had predicted in his 1905 theory. Bohr shared with Einstein his speculation that a controlled chain-reaction splitting of uranium atoms could produce an explosion far greater than any conventional chemical explosive could create. Leo Szilárd, a Hungarian physicist and, like Einstein, a Jewish refugee living and teaching in the United States, was also coming to this very conclusion. He feared that German scientists would indeed achieve a controlled chain reaction and would then work rapidly toward producing a nuclear weapon for Adolf Hitler. Alarmed, he and another physicist, Alexander Sachs, drafted a letter, which they mailed to Einstein in July 1939. Their purpose was to get the endorsement of the most famous and admired scientist in the world on a warning message to President Franklin D. Roosevelt.

On August 2, Szilárd, together with fellow Hungarian refugee physicist Edward Teller, went to see Einstein, who was spending the summer in a house at Peconic, Long Island. Einstein agreed to write a letter, which he dictated in German. Szilárd returned with it to his office at Columbia University, where he dictated a version in English to a stenographer. He then sent it back to Einstein, who read it, signed it, and posted it to President Roosevelt. Dated August 2, 1939, the letter read, in part:

> In the course of the last four months it has been made probable—through the work of Joliot in France as well as Fermi and Szilárd in America—that it may become possible to set up a nuclear chain reaction in a large mass of uranium, by which vast amounts of power and large quantities of new radium-like elements would be generated. Now it appears almost certain that this could be achieved in the immediate future.
>
> This new phenomena would also lead to the construction of bombs, and it is conceivable—though much less certain—that extremely powerful bombs of a new type may thus be constructed...

Einstein suggested that the president "may think it desirable to have some permanent contact maintained between the administration and the group of physicists working on chain reactions in America," and he concluded the letter on a more urgently ominous note: "I understand that Germany has actually stopped the sale of uranium from the Czechoslovakian mines which she [Germany] has taken over. That she should have taken such an early action might perhaps be understood on the ground that the son of the German Under-Secretary of State, von Weizsacker, is attached to the

Kaiser-Wilhelm-Institute in Berlin where some of the American work on uranium is now being repeated."

Such was Einstein's prestige that FDR, in February 1940, authorized the beginning of research, which was directed by a committee under the chairmanship of L. J. Briggs, head of the National Bureau of Standards. On December 6, 1941, the research project was transferred to the Office of Scientific Research and Development, headed by one of the most respected scientists in America, Vannevar Bush. The next day, the Japanese attack on Pearl Harbor thrust the United States into World War II, and, shortly after this, the War Department was given joint responsibility with the Office of Scientific Research and Development for the project. By the middle of 1942, researchers concluded that the military application of fission was indeed feasible, but that many facilities, including laboratories and industrial plants, would be required. Accordingly, the War Department assigned the U.S. Army Corps of Engineers to manage, on an accelerated basis, the necessary construction work. Because most of the early research was being conducted at Columbia University, in Manhattan, responsibility was assigned to the Corps' Manhattan Engineer District in June 1942. The army's direction quickly expanded beyond construction, and in September 1942 Brigadier General Leslie R. Groves, an army engineer who had directed design and construction of the brand-new Pentagon outside of Washington, was put in charge of all military and engineering aspects of what was now code-named the Manhattan Project.

While the work of creating fissionable materials was under way, a central laboratory capable of translating bomb theory into a working bomb had to be established. In 1943, J. Robert Oppenheimer, a charismatic American physicist, was chosen to create and direct the laboratory. Little more than two years later, at 5:29 on the morning of July 16, 1945, in the Jornada del Muerto desert some thirty-five miles Southeast of Socorro, New Mexico, the first nuclear device the Manhattan Project had produced was successfully tested. Less than a month after this, on August 6 and August 9, two fully weaponized versions of the device—the scientists referred to it simply as "the gadget"—were dropped on Japan, one on Hiroshima and the other on Nagasaki. The surrender of that nation followed, and on September 2, 1945, World War II came to an end.

Although Albert Einstein had played no active role in the Manhattan Project, his career led up to it, and his letter provided the impetus for its undertaking. After the use of the atomic bomb on Hiroshima and Nagasaki, Einstein became an eloquent voice in the quest for ways to prevent any future use of such weapons. After World War II, he turned away from physics—except for work on formulating a unified field theory, a single theory intended to explain all of physics—and became increasingly active in the World Government Movement, which, he hoped, would help to create world peace. In an interview with Alfred Werner, published in the April-May 1949 issue of *Liberal Judaism,* Einstein was asked what World War III would be like. "I know not with what weapons World War III will be fought," he responded, "but World War IV will be fought with sticks and stones." Einstein died on April 18, 1955, as the result of a ruptured aortic aneurism.

#10
J. ROBERT OPPENHEIMER

*As director of the Los Alamos Laboratory (1943-1945),
he led the science team of the Manhattan Project, which
created the atomic weapons used against Japan to end
World War II*

J. Robert Oppenheimer—the haunting face of the
charismatic scientific director of the Manhattan Project, pictured in 1944.
(credit: *Los Alamos National Laboratory*)

Born in New York City on April 22, 1904, to Julius Oppenheimer, a German Jewish immigrant who built a fortune as a textile importer, and his wife, Ella Friedman, an artist, Julius Robert Oppenheimer grew up in a house surrounded by the works of Picasso, Van Gogh, and others in his family's collection. He showed signs of genius early in life and was educated at New York's Alcuin Preparatory School before transferring in 1911 to the Ethical Culture Society School, an institution of the non-secular ethical culture movement. Oppenheimer moved through his elementary education quickly, skipping one and a half grades. After graduating from the Ethical Culture high school course, he was forced to take a year off because of colitis. Concerned about his son's health, his father asked his English teacher to take the boy to New Mexico, where, he believed, the exercise and salubrious Southwestern climate would help him recover. Young Oppenheimer fell in love with the landscape and developed a lifelong passion for horseback riding. He also became well acquainted with the Los Alamos Ranch School, which, on his recommendation, would become the center of the Los Alamos Scientific Laboratory, where the principal research for the atomic bomb was ultimately conducted.

Oppenheimer had excelled at the Ethical Culture School, with its broad liberal arts curriculum, and when he entered Harvard University at the age of eighteen, he studied English, French, Greek, and Latin literature in addition to Asian philosophy while pursuing majors in chemistry and physics. In 1925, after graduation, Oppenheimer was awarded a prestigious grant for study at Christ's College, Cambridge, England. He wrote to the legendary Nobel laureate physicist Lord Ernest Rutherford (1871-1937), asking to study with him at the University's Cavendish Laboratory. Rutherford, who is generally regarded as the father of nuclear physics, did not accept him as a student, but Oppenheimer went to Cambridge anyway, assuming he would find another mentor. Rutherford had rejected him because Oppenheimer admitted that he was a theoretician, rather than a laboratory physicist. Another Nobel laureate, J. J. Thomson (1856-1940), who discovered the first subatomic particle, the electron, did take him on—but on condition that he at least complete an introductory laboratory course. A naturally rebellious, somewhat arrogant, and, despite his charisma, even obnoxious young man, Oppenheimer feuded with the tutor Thomson assigned him, the experimental physicist and future Nobel laureate Patrick Blackett, on whose desk he once left an apple that had been dipped in a "noxious" chemical. For this, Oppenheimer narrowly escaped probation. Indeed, throughout his graduate work, those who became close to Oppenheimer noted what they considered self-destructive behavior, fits of violence, and periods of deep depression. Oppenheimer went for long stretches without eating—but never without smoking—and was a strikingly thin, haggard, and even gaunt figure. "Haunted" was a word often used to describe his appearance.

At Cambridge, he became increasingly interested in advanced atomic research and, in 1926, left the Cavendish Laboratory to study in Germany under yet another future Nobel laureate, the pioneer of quantum mechanics Max Born, at the University of Göttingen. Here he also met and was befriended by a veritable Who's Who of twentieth-century physics and the then-emerging field of quantum mechanics, including Werner Heisenberg (another Nobel-winning founder of quantum mechanics, who would take a leading role in Nazi Germany's unsuccessful effort to create a nuclear weapon), Pascual Jordan (a mathematician who made important contributions to quantum mechanics), Wolfgang Pauli (a 1945 Nobel laureate, whose "Pauli principle" is a key concept in quantum physics), Paul Dirac (whose Dirac equation predicted the existence of antimatter), Enrico Fermi (who would lead the Manhattan Project team that, in 1942, created the first sustained nuclear chain reaction), and Edward Teller (a Hungarian physicist who would not only be instrumental in the Manhattan Project, but who would lead postwar development of the hydrogen, or thermonuclear, bomb). It was from Göttingen, in 1927, that Oppenheimer received his doctorate, after which he returned to the United States, where he joined the faculties of the University of California at Berkeley and the California Institute of Technology (Caltech) and conducted advanced theoretical work based on the implications of quantum mechanics and relativity theory. Oppenheimer was especially interested in the energy processes of subatomic particles, including electrons, positrons, and cosmic rays.

Oppenheimer worked closely with Ernest O. Lawrence, who was conducting experimental work in particle physics using the cyclotron particle accelerator at the Lawrence Berkeley National Laboratory. Although this work was important, as was his research in theoretical astronomy and quantum electrodynamics, as well as relativistic quantum mechanics (Oppenheimer predicted two subatomic particles, the neutron and the meson, which were later found by others, and he also predicted the existence of neutron stars), he was better known as a brilliant lecturer and teacher than as a researcher.

Oppenheimer also gained notice for his anti-fascist and anti-Nazi political activism during the 1930s. When his father died in 1937, leaving him a large inheritance, he contributed generously to leftwing organizations. He flirted with membership in the Communist Party but neither joined it nor contributed to it, largely because of his objections to the oppressive policies of Joseph Stalin. In response to the Moscow Trials of 1936-1938, Oppenheimer publicly disavowed any ties with the Communists. But he was, like Leo Szilard, Edward Teller, Albert Einstein, and others, highly alarmed by rumors—which he believed were quite true—that German physicists were at work developing nuclear weapons for Hitler.

After World War II began in Europe on September 1, 1939, Oppenheimer turned his own professional work toward an effort to beat the German researchers to finding a process for separating fissionable uranium 235 from natural uranium. He also embarked on research to determine how much fissionable U 235 was required to make an atomic bomb. The nature of this work, along with his reputation as a charismatic teacher, brought Oppenheimer to the attention of Brigadier General Leslie R. Groves, director of the Manhattan Project. A brash, charmless, overweight military martinet, a straight-arrow engineer rather than a freewheeling scientist, Groves had a personality and political orientation 180 degrees opposite that of Oppenheimer. Nevertheless, Oppenheimer was Groves's first choice as science director of the Manhattan Project. He set aside the man's leftwing views and the fact that he was not a Nobel laureate. Although most of his work had been in the field of theoretical physics, and the impenetrable area of quantum mechanics at that, Oppenheimer demonstrated a grasp of the practical aspects of the atomic bomb problem. Moreover, Groves, a keen judge of human capital, saw that he and Oppenheimer had one trait in common: boundless ambition. Groves, who had just built the Pentagon in eighteen months from plans to completion, saw in Oppenheimer his own intensity and drive, qualities he believed were indispensable to rapidly turning theoretical physics into a working bomb.

Oppenheimer took the assignment, and in November 1942, Groves, at Oppenheimer's instigation, scouted the Los Alamos area as the site for the Manhattan Project's principal laboratory. Groves agreed with him that the site was sufficiently remote to afford secrecy, yet was close to water and transportation. It was also near an area that could be used as a proving ground. Oppenheimer was now charged with the task not merely of turning physics into a weapon, but of both creating and administering a laboratory to carry out the major research. He personally reached out to assemble the team of scientists required for the work. It was a group who collectively possessed unprecedented scope and depth.

While Groves attended to the titanic task of creating the massive manufacturing facilities to produce fissionable material, Oppenheimer oversaw the construction and staffing of the Los Alamos research complex. To this remote New Mexico mesa, some of the nation's greatest physicists and chemists came to live and work. A combination top-secret military installation and research laboratory, Los Alamos required a unique compromise between the creative freedom and openness necessary for scientific research and the high degree of discipline and security required in top secret weapons production. Oppenheimer, who could be moody and difficult, rose to the occasion and forged an excellent working relationship with Groves on the one hand and the scientists on the other.

His technical and scientific task was to supervise the invention of methods for reducing the fissionable materials that emerged from Groves's production plants to pure metal that could be fabricated into the precisely machined shapes that would enable an explosive chain reaction. The goal was to bring together very rapidly sufficient amounts of fissionable material to achieve a supercritical mass—resulting in a detonation. Moreover, this exquisitely difficult feat of materials engineering had to be carried out within a device that could be carried on board a bomber, dropped over a target, and detonated at precisely the proper altitude above the target; explosion on impact was not desirable, because much of the explosive force would be absorbed by the earth and therefore dissipated. To further complicate the task, these problems had to be solved well before much fissionable material was available. The idea was to conserve as much of what could be produced for use in the finished bombs.

By the summer of 1945, when enough Plutonium 239 had emerged from the secret plant in Hanford, Washington, to produce a nuclear explosion, the Los Alamos scientists had created a weapon they believed was ready to field test. Oppenheimer assembled observation and monitoring equipment to ensure that they would have accurate data on the performance—or failure—of the bomb. At Alamogordo, 120 miles south of Albuquerque, a special tower was constructed, from which the test bomb—the scientists dubbed it "the gadget"—was suspended. Although the site was remote from population centers, the scientists were far from certain as to the "yield" (the energy and extent) of the explosion that would be produced. There was even a chance, some believed, that the detonation of the bomb could set off a chain reaction in the atoms of the air itself, perhaps destroying a vast area. Theoretically, it was even possible that the blast would ignite the very atmosphere of the earth.

The test bomb was detonated at 5:30 a.m. on July 16, 1945. Scientists and a handful of VIPs observed from bunkers and trenches ten thousand yards distant. All who witnessed the explosion were awed. A blinding flash was followed by a heat wave and, finally (since sound travels much more slowly than radiated energy), by a roar and shock wave. The blast produced a great fireball, followed by a mushroom-shaped cloud (rising to an altitude of forty thousand feet), which would become a dreaded emblem of the "atomic age." This first bomb was calculated to have produced an explosion equivalent in energy to 15,000-20,000 tons of TNT. Oppenheimer later recalled, on a 1965 television program, what the moment was like:

> We knew the world would not be the same. A few people laughed, a few people cried. Most people were silent. I remembered the line from the Hindu scripture, the Bhagavad Gita; Vishnu is trying to persuade the Prince that he should do his duty and, to impress him, takes on his multi-armed form and says, 'Now I am become Death, the destroyer of worlds.' I suppose we all thought that, one way or another.

In August, two fully weaponized bombs, one using Uranium 235 and the other using Plutonium 239, were dropped on the Japanese cities of Hiroshima (August 6) and Nagasaki (August 9). Within days, the Japanese agreed to unconditional surrender, and World War II was formally ended on September 2, 1945, in a signing ceremony aboard the USS *Missouri*, at anchor in Tokyo Bay.

In October, Oppenheimer resigned as director of Los Alamos and, in 1947, was appointed to head the Institute for Advanced Study at Princeton University. Concurrently, from 1947 to 1952, he also served as chairman of the General Advisory Committee of the Atomic Energy Commission, which, under his leadership, in October 1949, announced its opposition to the development of the hydrogen bomb, which was many times more powerful than the fission bombs dropped on Japan. Oppenheimer had profound reservations about nuclear weapons, and he regarded thermonuclear—or hydrogen—weapons as capable of ending civilization. At this time, the height of the Cold War, Oppenheimer's opposition to the hydrogen bomb created enormous controversy, and, on December 21, 1953, he learned of a military security report that accused him of having had Communist ties in the past, of having interfered with the investigation of Soviet espionage agents, and of opposing the building of the hydrogen bomb not on moral grounds but in a deliberate effort to undermine national security. Although a subsequent hearing cleared him of treason, it also ruled that his access to military secrets should be terminated, and he was removed as adviser to the Atomic Energy Commission.

J. Robert Oppenheimer had sought fame. Heading the atomic bomb project had been his substitute for a Nobel Prize. Now, however, he became celebrated as a martyr, having suffered the fate of a liberal scientist in a frightened age. His work resulted in a weapon with profound moral consequences. When he made his own moral convictions public, he was condemned. A kind of mythology quickly grew up about him—the scientist as haunted genius, a modern Prometheus punished for the great force he brought into the world, the wizard who liberated the atomic genie and then struggled tragically to put it back into the bottle.

Oppenheimer spent his later years less immersed in theoretical physics than in the moral and philosophical questions relating to the place of science in society. He received the Enrico Fermi Award of the Atomic Energy Commission in 1963, retired from Princeton in 1966, and, a lifelong chain smoker, succumbed on February 18, 1967, to throat cancer.

#11
Harry S. Truman

Decided to use the ultimate weapon

President Harry S. Truman is flanked by Joseph Stalin (left) and Winston Churchill (right) on July 17, 1945, at the Potsdam Conference, held outside of Berlin after Germany's surrender. (credit: *Truman Library*)

At 7:09 on the evening of April 12, 1945, two hours and twenty-four minutes after Franklin Delano Roosevelt succumbed to a cerebral hemorrhage while sitting for a portrait at the "Little White House" in Warm Springs, Georgia, his vice president stood in the Cabinet Room of the White House in Washington, raised his right hand, put his left on the cover of a Gideon Bible (quickly borrowed from Howell Crim, head usher of the White House), and swore the presidential oath.

No one ever thought Harry S. Truman would become president—not the late president, not the American people, and, least of all, not the man with his hand on the Bible. Sixty-one years earlier, on May 8, 1884, in a tiny bedroom off the parlor of their home in the market hamlet of Lamar, Missouri, the newly sworn-in chief executive was born to John Anderson Truman and Martha Ellen Young. John was a mule trader and farmer, and when the mule business went sour in 1885, he moved the family to a farm near Harrisonville and, two years later, to another farm, near Grandview. At just under six feet, Harry was not a small man, but he was slightly built and so nearsighted that he required thick eyeglasses from the age of nine. He was not well suited to farm life, and he was pleased when the family, which now included his brother, John Vivian Truman (always called Vivian), moved to the city of Independence in 1890. There his sister, Mary Jane, would be born, and there he would receive most of his schooling.

Harry's favorite activities were reading and playing the piano. As he approached adolescence, he decided he would become either a historian or a pianist. But the family never had the money to finance a college education or advanced music lessons; therefore, after completing high school, Harry briefly attended business college but soon sought work and found a job in the mail room of the *Kansas City Star*. He moved on next to the position of timekeeper for a Santa Fe Railroad construction project and, in 1903, started clerking and then bookkeeping at a Kansas City bank. He might have carved out a decent banking career, but, in 1905, his father summoned him to work on the family's new 600-acre farm at Blue Ridge, near Grandview. Like it or not—and he did not—Harry Truman became a farmer. When his father died in 1914 and he inherited the farm, it seemed to him that he was doomed to a farmer's life.

The one benefit of having a substantial family farm was that it gave young Harry the nerve to begin, about 1911, courting Elizabeth—Bess—Wallace, with whom he had been in love ever since meeting her in 1890, at Sunday school. They were not engaged until November 1913—and secretly at that. By early 1917, they were ready to get married at last, but in April the United States entered World War I, and Truman, determined to serve in the army, did not want to risk making Bess a widow. He postponed the marriage.

Some thought him foolish. At thirty-three, he was three years beyond draft age. Add to that his bad eyesight, and no one expected him to enlist. But he felt compelled, volunteered, and was sent to France in 1918 as the captain of a field artillery battery that saw intense action at St. Mihiel and the Meuse-Argonne, the two great American offensives in the Great War. While he failed to acquire a taste for military life, he did discover that he had an aptitude for service and for leadership. Yet, after returning to the States in 1919 and finally marrying Bess Wallace, Truman did not aim to lead anyone or anything. Instead, he opened a haberdashery on Kansas City's 12th Street in partnership with an army buddy, Eddie Jacobson.

The shop got off to a fine start, and Harry was content to see himself making a life as a small businessman in Kansas City. But a postwar recession swept the United States—especially in predominantly agricultural regions—early in the 1920s, and Harry soon found himself out of business. Married, deeply in debt, and having lost his formerly clear direction, he accepted a friend's offer to introduce him to Thomas J. Pendergast, boss of the Kansas City Democratic political machine. Backed by Pendergast, Truman was elected county judge in 1922. He failed to win reelection two years later but was elected presiding judge of the county court in 1926. Despite the judicial-sounding title of these offices, they were administrative, and Truman was, in effect, commissioner of Jackson County, Missouri. Friends feared that Truman would doggedly follow Pendergast into the depths of political corruption that was a national scandal. He surprised all, however, by building a reputation, during two four-year terms, for his honesty, public service, and highly competent management.

Truman's honesty moved Boss Pendergast to throw his support behind other candidates for higher office. The problem was that nobody Pendergast asked wanted to run in the 1934 Democratic primary for a seat in the U.S. Senate. After receiving multiple "no thank yous," Pendergast turned to Truman as a last resort. Truman accepted, and he handily won the Democratic primary, which, in the "Solid South" Missouri of the 1930s, virtually assured winning the office. He entered the Senate in 1935 under the inevitable cloud of Pendergast corruption, but his plain-spoken, friendly, yet blunt manner and his earnest work ethic quickly won respect, trust, and affection from Senate colleagues as well as his constituents. He compiled a respectable record of achievement during his first term, but in his second, he captured the national spotlight when he created and chaired a committee to uncover waste and fraud in the U.S. military and its suppliers.

The Truman Committee, as it was universally called, was dogged in exposing waste due to institutional inefficiency and stupidity as well as instances of deliberate fraud. Even more important than finding the problems, however, was Truman's emphasis on correcting them. He held military officers, civil administrators, and, most of all, defense contractors to the highest standards of performance, both to equip the military with the best and to deliver value for money. Truman showed himself less interested in meting out comeuppance and punishment than in motivating excellence. His committee made it a practice to issue draft reports of its findings to the corporations, unions, and government agencies under investigation to prompt voluntary correction of abuses before the government resorted to disciplinary action or prosecution. In a memorable instance, which occurred on the eve of American entry into World War II, Truman challenged aircraft innovator and manufacturer Glenn Martin to redesign his company's twin-engine B-26 Marauder *after* it had gone into production with wings that had been judged too short to achieve maximum performance. More urgently, reports suggested that the design flaw had already sent several airmen to their deaths.

Summoned to testify before the Truman Committee, Martin defiantly stated that, with the design already in production, it was too late to make changes. Truman responded with his trademark directness: "If the lives of American boys depended upon the planes that were produced for the United States Army Air Force, the committee would see to it that no defective ships were purchased."

It was a moral argument instantly translated into business terms, and this brought a single sentence in reply from Martin: "Well, if that's the way you feel about it, we'll change it." It was straightforward Truman at his best.

When Franklin Roosevelt ran for an unprecedented fourth term following his unprecedented third, he decided that he needed a running mate to replace Henry A. Wallace. A vital supporter of FDR's New Deal, Wallace had served as secretary of agriculture from 1933 until September 1940, when the president tapped him as running mate for his third-term bid. It had been a controversial choice, with many party members objecting that Wallace was too far left. The president stood firm, and FDR was vindicated by a landslide victory. But in the course of the third term, Wallace espoused views that were increasingly socialist in orientation. He had gone too far even for Roosevelt, and, the president believed, the voters would at last reject him. Some in the party continued to push for Wallace, but Roosevelt responded with an ultimatum. He would accept either Supreme Court Justice William O. Douglas or Senator Truman as his fourth-term running mate. Although Truman expressed no interest in the job, he secretly cherished the opportunity to finally shed any lingering taint attached to being "the senator from Pendergast." State and city party leaders preferred Truman over Douglas, and the man's Senate record made him reasonably attractive. Yet when the question was finally popped, Truman demurred. "Senator from Pendergast" or not, he realized that he deeply loved the Senate and its camaraderie. With the Democratic National Convention underway and Truman still playing hard to get, Roosevelt phoned his convention hotel room. Party worker Robert Hannegan picked up, and FDR gave him a message for Truman—in a voice sufficiently loud and angry to be heard by everyone in the room, without having to be relayed: "You tell the Senator that if he wants to break up the Democratic party in the middle of the war, that's his responsibility."

One witness in the room recalled that Truman replied, "Well, if that's the situation, I'll have to say yes." Truman himself remembered it quite differently as just two words: "Oh, shit!"

At sixty-three, President Roosevelt, afflicted with adult-onset polio (some modern medical investigators believe he actually had Guillain-Barré syndrome) and suffering from runaway hypertension, burdened by a presidency that had spanned the Great Depression and more than three years of World War II, was clearly a sick man. So much was apparent to everyone, including Truman, but no one, Truman included, could imagine a world without Franklin D. Roosevelt.

And then he died. During the mere eighty-two days of his vice presidency, Truman met with FDR only twice. Neither meeting was substantive, and the president certainly did not prepare him for possible succession to office. Truman kept himself informed as to the progress of the war, but he received no special briefings, and of the top-secret Manhattan Project, the massive and massively successful effort to build an atomic bomb, he was told nothing at all.

Truman's elevation to the presidency could not have come under worse or more critical circumstances. He found himself successor to a chief executive who had been worshiped. Although victory had been all but completely won in Europe—VE Day would come in less than a month—the Pacific war raged on. In strictly military terms, the Japanese had been defeated, but they not only kept fighting, they were taking more American lives than at any other time in the war. Add to this that the Missouri senator who had made his reputation fighting inefficiency and corruption in war production was now expected to deal with military brass hats from the U.S. military and all the Allied countries as well, as such towering figures as Winston Churchill, the ruthlessly enigmatic Joseph Stalin, and the ever-obstinate Charles de Gaulle.

World War II saw uncounted horrors, but it also occasioned a few miracles. Among these was the rapid rise of Harry S. Truman to wise and courageous leadership in an incredibly complex time of unparalleled danger. A president doesn't fight a war; he or she makes the decisions that determine how the war will be fought. Those decisions facing Truman were world changing, world building, and, potentially, world destroying. Immediately after taking the oath of office, Truman spoke briefly to the Cabinet, told them that he hoped all would stay on the job, telling them that they would inevitably disagree with one another from time to time, but that all decisions would, in the last measure, be his and his alone and that, once those decisions were made, he expected their full support. With that, the Cabinet members filed out, except for Secretary of War Henry Stimson, who approached the new president to tell him that they needed to speak very soon concerning a "new explosive" of unimaginable power. Twelve days later, on April 24, Stimson and Major General Leslie Groves, director of the Manhattan Project, briefed Truman on the bomb.

He knew that, assuming the weapon tested out successfully, it would fall to him to decide whether to use it. It was one of many wartime decisions he made. Some were unpopular, and Truman garnered little support from the press—the "sabotage press," he sometimes called it. Mostly Republican in orientation, the nation's newspapers continually sniped and second-guessed the president in ways they would not have treated Roosevelt. One journalist famously quipped, "To err is Truman."

Truman let it all roll off his back and went about making some of the most difficult and important decisions any president has ever made. The most famous, of course, was the decision to use the atomic bomb against

Japan. Although Truman later claimed that many other decisions were far harder, none was of greater consequence for World War II and for the world as it evolved after the war. In a question-and-answer session following a Columbia University lecture in 1959, Truman said that the decision to use the atomic bomb "was no 'great decision'" because the bomb "was merely another powerful weapon in the arsenal of righteousness. The dropping of the bombs stopped the war, saved millions of lives. It was a purely military decision."

The atomic bomb had been successfully tested at 5:29 a.m. on July 16, 1945, in a remote stretch of the Alamogordo Army Air Base in the New Mexico desert. At the time, Truman was attending the Potsdam Conference with Churchill and Stalin just outside of the ruined city of Berlin. When he received word of the successful test, he felt nothing more than relief that the device, which had eaten up two billion 1940s dollars, had worked. On July 20, he told Generals Dwight Eisenhower and Omar Bradley about the test, and he discussed the role of the bomb in the Pacific war. Eisenhower voiced his opposition to its use, arguing that the United States should not be the first nation to deploy such a horrific weapon. Others were also opposed, including some of the very scientists whose work had created the device. Among these was Leo Szilard, a Hungarian refugee physicist who might be called the father of the Manhattan Project. He was the man who, back in 1939, persuaded Albert Einstein to write to President Roosevelt, urging him to authorize a crash program of atomic weapons research with the goal of beating the Nazis to the bomb. Yet a majority of the Manhattan Project scientists, including the project's scientific director, J. Robert Oppenheimer, and Enrico Fermi, leader of the team that had created the world's first sustained nuclear chain reaction, issued a report finding "no acceptable alternative to military use" of the bomb. A few days after this, on June 27, Undersecretary of the Navy Ralph A. Bard wrote a memorandum warning that using the weapon without warning would undermine "the position of the United States as a great humanitarian nation." Szilard circulated two petitions, signed by a total of 128 Manhattan Project scientists, appealing to President Truman to forbid the use of the atom bomb. More petitions followed, yet a majority of Manhattan Project scientists polled at the University of Chicago voted for its immediate military use.

In the end, while Truman was aware of the petitions, they did not figure in his decision. He considered alternatives to using the weapon. They boiled down to just two.

The first was to continue the conventional aerial bombing of Japan, along with a naval blockade. The strategic bombing of Japan had already destroyed most of the nation's major cities. The horrific firebombing of Tokyo had killed at least 120,000 persons—a death toll unprecedented and one, in fact, that would not be eclipsed by either of the two atomic weapons that would be used. The combination of unremitting air raids and the naval blockade was intended to beat and starve Japan into surrender. Many American strategists believed that this brutal combination would kill more and more Japanese, but it would never produce unconditional surrender. In the meantime, Allied lives and treasure would continue to be poured into the war.

Japanese history supported the assessment that Japan would die before surrendering. In all of its history, Japan had never surrendered, and in the entirety of World War II, no Japanese military unit had ever laid down its arms. None of the Japanese-held Pacific islands had been taken until nearly every Japanese defender had been killed. Iwo Jima was a prime example. The most optimistic American military strategists believed the war would not end before June 1946 and it would cost a minimum of 250,000 Allied lives, mostly American. Total Allied invasion casualties, killed and wounded, were expected to approach a half million, but General Douglas MacArthur put the figure at a million. For Truman, these numbers outweighed every moral objection, even the risk posed to the future of civilization itself. Moreover, Truman and Churchill, having at long last persuaded Stalin to commit the Soviet Union to make a declaration of war against Japan, now believed that a Russian presence in Japan would result in that country (at least the northern part of it) becoming a Soviet satellite after the war. If atomic weapons ended the war before the Soviets invaded, they would preempt any Russian postwar claim on the country.

If continuing conventional warfare was unacceptable, a second alternative to dropping the bomb on Japan might suffice. Some proposed a demonstration of a detonation on an uninhabited island—a demonstration that top officials of the Japanese military and government would observe. The counterarguments to this were several: First, the device might simply fail, an outcome that would only strengthen the Japanese resolve to fight on. Second, the test might succeed but fail to make a sufficient impression, since the target would be uninhabited. Third, the test would warn the Japanese to heavily defend against any incoming air raid. Fourth, the test would expend one of only two operational weapons currently in the arsenal. For Truman, any one of these outcomes made this alternative a non-starter.

Still, some of Truman's advisors, Eisenhower among them, insisted that Japan was so close to surrendering that there was no need either to use or demonstrate the bomb. Truman understood, however, that during the three months between April 12, when he took office, and the successful test of the atomic bomb on July 16, a Japan that was supposedly about to surrender had inflicted American battle casualties amounting to almost half the total from three full years of the Pacific war. He concluded that military defeat alone would not bring Japan's surrender.

And that brought up another problem, as some close to the president theorized that the Japanese refusal to surrender was less an act of will than of cultural inability. Having never been successfully invaded and having never surrendered, they argued, the Japanese did not *know* how to do it. It was a concept that did not exist in their cultural vocabulary. To end the war, it was argued, the Allies needed to settle for something less than unconditional surrender. Secretary of War Henry Stimson suggested demanding an end of resistance rather than an unconditional surrender. Truman rejected this—but then came up against the final argument against using the atomic bomb: It was an apocalyptic act. No matter how terrible the current war was, the argument went, using atomic weapons was worse—a war crime on an unparalleled scale and an act that would introduce into warfare a weapon capable of ending civilization itself.

Truman was an eminently intelligent and moral leader. He understood the objections based on morality and apocalyptic risk. The war, however, had redrawn the moral map, and the vision of apocalypse was hypothetical, whereas the reality of war was real and present. As he wrote to his wife, Bess, Harry Truman believed the atomic bomb would "end the war a year sooner...and think of the kids who won't be killed! That's the important thing."

In the end, of course, two atomic weapons were dropped. The first, used against Hiroshima on August 6, 1945, resulted in eighty thousand immediate fatalities, with another fifty thousand to sixty thousand deaths due to injury or radiation poisoning over the next several months. The second bomb, dropped on Nagasaki, August 9, produced some seventy thousand deaths in total.

On August 10, Truman received a message from the Japanese government, declaring that it would accept unconditional surrender as stated in the Allies' Potsdam Declaration, but with the understanding that the emperor would remain on the throne. It was, therefore, an offer of "unconditional surrender" subject to one condition. As such, some advised Truman to reject it. By this time, a third atomic bomb was ready to use. Those who counseled rejection advised the president to order the third bomb deployed. Truman told Henry A. Wallace—who served as his secretary of commerce—that he could not tolerate the thought of killing "all those kids," by which he meant, this time, *Japanese* kids. On August 10, he wrote in his diary that the Japanese "wanted to make a condition precedent to the surrender. Our terms are 'unconditional.' They wanted to keep the Emperor. We told 'em we'd tell 'em how to keep him, but we'd make the terms." Told he could have unconditional surrender on one condition, Truman replied (in effect) that the Allies would agree to that condition on terms the Allies would dictate. While waiting for the Japanese reply, Truman ordered conventional air raids against Japan to recommence on August 13. Japanese acceptance came on August 14. World War II was over, and the "Atomic Age" had begun.

#12
GEORGI KONSTANTINOVICH ZHUKOV

Icon of Soviet victory in the "Great Patriotic War"

Marshal Georgi Zhukov decorates Field Marshal Bernard Law Montgomery with the Russian Order of Victory. From left: Montgomery, Dwight D. Eisenhower, Zhukov, and British Air Chief Marshal Sir Arthur Tedder. The photograph was taken at Frankfurt on June 5, 1945.
(credit: *U.S. Office of War Information via Wikimedia Commons*)

Georgi Zhukov rose to the rank of Marshal of the Soviet Union during World War II, which the Russians, to this day, call the Great Patriotic War. A commander of considerable courage and fortitude, he exhibited tactical and strategic talent in leading or coordinating Red Army forces in numerous World War II campaigns and battles. It fell to him to command the 1st Belorussian Front, a massive army group consisting of thirteen Soviet armies, which formed the lead force (along with the 2nd Belorussian Front and the 1st Ukrainian Front)—2.5 million soldiers in all—that fought the Battle of Berlin (April 16-May 2, 1945). The culminating clash in the European war, it brought about the final defeat of Nazi Germany. With ample justification, Stalin capitalized on Zhukhov's role in the Berlin victory and chose him to accept the German instrument of surrender and to inspect the great Moscow Victory Parade of 1945. Zhukov emerged from World War II as by far the most famous of Red Army commanders—and perhaps the only Soviet officer whose name had become universally known throughout the West. Indeed, he may have been the finest of the Red Army's principal commanders in World War II.

The village in which Zhukov was born, on December 1, 1896, to a poor peasant family, was small, obscure, and quite indistinguishable from the many other impoverished hamlets of tsarist Russia. Called Strelkovka, in Maloyaroslavsky Uyezd, Kaluga Governate, it has since been renamed Zhukov in a district now called Zhukovsky, about sixty miles east of Moscow in the Kaluga Oblast. In 1908, when young Zhukov came of age in Strelkova, he was apprenticed to a fur trader and pursued this trade until 1915, when he was drafted into the Imperial Russian Army for service in World War I. Zhukov was attached to the 106th Reserve Cavalry Regiment (initially designated the 10th Dragoon Novgorod Regiment) and immediately distinguished himself in combat. He was twice decorated with the Cross of St. George—presented to soldiers of the lower ranks for exhibiting "undaunted courage"—and was promoted from private to non-commissioned officer on account of his valor.

After the October Revolution of 1917, Zhukov joined the Bolsheviks and, after recovering from a dangerous bout of typhus, fought in the Russian Civil War from 1918 to 1921, achieving command of a unit of the 1st Cavalry

Army. Zhukov was enrolled in a junior officers' military school in 1920, from which he graduated later that year. In 1921, he was awarded the Order of the Red Banner for his role in the suppression of the Tambov Rebellion, an anti-Bolshevik peasant uprising centered on the town of Tambov and spanning the summer of 1920 to the summer of 1921. With the conclusion of the Civil War, he was enrolled in an intermediate-level cavalry officer course, which he completed in 1925. From here, the young officer was sent to Germany, to study advanced military science in the *Kriegsakademie* (war college), a clandestine institution created in violation of the disarmament provisions of the Treaty of Versailles. Zhukov's enrollment was part of a secret military collaboration that took place between the Soviet Union and the Weimar Republic during the late 1920s, and it gave him invaluable insight into the strategic and doctrinal thinking of the German military on the cusp of the Nazi rise.

Zhukov returned to the Soviet Union in 1928 and entered the prestigious Frunze Military Academy that year. He graduated from the academy in 1931, having been appointed the preceding year to command the 2nd Cavalry Brigade of the 7th Cavalry Division. In February 1931, he was named Assistant Inspector of Cavalry of the Red Army—his first army-wide office. In May 1933, Zhukov was given command in the 4th Cavalry Division and, four years later, was made commander of the 3rd Cavalry Corps. Command of the 6th Cavalry Corps followed soon after. In 1938, he was appointed deputy commander of the entire Byelorussian Military District. At this high point, however, it appeared that he was about to suffer the same fate that befell many other top-level Soviet military officers during the great purges instigated by a politically paranoid Joseph Stalin. Indeed, many believe that Zhukov escaped the purge and its consequences—imprisonment, Siberian exile, and even execution—because of an administrative oversight. It might also have been the case that Stalin recognized an urgent need for his talent. He was assigned in 1938 to head the Soviet First Army Group in the undeclared Soviet-Japanese Border War of 1932-1939.

Zhukov played a major role in what became the strategically decisive Battle of Khalkhin Gol with what he called his "Soviet Offensive," which was launched on August 20, 1939. Like the great offensives of World War I, it began with a massive artillery barrage, but then Zhukov took a far more dynamic approach. He followed the barrage with an advance of some five hundred tanks. Simultaneously, in an action that anticipated the German "Blitzkrieg" tactics soon to be used against Poland in the commencement of

World War II, Zhukov supported his ground forces with some five hundred fighter and bomber aircraft. The combination of fighters and bombers in a single ground-support operation was boldly innovative, a first demonstration of Zhukov's out-of-the-box tactical thinking.

And there was yet more. The massive offensive began as a conventional frontal attack. But Zhukov soon revealed himself as a masterful strategist by holding back two complete tank brigades, which were not released into the advance until after full contact had been made by the frontal assault. At that point, the two reserve brigades swept around both Japanese flanks, with the support of mechanized artillery and infantry, as well as additional tanks. This double envelopment encircled the Japanese 6th Army, quickly capturing its rear-echelon supply depots. By the last day of August, the Japanese 6th Army had been cleared from the border region.

Since the Soviet-Japanese Border War was undeclared, the world paid little attention—especially amid the escalating crisis of Nazi German aggression. But much as the Spanish Civil War of 1936-1939 provided the German Luftwaffe with a testing ground for tactics it would use in World War II, the conflict with Japan gave Zhukov an opportunity not only to test but to exhibit tactics he would use in counterattacking the German invaders during World War II. Of special value was Zhukov's practice of continually injecting battle-hardened troops into newly created military formations to improve general morale and performance. Zhukov also closely observed the performance of the early generation of post-World War I Soviet tanks and drew up a long list of recommendations for improvements. These were soon incorporated into the T-34 medium tank, which not only became the mainstay of Red Army armor during World War II but quickly earned a reputation as the greatest tank of that war. Finally, at Zhukov's suggestion, the veterans of Khalkhin Gol were widely distributed to Red Army units that had not seen action against the Japanese. Zhukov's idea was to disseminate the benefits of combat experience quickly and widely throughout the Red Army. As for Zhukov himself, he received the USSR's highest decoration, the title of Hero of the Soviet Union.

After his magnificent victory against the Japanese, Zhukov was appointed deputy commander (1939) and then commander (1940) of the Kiev Military

District. In the fall of 1940, he began planning an exercise intended to perfect a plan for defending the Soviet western border. He decided to test the efficacy of a preemptive offensive. In war games, this approach proved highly successful—an outcome Stalin used to create powerful military propaganda. Unfortunately, the propaganda represented an inflated estimate of the efficacy of Zhukov's approach and thus instilled a dangerous complacency about the Red Army's readiness to deal with an invasion. For now, however, Zhukov was riding the crest of the great wave created by his actual success magnified by relentless propaganda, and on February 1, 1941, he was named chief of the Red Army's General Staff and Deputy Minister of Defense of the USSR. He now set about creating a "Strategic Plan for Deployment of the Forces of the Soviet Union in the Event of War with Germany and its Allies." Although the plan was completed by mid-May 1941, weeks before Operation Barbarossa, the German invasion of Russia, it is unclear whether Stalin accepted or rejected it. Long after the war, in the 1960s, Zhukov claimed that Stalin never approved the plan, but he did not make clear whether, in part or in whole, the plan was nevertheless executed.

When the Germans began the Russian invasion on June 22, 1941, Zhukov immediately ordered a full counteroffensive intended to encircle and destroy the invaders. By sheer numbers, the Red Army should have been able to do this, but the grand envelopment failed, and the Germans advanced at great cost to the Red Army and the Soviet people. Stalin removed Zhukov as Chief of the General Staff, probably because he had proposed abandoning Kiev in a bid to avoid envelopment by the advancing German juggernaut. Zhukov was now relegated to command of the Reserve Front, but on September 10, 1941, was sent to command the Leningrad Front as well. He took charge of the desperate defense of the city, which was held under siege for nine hundred days.

As the war continued, Zhukov was incrementally restored to positions of greater and greater responsibility. He was made representative to the Stavka (Supreme Command, headed by Stalin himself) for both the Reserve and Western Fronts on October 6, 1941, and four days later, the two commands were merged as the Western Front under his command. Thus, Zhukov came to lead the Battle of Moscow (October 2, 1941-January 7, 1942) and the Battles of Rzhev (January 8, 1942-March 31, 1943).

In August 1942, Zhukov was elevated to Deputy Commander-in-Chief of the Red Army and dispatched to Stalingrad to plan the defense of Stalin's namesake city. He then collaborated on the plan for the all-out Stalingrad counteroffensive, which brought about the turning point in the war on the Eastern Front. (The entire Battle of Stalingrad spanned August 23, 1942 to February 2, 1943.)

In November 1942, Zhukov was assigned to coordinate the Western Front and the Kalinin Front in Operation Mars (November 25-December 20, 1942), the first great Soviet offensive launched against the Germans. Just after New Year 1943, he returned to the Leningrad Front in a counteroffensive there. During July 1943, he was assigned as the Stavka officer charged with coordinating the epic Battle of Kursk (July 5-16, 1943), and he planned the highly effective offensive that was mounted in the wake of the battle. (Some contemporaries report that Zhukov claimed more credit for Kursk than he deserved.)

In 1944, Zhukov coordinated the offensive of the 1st Ukrainian and 2nd Ukrainian Fronts and on March 1 was named commander of the 1st Ukrainian Front. He was then assigned to coordinate the 1st Belorussian and 2nd Belorussian Fronts and, later, the 1st Ukrainian Front in Operation Bagration, the massive Belorussian Strategic Offensive Operation of June 22-August 19, 1944, which liberated all of Byelorussia and gained a wide foothold in Poland. Bagration positioned the Red Army for its final push into Germany and against Berlin. In August, at the successful conclusion of Operation Bagration, Zhukov was transferred to the 3rd Ukrainian Front to prepare it for the Red Army advance into Bulgaria.

On November 16, 1944, Zhukov was again shifted to a new command, that of the entire 1st Belorussian Front in the great Soviet Vistula–Oder Offensive, which set up the Red Army for the culminating operation of the European war, the Battle for Berlin. With a fiercely stirring oration broadcast to the troops, Zhukov rallied his armies to take bloody vengeance for all that the German invaders had done to "our brothers and sisters, our mothers and fathers, our wives and children." He exhorted the soldiers to "exact a brutal revenge." The men and women of the Red Army followed Zhukov's orders zealously, all along the advance to Berlin looting and burning German cities and towns, raping and murdering German civilians.

Despite the deliberate brutality of the advance, Zhukov proceeded methodically in closing in on the German capital. Once within the city, his soldiers engaged in fierce street-by-street, house-to-house fighting, taking an incredibly heavy toll on the German forces, which lost some one hundred thousand killed, more than twice that number wounded, and nearly a half-million captured. (Red Army losses were more than eighty-one thousand killed and 280,251 wounded or sick.) The Battle of Berlin earned Zhukov the honor of overseeing and accepting the surrender of the city and, subsequently, the surrender of what remained of the German army. After receiving that final surrender on May 8, 1945, he was assigned to administer the military occupation of the Soviet Zone of Germany from May 1945 to March 1946.

Zhukov's popularity following the end of World War II did not sit well with Stalin, who understood that a cult of personality, which was the very foundation of his dictatorship, could not support more than one personality. Accordingly, Stalin saw to it that Zhukov was assigned a series of obscure regional commands, most notably the Odessa Military District, which kept him well out of the public eye and the Kremlin power center. After Stalin's death in 1953, Zhukov was instantly elevated to deputy minister of defense. He supported Nikita Khrushchev in his opposition to the chairman of the Council of Ministers, Georgy Malenkov, who sought a reduction in military spending. After Khrushchev forced Malenkov to resign and replaced him with Nikolay Bulganin in February 1955, Zhukov succeeded Bulganin as minister of defense. He was also elected an alternate member of the Presidium.

As minister of defense, Zhukov vigorously applied all that he had learned in the perilous early days of World War II. He initiated programs that introduced greater professionalism throughout the Soviet armed forces. This meant reducing the Communist party's role in military affairs and elevating non-political, militarily qualified officers to positions of greater power. Inevitably, therefore, he fell out of favor with Khrushchev, who was now Soviet premier. However, Zhukov temporarily redeemed himself in Khrushchev's eyes through his effort to keep the premier in power when a majority of the Presidium tried to oust him. Zhukov ordered aircraft to transport members of the Central Committee from far-flung regions of the country to Moscow to restore the political balance in Khrushchev's favor in June 1957. This timely intervention prompted Khrushchev to promote Zhukov to full membership in the Presidium in July 1957. Nevertheless, the premier continued to oppose Zhukov's efforts to replace party officials with military officers in the administration of the armed forces. Finally, on October 26, 1957, Zhukov was formally dismissed as minister of defense and, a week later, was removed from his party posts.

The marshal of the Soviet Union retired into quiet obscurity until Khrushchev himself fell from power in October 1964. Two years later, Zhukov was awarded the Order of Lenin and was permitted to publish his autobiography in 1969. He died on June 18, 1974, not nearly as appreciated in the Soviet Union as he should have been and, given the magnitude of his achievements in the war against Hitler, also deprived by the Western Allies of the recognition he so richly merited.

#13
PHILIPPE PÉTAIN

The Frenchman who bargained with the devil

Philippe Pétain, briefly prime minister of France and then Chief of the French State (Vichy France). (credit: *Harris & Ewing Collection, Library of Congress*)

The long history of France and its leaders is filled with the very highest of drama. In the case of Marshal Henri Philippe Pétain, the drama was darkest tragedy and the role he played in it was the hero who suffered a tragic fall. In World War I, Pétain emerged as one of a precious handful of capable, competent, humane, and truly heroic French commanders. His leadership through the grimmest passages of the 1914-1918 war, especially during the enormously costly Battle of Verdun (February 21-December 18, 1916), elevated him to the richly deserved status of national hero. Many considered him a savior of France. Some two decades later, in another time of dire national need, the people of France once again turned to Marshal Pétain, now an old man of eighty-four. Faced with total defeat in the Battle of France (May 10-June 25, 1940), French President Albert François Lebrun appointed Pétain prime minister. In this office, he quickly led the government to "come to terms" with Hitler. This meant the partition of France into a German-occupied north (Paris included) and an unoccupied, nominally sovereign German puppet state in the south with its capital in the spa town of Vichy. For this, the sometime savior of France was forever dishonored in the eyes of his nation and history itself. France's stirring revolutionary motto, *"Liberté, égalité, fraternité"* ("Liberty, equality, fraternity"), was effaced and replaced by the stunted motto of Vichy France: *"Travail, famille, patrie"* ("Work, family, fatherland"). Until the French liberation of September 7, 1944, Vichy was the searing emblem of the heartbreak of France and the terrible cost of submission to the Nazi tide.

Henri Philippe Pétain was born on April 24, 1856, in the town of Cauchy-à-la-Tour, Pas de Calais, France. He was the son of a farming family, with no military tradition—other than the experience of a great-uncle of Philippe, Father Abbe Lefebvre, who, as a young man, had served in the Grande Armée of Napoleon. The old gentlemen went on to become not a soldier by profession but a Catholic priest, yet he nevertheless regaled young Philippe with tales of travel, battle, and, above all, glorious victory. This was enough for the young farm lad, who, with visions of Napoleonic glory, set his sights on a military career. He studied diligently in school, joined the French army in 1876—five years after France's humiliation in the Franco-Prussian War

(1870-1871)—and was admitted in 1887 to the prestigious *École spéciale militaire de Saint-Cyr*, the nation's foremost military academy. In view of his superior performance, he was sent on to the *École Supérieure de Guerre*, the army war college, where those destined for high command were educated.

After early service in the *Chausseurs à pied*, the elite infantry, Pétain was variously assigned to staff and field duties. He was dismayed to discover that his progress up the ladder of command was agonizingly slow. In part, this was the nature of the peacetime French army, but it was also the product of his own individualistic defiance of accepted French army doctrine. In the years before World War I, French officers and their troops were inculcated with the gospel of the maximum offensive, often called "*Attaque à outrance*"— "attack to the uttermost." The idea was that only a furiously violent, all-out, head-on infantry assault creates victory. This notion was founded less on rational military theory than on an admixture of patriotic zeal, a notion of the inherent superiority of Gallic warrior blood, and the existence in the French soul of a kind of animal spirit or "vital impetus" the French philosopher Henri Bergson called *élan vital*.

Like so many beliefs based in the gut rather than in the brain, *Attaque à outrance* became an article of faith that was not to be questioned. Pétain questioned it. Although he was not promoted to major until 1900, his intelligence was highly respected, and his abilities as a theorist were recognized by an instructor's appointment to the *École de Guerre* in 1906. His conservative, methodical, and essentially defense-oriented ideas concerning the destructive effect of firepower were summed up in his mantra: "*Le feu tue!*"—"Firepower kills!" But this was squarely at odds with what the highly influential Colonel Louis Loyzeau de Grandmaison believed. "In the offensive," Grandmaison declared to his *École* students, "imprudence is the best of assurances.... Let us go even to excess, and that perhaps will not be far enough.... For the attack only two things are necessary: to know where the enemy is and to decide what to do. What the enemy intends to do is of no consequence."

The majority of the French officer corps, including most of those who would go on to lead the fight in World War I, such as Ferdinand Foch, were of the party of Grandmaison. Pétain nevertheless had some important followers, including one destined to lead the Free French in World War II, Charles de Gaulle. He credited Pétain with having taught him the very art of command.

At the outbreak of World War I in August 1914, Pétain was a colonel in command of the 33rd Regiment and quickly distinguished himself, achieving promotion to brigadier general by the end of the month. Brilliant performance at the First Battle of the Marne (September 6-10, 1914) earned him promotion to general of division, and by October 25 he was in command of XXXIII Corps in Artois. Again, Pétain performed superbly, this time during the Arras offensive of May 9-16, 1915, and was given command of the Second Army in June.

Pétain was in command of the Second Army at the start of the Battle of Verdun in February 1916. The complex of forts and strong points in and around Verdun had been stripped of men and movable artillery in the early days of the war in mindless pursuit of the Grandmaison doctrine that called for everything to be thrown into offense and virtually nothing devoted to defense. Now, the French army and people were paying the price. Suddenly, Verdun emerged as not only an important strategic objective, but as a "fortress" symbolic of the defense of France itself. It must *not* be lost.

In view of his outstanding performance in the war thus far and in acknowledgment that his long-held doctrinal beliefs were being vindicated, Pétain was promoted to Commander of the Army Group Centre—fifty-two divisions. Recognizing the struggle at Verdun was a matter of endurance, Pétain radically departed from the accepted practice of holding down the same infantry divisions on a given front for many weeks and even months. Pétain instead began rotating divisions out at two-week intervals. This not only greatly lifted morale, it ensured that fresh, rested troops were always in the critical positions. In addition, he created a massive logistical plan with continuous truck transport convoys moving over a well-maintained route called the "*Voie Sacrée*," the Sacred Way, which brought a never-ending supply of munitions, food, and troops. All was aimed at applying his controversial *École de Guerre* doctrine of "*le feu tue!*," *firepower kills!* The Sacred Way fed the guns that hammered the Germans attacking Verdun.

Pétain reinvigorated the Battle of Verdun, famously alluding to the phrase Joan of Arc used to rally the French army against the English: "*On les aura!*"—"We'll get 'em!" And although his successor to command of the Second Army, General Robert Nivelle, uttered the much-repeated pledge "*Ils ne passeront pas!*" ("They shall not pass!"), that it was almost universally attributed to Pétain reveals the esteem in which he was held. He had become a national hero.

His status was gravely tested when, beginning in May 1917, the French army was swept by a wave of mass mutinies, so extensive that they threatened to bring defeat on France. Pétain responded with strength and compassion, aggressively prosecuting the ringleaders of the mutiny, even as he set about addressing the soldiers' many just grievances. His reforms brought greater humanity to the French army and substantially improved the lot of the common soldier. As commander-in-chief of the French army, Pétain conducted the closing months of the war with great skill, always stressing preparedness and the setting of achievable goals rather than the often debilitating, even suicidal policy of unconditional all-out attack. Notably, however, it was the far more aggressive Ferdinand Foch, not Pétain, who was chosen as generalissimo of the Allied Supreme Command, which coordinated the combined French, British, Italian, and American forces. Nevertheless, by war's end, Pétain was elevated to the office of marshal of France, and in 1920 he was named vice president of the Supreme War Council. He became inspector general of the army in 1922 and served as minister of war during the brief government of Gaston Doumergue in February-November 1934.

Having made the transition from service in uniform to civilian politics, Pétain, unafraid to speak out in criticism of the military establishment, now became an outspoken critic of civilian politicians, whom he accused of neither leading nor governing. During the 1930s, he made clear his increasing disdain of liberalism and his advocacy of strong, even autocratic government. Appointed ambassador to Fascist Spain in March 1939, he was recalled to France in May 1940 as his nation faced defeat at the hands of the Nazis in what was now World War II.

After the Battle of France—the German invasion—had pushed the northern French forces and the entire British Expeditionary Force (BEF) to the English Channel port of Dunkirk on June 5, Prime Minister Paul Reynaud began to advance his argument for an armistice—that is, French surrender. On June 8, Charles de Gaulle, Pétain's former student and now a newly promoted brigadier-general as well as under-secretary for war, argued for fighting on. Pétain disagreed. Moreover, when Reynaud pointed out that the French government was bound by treaty to secure Britain's ascent before seeking an armistice, Pétain countered that Britain had gotten France into its present position and therefore had forfeited its right to be consulted. On June 10, General Maxime Weygand, now the French supreme commander, joined in the call for an armistice, declaring that further fighting had become "meaningless." The following day, June 11, Winston Churchill visited Tours, to which the government had evacuated. He called on France to resist by any means necessary, including guerrilla warfare. Pétain responded that this would merely destroy the nation. On June 12, citing among other things the danger of a Communist uprising in Paris, Pétain affirmed his support for Weygand's proposal of an immediate armistice. When Churchill returned on June 13 for another conference, he was told that the position of France was entirely hopeless.

Pétain argued against setting up a French government in exile. "Duty," he insisted, dictated that the government remain in France—although it now evacuated to Bordeaux. It was here, on June 14, that de Gaulle shook Pétain's hand before he set off for London, from which de Gaulle would lead the Free French Movement. Pétain would pursue a very different course.

Meeting with the Cabinet on June 15, Prime Minister Reynaud proposed that France emulate the Dutch. The French army, he said, should lay down its arms and continue the war from abroad. Weygand convinced Pétain that this course would be, in fact, an abandonment of the French people and a more shameful form of surrender. In the end, the Cabinet voted a kind of waffling course. They would neither surrender nor fight on, but ask the Germans for terms. On the next day, eager to force the armistice issue, Pétain threatened to resign from the Cabinet, knowing that this would bring down the Reynaud government. Churchill, in the meantime, presented a kind of Hail Mary proposition to Reynaud, by which the British proposed to create a Franco-British Union with joint nationality for the British and the French. Reynaud liked the idea, but others found it insulting. Ultimately, a majority of the Cabinet voted to seek an armistice separate from Britain, whereupon Reynaud resigned as prime minister, and President Lebrun appointed Pétain in his place.

A half hour after midnight on June 17, Pétain made a radio broadcast to the people of France, the majority of whom greeted his ascension with great enthusiasm. In this dark hour, he truly did appear to be their savior. Having flown to London, Charles de Gaulle broadcast his call for resistance. At the time, very few listened.

Under Pétain, on June 22, France signed an armistice in the very same place, Compiègne, and in the very same rail car in which the German representatives had signed the humiliating armistice of November 11, 1918. With the shoe now on the other foot, France turned over to Germany occupational control of the north and west of the country, including Paris and all of the Atlantic coastline. The remainder of France was unoccupied. Although occupied Paris legally remained the capital of this unoccupied portion of the nation, the government moved on July 1, 1940, to the spa town of Vichy, from which the new "French State," as unoccupied France was officially designated, was to be governed. Henceforth, everyone referred to unoccupied France as Vichy or Vichy France. As for Third French Republic, the Chamber of Deputies and Senate, meeting in Vichy, voted it into extinction and appointed Pétain as "Head of State" for Vichy.

Although the Deputies and Senators specified that the new state would be republican in form, Pétain was granted quasi-dictatorial powers. He did not object. The old man was an autocrat by disposition and political belief. Accepting no responsibility for the surrender, he blamed it on the government of the "corrupt" Third Republic. He quickly promulgated new laws enshrined in a "constitution" that abolished the presidency, adjourned parliament indefinitely (so much for representative republicanism), and gave him carte blanche in hiring and dismissing all ministers and civil servants. He also empowered himself to pass laws through the Council of Ministers and to choose his own successor. As one of his minions commented, Pétain now had more power than any French ruler since the Sun King, Louis XIV.

Perceiving receptivity at the top, fascist elements within French government and society launched a *Révolution nationale* ("National Revolution") from the Vichy platform. Gone was the democracy of the Third Republic. The new government would be authoritarian and quasi-theocratic—that is, Catholic. In the move from a "Republic" to a "State," France would spurn as false the idea that all men were created by nature equal. Pétain sanctioned the wholesale dismissal of Third Republic civil servants, the creation of special courts, the imprisonment of refugees and opponents, and, most important, a slate of antisemitic laws. The government seized control of the media, censored the press, and abolished freedom of expression. A cadre loyal to Pétain and his new fascism was created, the *Légion Française des Combattants*. As for relations with Hitler's Third Reich, Pétain enthusiastically led the government in a policy of collaboration and delivered to Hitler an army of volunteers eager to serve on the Russian front. Despite the extremity of the new state, most nations recognized its legitimacy, the United States included. And yet, as a matter of record, a formal state of war continued to exist between Germany and France.

The British attacked France's North African colonies, which were nominally controlled by Vichy. This prompted Pétain to authorize the establishment of a collaborationist militia (the *Milice*), which opposed the underground French resistance (called the *Maquis*). Thus, under Pétain, Vichy became an active ally of Germany, even as it officially continued to be the enemy of Germany.

Under the National Revolution, which Pétain approved, Vichy police officials and the Milice rounded up Jews, various immigrants (mostly from the Mediterranean countries), gypsies, Freemasons, Communists, and homosexuals. Some were variously persecuted, and many were consigned to Vichy-run concentration camps, which also housed political prisoners. All of this was done on the initiative of Vichy and without coercion from the Germans. In occupied France, the round-up and persecution of the Jews was instigated by the Germans, but to a large extent executed by the French police. In Vichy, all of this was handled by the French State. Because Pétain and Vichy had instigated and executed the abolition of the Third Republic, however, officials in occupied France, after the war, claimed that Vichy had been responsible for all of the war crimes in which French officials participated. In all, about 90,000 Jews who had been living in France died in concentration camps. This was about 25 percent of the prewar Jewish population of the country.

In August 1944, after the Allies had liberated Paris and were well on their way to liberating all of France, Pétain wrote a letter to Joseph Darnand, prominent in the *Légion Française des Combattants*, condemning Légion "excesses." Darnand refused to accept blame, replying to Pétain that he should have "thought of this before." In any event, the Germans did not abandon Pétain to the Allies—or allow him to surrender to them. After France was liberated, on September 7, 1944, Pétain and his Vichy cabinet were evacuated to Sigmaringen in Germany as a government-in-exile. Because this was a forced violation of his pledge never to leave France, Pétain refused to participate in the government. On April 5, 1945, Pétain wrote to Hitler, requesting that he be allowed to return to France. The Führer did not reply. Before the month was out, however, Pétain was transported to the Swiss border, which he crossed, continuing to the French frontier.

De Gaulle later called Pétain's return to France, where he knew he would face trial, "courageous." Yet honorably throwing himself on the mercy of French justice did not save him, and the postwar provisional government of France, headed by De Gaulle himself, put the ancient Marshal on trial from July 23 to August 15, 1945. The charge was treason. Although he denied the right of the court to try him, he remained stoically silent throughout the proceedings. Convicted, Pétain was sentenced to death—by a one-vote jury margin. The Court itself requested that the sentence be stayed, and, ultimately, De Gaulle personally commuted the sentence to life imprisonment, citing not only Pétain's age, but his military contributions in World War I. Eager to put Pétain out of sight and out of mind, De Gaulle ordered his immediate incarceration at Fort du Portalet in the Pyrenees. Later, he was transferred to the Fort de Pierre-Levée on the Île d'Yeu, off the French Atlantic coast.

Despite subsequent pleas from several nations to show clemency by releasing the old man, he remained incarcerated on the Île d'Yeu, increasingly slipped into senility, and died on July 23, 1951, at ninety-five.

The career of Marshal Henri Phillipe Pétain was a personal and national tragedy. The most favorable interpretation of his role in the French surrender and the creation of Vichy was that he wanted to spare the French people the devastation the Germans had already visited upon nations in eastern Europe. Yet it is also true that Pétain's authoritarianism was not far out of tune with the governing style of no less than Hitler, Mussolini, and the other fascist dictators, and Vichy, under his regime, voluntarily—even avidly—collaborated in the persecution of French citizens, including the deportation, forced labor, and death of thousands of French Jews. Without question as well, Pétain's government sacrificed French national identity and honor. With considerable wisdom, one of his aides criticized him for thinking "too much about the French and not enough about France."

#14
CHARLES DE GAULLE

Exiled Champion of Free France

Charles de Gaulle is seated at his desk in London, from which he served, in exile, as commander of the Free French Forces resisting Germany. Note the Lorraine Cross pinned above his left coat pocket—symbol of Free France.
(credit: *Imperial War Museums, London*)

German forces invaded France during the very first month of World War I, sweeping in a great wheeling arc to the north, through Belgium, and then descending on the flank and rear of the French army. The German Kaiser promised his people that their fathers and sons in the field would be home "before the leaves have fallen from the trees." And, through most of August 1914, it looked as if the Kaiser would be able to keep his promise—but then the French took a stand on the Marne, Paris was saved, and the war was not over in a month but had to be fought out over four unimaginably bloody years, ending in the devastation of France and the defeat of Germany. Just shy of twenty years after that first war ended, Adolf Hitler invaded Poland on September 1, 1939, and then he took the war to France on May 10, 1940. A few weeks later, on June 23, an Armistice was signed, and, two days after that, the Battle of France ended—this time in a resounding victory for Germany.

The defeat of France was absolute and ignominious. The terms of the Armistice established German occupation of three-fifths of France north and west of a line through Geneva and Tours, extending to the Spanish border, and France was obliged to pay Germany the costs of the occupation, to the tune of four hundred million French francs a day. Two-fifths of France, essentially the territory south of the Loire River, was renamed the French State but universally called Vichy and administered as a nominally sovereign German puppet by the Marshal Philippe Pétain.

As for the French military, the surrender had been all but total. A small fraction of the French army had been evacuated to England from Dunkirk along with survivors of the British Expeditionary Force. At large as well was one senior officer, a newly created brigadier general named Charles de Gaulle. He had fought in the Battle of France and simultaneously served briefly as Under-Secretary of State for National Defense and War, a post that gave him almost complete responsibility for coordinating French military action with that of the British. In May 1940, General Maxime Weygand was summoned from duty in Syria to replace the feckless General Maurice Gamelin as the French army's supreme commander. He took over on May 17, but by June 8 he was telling de Gaulle that the situation was hopeless, the end was near, France was defeated, and Britain would have no choice but to capitulate as well. Hitler would rule Europe, and Weygand looked toward an armistice with the Germans that would give him a skeleton army large enough to maintain order among the conquered French people within a conquered continent. When de Gaulle responded by urging him to fight on, Weygand laughed, a laugh de Gaulle later recalled as "despairing."

Refusing to give in or give up, de Gaulle flew to London the very next day, June 9, to meet with Prime Minister Churchill, and then returned to France. On June 10, Italy invaded southern France. De Gaulle once again tried to persuade Weygand to continue the fight by making a last-ditch stand at Paris. Instead, the government declared the capital an open city. To spare its destruction, it would not be defended. On June 11, the government evacuated Paris, and de Gaulle sought General Charles Hunziger, French commander of the Central Army Group, so that he could offer him Weygand's position as supreme commander—even though Weygand had yet to resign.

It was to no avail. The French leadership continued to dissolve into defeatism. On June 14, de Gaulle accepted a mission to go once again to London to discuss the idea of evacuating the remaining French forces to the North African colonies. That evening he happened to dine in the same restaurant as Pétain and there said goodbye to him for the last time. Unable to get a flight out of France, de Gaulle took a boat to Plymouth on June 15 and, on the next day, met with Churchill at 10 Downing Street to discuss a proposed Anglo-French Political Union, a temporary nation by which the war against Germany might be continued. He was flown in a British aircraft back to France, only to learn on landing that, in his brief absence, he had been removed from the government and Pétain had been named prime minister, charged with immediately securing an armistice.

It was now late in the day of June 16, 1940, the day the French armies surrendered in the field. A British general named Edward Spears was in Bordeaux. Fluent in French, he had served as special aide to Churchill, who had given him an urgent assignment: retrieve de Gaulle and bring him back to Britain. It was clear that he was the only French general officer willing to continue the fight against Germany.

So the curtain went up on the opening act of Charles de Gaulle's campaign to redeem France from an infamous collaboration with Nazi Germany and what de Gaulle saw as the enslavement of the French people.

He knew he was in imminent danger of arrest either by the German soldiers or by French police, who were now collaborating with them. Determined to stay in the fight, he quietly announced, on the morning of June 17, that he was driving General Spears to the Bordeaux airfield to see him off on his return flight to Britain. France was no longer allied with England, and it was time for Spears to leave. De Gaulle told no one that he intended to go with him.

In addition to the British and French general, the car carried de Gaulle's aide de camp, Lieutenant Geoffroy de Courcel, and a trunk of top secret documents snatched from the French war ministry. They contained the names of officers who could be recruited for a military resistance in occupied France. The drive to the airfield was perilous in the extreme—and painfully slow, as the vehicle maneuvered past abandoned wrecks and endless oozing lines of despairing refugees. At every crossroad, gendarmes loyal to Marshal Pétain stood guard. It was likely that any or all of them by now had received orders to arrest Charles de Gaulle. Yet the car was never even stopped, not once, until it finally reached the airport gate. There, a police officer peered into the vehicle, demanding to know why a *British* officer was seated with two *French* officers in an automobile headed for the runway. De Gaulle replied that he was escorting the Englishman to a flight bound for his homeland. Within another day or two, no face in Europe, except for that of Adolf Hitler, would be more universally recognizable than Charles de Gaulle's. What is more, at six-foot-five, he had been an imposing presence. For now, tall though he was, he was just an officer on an errand. The gendarme waved the car through, and the party drove up to the waiting De Havilland Dragon Rapide biplane.

It was a small, fragile-looking civilian airliner, next to which its pilot frantically waved to the approaching passengers. He strode up to the car to work out plans for an immediate departure. When he saw the heavy trunk laden with documents, he pointed out that it was liable to shift in flight, unbalancing the light biplane, and sending it into a tailspin. Better tie it down inside the fuselage.

But no one had a rope.

Anxious to get away before everyone would be subject to arrest, the pilot suggested leaving the trunk behind. Hitherto calm, General de Gaulle suddenly became animated.

Non!

The papers the luggage contained could not be left behind. The future of France depended on the contents of the trunk. De Gaulle ordered Lieutenant de Courcel to find a rope and bring it back. With that, de Gaulle leaned back in the rear seat of the car, chain-smoking the gold-tipped cigarettes he favored while Spears paced outside, anticipating the arrival of French or German agents.

At last, he spied de Courcel, running, a ball of twine tightly clutched triumphantly in one hand. With its cargo tied down, the little London-bound plane took off, and until August 25, 1944, the day Paris was liberated by the Allies, Charles de Gaulle would be, in exile, the heart, soul, and mind of something he called "Free France."

Charles-André-Marie-Joseph de Gaulle was born on November 22, 1890, into an intensely nationalistic family in the industrial city of Lille, France. His father, Henri, a professor of history in a Jesuit college, would later found his own school. His mother was from a prominent family of Lille industrialists. Her most prominent memory was of the shameful French defeat by the Prussians at Sedan in 1870 during the Franco-Prussian War. Her telling and retelling of that event made a deep impression on her son—the third of five children—and it prompted him to train for a military career at the Academy of Saint-Cyr. After graduation and commission as a second lieutenant in 1913, he was attached to an infantry regiment under the command of Colonel Philippe Pétain.

De Gaulle made an immediate impression on the colonel as a young officer of extraordinary intelligence and initiative. As for de Gaulle, he readily reciprocated his colonel's high regard. To him, Pétain seemed an ideal officer, and he revered him as a mentor. When World War I commenced in the summer of 1914, the young second lieutenant displayed great courage, especially during the bloody defense of Verdun, a campaign in which de Gaulle was wounded three times and made a prisoner of war after he was knocked unconscious by the close detonation of an artillery shell on March 2, 1916, and then bayonetted in the thigh. He spent the next two years and eight months as a POW, making five valiant, albeit unsuccessful, attempts to escape. In letters to his parents, he called his confinement a "shameful misfortune," and he was not released until the armistice.

Following the war, de Gaulle served briefly as a member of a military mission to Poland. He then taught at his alma mater, Saint-Cyr, before being chosen for two years of special training in strategy and tactics at the *École Supérieure de Guerre* (the French War College). After graduating in 1925, he was promoted by Marshal Pétain to the Staff of the *Conseil Supérieur de la Guerre*, the Supreme War Council.

Holding the rank of major, de Gaulle served from 1927 to 1929 in the French army, assigned to occupy the Rhineland, per the Treaty of Versailles. During this service, he grew increasingly alarmed by the continued danger he saw posed by German aggression, which increased in volume and intensity throughout the 1920s. Following the Rhineland assignment, he served for two years in the Middle East and then, as a lieutenant colonel, served for four years as a member of the secretariat of the *Conseil Supérieur de la Défense Nationale.*

In addition to his work as a field and staff officer, de Gaulle, a skilled writer, was a compelling military theorist, who, in 1924, wrote a study of the relation of the civil and military powers in Germany, a provocative and well-received book titled *Discord Among the Enemy.* He also lectured on military leadership, collecting his talks in *The Edge of the Sword,* a widely read book published in 1932. Two years later, he published another book, this one a study of military theory titled *The Army of the Future.* In this work, he developed and defended the idea of building and maintaining a small professional army designed to have a high degree of mechanization for maximum flexibility and mobility. This concept bore a resemblance to the post-World War I German idea of the *Führerheer,* the "leader army," a small professional army that would serve as the core around which a massive conscripted fighting force could be quickly raised in time of war. De Gaulle's idea ran directly contrary to the prevailing French strategy of the interwar period, which was based on maintaining a defensive force consisting of soldiers conscripted for a required term of service. The Maginot Line, a set of forts and hardened defensive positions built along France's eastern border, was part and parcel of prevailing French military policy. While it was actually intended to do nothing more than slow an enemy invasion to buy time to mount a counterattack, French military planners came to think of it as an impregnable substitute for a more active and aggressive military policy.

De Gaulle was not content with allowing his ideas to be taken as merely academic. He became politically active, continually appealing to government leaders in an effort to win them to his point of view. This provoked a good deal of discord with de Gaulle's military superiors, including Marshal Pétain himself, who protested de Gaulle's right to publish a historical study titled *France and Her Army*—a work that appeared, after much delay, in 1938.

❖

Post-World War I France, like the other major Western European democracy, Britain, was desperate to avoid a new major war. Although the Allies had been victorious in the 1914-1918 war, they had suffered great devastation, especially France. Charles de Gaulle's appeals to prepare for the coming war and to do so aggressively, by building a professional army capable of delivering a strong counterattack or even a preemptive attack, were stoutly resisted. Thus, when Hitler made war, the France he confronted lacked both the heart and the stomach to fight effectively. The French army was considerably larger than the German army, and it was well equipped. What it lacked was top-notch leadership and the popular and political will to wage an all-out war.

Two days after General de Gaulle was spirited out of France in General Spear's aircraft, he made the first of many radio broadcasts to the French people from a BBC radio studio in London. *"À tous les français"* ("To all Frenchmen"), he began:

France has lost a battle! But France has not lost the war! The government of the moment has capitulated, giving way to panic and delivering the country into servitude. However, not all is lost. Out in the free world, immense forces have not yet entered the fray. One day, these forces will crush the enemy. It is necessary that on that day France is present at the victory. Then she will recover her liberty and her grandeur. Such is my goal, my only goal!

That is why I invite all French people, wherever they find themselves, to join with me in action, in sacrifice, and in hope.

Our nation is in danger of dying. Let us struggle to save her!

Vive la France!

His brief broadcast was printed up in the form of posters, and some of the French who joined de Gaulle in London—mostly survivors of Dunkirk—smuggled these back into France and saw to their distribution.

De Gaulle's speech was considered the founding of the French Resistance. To be sure, the June 18 broadcast did not produce a flood of volunteers, but it was a stance, and over the succeeding months, more and more French men and women rallied to de Gaulle and the Free French cause.

General de Gaulle remained in England, directing the Resistance and working with the British and, later, the Americans as well as coordinating the Free French forces attached to the Allied armies. He continued broadcasting from London, prompting a Vichy military court to try him in absentia for treason. Found guilty of treason on August 2, 1940, he was sentenced to death, loss of military rank, and confiscation of property. With the die cast, he threw himself with great skill, energy, and determination into organizing the Free French Forces and a shadow Free French government-in-exile. It was an extraordinary task, since the brigadier general was all but unknown outside of French military circles. Even the people of France did not recognize him as a political figure until well into the course of the war. All that sustained him was his supreme self-confidence, his strength of character, his ability to lead, and a conviction that France was far greater than the handful of leaders who had betrayed her. Throughout the war, until the liberation of his country, de Gaulle continued to broadcast from exile, first from London and then, in 1943, from Algiers, which had been liberated from the control of collaborationist Vichy officials. He worked closely, but often contentiously, with the British and American high command. The resistance movement coordinated with the SAS—Special Air Service (British Special Forces)—although the effort did always go smoothly.

It was friction directly with Winston Churchill and his government that motivated de Gaulle to transfer his headquarters to Algiers as soon as that French colony had been secured. In Algiers, without interference from the British, he became president of the French Committee of National Liberation. He served at first with General Henri Giraud, but then skillfully engineered Giraud's ouster so that he might emerge as sole leader of the committee. It was de Gaulle, now the unquestioned head of the Free French government-in-exile, who returned in triumph to Paris on September 9, 1944, after the capital's liberation.

❖

After the war, Charles de Gaulle was the obvious choice to lead two successive provisional governments. Nevertheless, on January 20, 1946, he resigned over a dispute with the political parties forming the permanent coalition government. The surrender to Germany had brought an end to the Third French Republic, and when the Fourth French Republic was formed after the war, de Gaulle found deep fault with it, condemning it as very likely to repeat the errors of the Third Republic. This moved him to found, in 1947, the *Rassemblement du Peuple Français* (Rally of the French People), which won 120 seats in the National Assembly in the 1951 elections. The RPF soon disappointed him as well, however, and the always prickly de Gaulle severed his connection with it in 1953. Absent his leadership, the RPF disbanded two years later, and de Gaulle withdrew from both the civilian government and the military during 1955-1956. During this interval, he wrote three volumes of memoirs.

When insurrection broke out in Algiers in 1958 and threatened to bring civil war to France, Charles de Gaulle was thrust back into the national arena as prime minister designate. On December 21, 1958, he was elected president of what was now the Fifth French Republic, a government that has endured for nearly sixty years and counting. He served as president for the next ten years, amid much turbulence, controversy, and opposition from the nation's leftwing political leaders. Upon his retirement, de Gaulle resumed writing his memoirs but succumbed to a heart attack on November 9, 1970, a year after leaving office. He was eighty years old.

#15
HERMANN GÖRING

Nazi Reichsmarschall (Imperial Marshal), who was architect of the powerful German Luftwaffe (air force) in World War II and who initially authorized the Holocaust

Hermann Göring, in the dock at the Nuremberg Tribunal. Beside him are fellow defendants Rudolf Hess (Hitler's deputy Führer), Joachim von Ribbentrop (ex-German foreign minister), and Wilhelm Keitel (chief of the German Armed Forces High Command, or OKW). Behind him are (from left) Karl Dönitz (admiral of German navy and Hitler's appointed successor as head of state), Erich Raeder (commander of Germany's submarine fleet), Baldur von Schirach (head of the Hitler Youth), and Fritz Sauckel (ex-Plenipotentiary for Labor Deployment— Germany's master of slave labor). (credit: *U.S. Army via Wikimedia Commons*)

Hermann Göring's zeppelin-like girth, his flamboyant uniforms—including the sky-blue ensemble he designed for his role as head of the *Luftwaffe*—his corruption, his insatiable kleptocratic looting, and his drug habit have long prompted some historians of Nazism to take him less than seriously. Outwardly, he could indeed be a buffoon, but he was deadly serious about National Socialism. An early Nazi Party member, he was wounded in the failed Beer Hall Putsch of 1923, showed Hitler slavish devotion, founded the *Gestapo* (secret police), built the *Luftwaffe* (air force), was president of the Reichstag, and mobilized all sectors of the German economy for war. In all, from the beginning to the end of the Nazi regime, he vied with Heinrich Himmler for the status of second most powerful man in Germany.

And he was, first to last, a true Nazi believer. Captured after the war, Himmler was bound over for trial by the war crimes tribunal at Nuremburg. He showed no remorse but defended himself with great skill and unflagging enthusiasm. He nominated himself as the leader of the other defendants and sincerely believed he was a martyr to a great cause and, more important, would be remembered as such. In the end, sentenced to hang, he cheated the hangman by swallowing cyanide he had successfully hidden through his long incarceration. While he died unmourned, he was—and remains—a symbol of Nazism second in prominence only to Hitler.

❖

Born January 12, 1893, at Rosenheim, Bavaria, to Heinrich Ernst Göring and his second wife, Franziska Tiefenbrunn Göring, Hermann was one in a family of ten children. His father had had five by his first wife and would have five more by the second. Hermann was the fourth of that latter group. A former cavalry officer, Heinrich Göring had been the first governor-general of South-West Africa (today Namibia), at the time a German protectorate. When Hermann was born, Heinrich was serving as German consul general in Haiti. Franziska had returned to Germany to give birth to Hermann, nursed him for six weeks, and then left her newborn with a friend in Bavaria. She would not see him again for three years, when Heinrich returned with her to Germany.

When Heinrich did return, he retired from government service, and the large family would have been reduced to living on his pension had it not been for young Hermann's namesake and godfather. In one of the more profound ironies in the life of Hermann Göring, the godfather, Dr. Hermann Epenstein, was a prosperous *Jewish* physician and businessman, who had met Heinrich in Africa. He provided the family with a home in Berlin-Friedenau and, later, Veldenstein, a small castle near Nuremberg. Heinrich seems also to have been complicit in furnishing his wife as Epenstein's mistress, an apparently voluntary cuckolding relationship that lasted some fifteen years.

As for young Hermann, he had been attracted to things military since early childhood. He enjoyed dressing up in the uniform of a South African Boer, and he played with toy soldiers. He read military history avidly and enrolled at the Karlsruhe Military Academy in 1905, followed by the main cadet school at Lichterfelde in 1909. Upon graduating in 1912, he was commissioned a lieutenant in the Prince Wilhelm Regiment (112th Infantry) of the Prussian Army. At the outbreak of World War I in 1914, Göring was sent to Mulhouse with the 112th and served there for a year before he was hospitalized for severe rheumatism. Trench warfare did not agree with him. A friend, the pilot Bruno Loerzer, persuaded him to transfer to the more comfortable and exciting air service. Turned down for a transfer, he nevertheless flew as Loerzer's observer. Although he was discovered and sentenced to three weeks' confinement to barracks, the sentence was waived and his observer's status made official.

Göring served with distinction as an observer, earning, along with Loerzer, the Iron Cross, first class. He went on to pilot training and flew with *Jagdstaffel* (Squadron) 5 until he was shot in the hip during an aerial dogfight. This took him out of the war for a year, but in February 1917, he was assigned to *Jadgdstaffel* 26, which was commanded by Loerzer. He proved himself a natural pilot and, even more important, a natural dogfighter. He scored one aerial victory after another and rose to command *Jadgdstaffel* 27. Among his many decorations was the so-called Blue Max, the *Pour le Mérite* that had been established by Frederick the Great in 1740 and was among the highest of Imperial German honors. But the crowning achievement of his World War I career was his being named, on July 7, 1918, to command *Jagdgeschwader* 1, the legendary "Flying Circus" that was originally led by the late Red Baron himself, Manfred von Richtofen.

As the war ground to its end in November 1918, Göring repeatedly refused to obey orders to withdraw his squadron from action. On the day of the Armistice, November 11, 1918, he was ordered to surrender his unit's aircraft to the Allies. Believing, like many other German military officers, that the German capitulation was an act of betrayal, he refused. Like others under his command, he purposely crash landed to keep his plane out of enemy hands. He left the military, convinced that he and his comrades at arms had been "stabbed in the back" by weak civilians, Jews, Marxists, and the Republicans who had conspired to overthrow Kaiser Wilhelm II and send him fleeing into Dutch exile.

Although Göring left the military, he continued flying. After struggling to make ends meet as a barnstormer, he accepted an offer to fly as a test pilot for the Dutch Fokker aircraft manufacturing firm and the Swedish Svenska Luftraflik (1919-1920). He enrolled at Munich University in 1921 and, in that city, met Adolf Hitler. Impressed with his charismatic oratory, Göring joined the fledgling Nazi Party in 1922. In 1923, Hitler named him to command the paramilitary *Sturmabteilung* (SA), the Storm Troopers. He was quickly promoted from *Oberster SA-Führer* (colonel) to *Gruppenführer* (lieutenant general). In the meantime, he married Baroness Carin von Kantzow, a Swedish noblewoman, who grew fond of young Hitler and, with Göring, hosted him and three other principals of the early Nazi Party: Ernst Röhm, Rudolf Hess, and Alfred Rosenberg. Göring further cemented his relationship with Hitler by participating in the Beer Hall Putsch of November 8-9, 1923, in which he sustained a serious leg wound. His wife spirited him out of Germany and to Innsbruck, Austria, where he was operated on. Given morphine to control the pain, he instantly became a lifelong addict.

A hunted man in Germany, Göring moved with Carin to Venice and, in May 1924, visited Rome, where they met with Benito Mussolini, who told Göring that he very much wanted to meet with Adolf Hitler—at the time serving a sentence in Landsberg prison while also composing his memoir, *Mein Kampf.* Until 1927, the Görings were fugitives in Europe, with Hermann in the throes of an uncontrollable addiction punctuated by periods of violence so extreme that he was more than once confined to an asylum and forced to wear a straitjacket. A declaration of amnesty in Germany brought him back in 1927, and he returned to work in the aircraft industry. Carin, however, ill with tuberculosis and epilepsy, died in October 1931.

As the Nazi Party was rebuilding itself and then expanding, Göring won election to the Reichstag (German parliament) in 1928 as a representative from Bavaria. He was one of only twelve Nazis to gain a seat, but in 1930 he became one of 107. Hitler sent Göring to meet with the future Pope Pius XII in the Vatican during May 1931, and in 1932, with the Nazi party now firmly entrenched on the German political scene, Göring became president of the Reichstag.

The following year, 1933, President Paul von Hindenburg named Hitler chancellor. On the night of February 27, fire broke out at the Reichstag. Among the first to arrive on the scene was Göring, who, after the arrest of Marinus van der Lubbe, a communist radical, who claimed responsibility for the fire, Göring, in his capacity as president of the Reichstag, demanded a roundup of all communists. He ushered through passage the so-called Reichstag Fire Decree, which suspended basic rights and authorized detention without trial. Some four thousand Communist Party members were arrested. When Göring demanded that they be summarily shot, Rudolf Diels, head of the Prussian political police, ignored him. This affront prompted Göring to create the Gestapo, a secret police force. Appointed *Reichsminister*—minister without portfolio—as well as Minister of the Interior for Prussia, and Reich Commissioner for Aviation, Göring ordered construction of the first concentration camps, which were originally used to detain political dissidents but were before long greatly expanded to confine Jews and others the Reich deemed "undesirable." By April 1934, Göring turned over management of both the Gestapo and the camps to Heinrich Himmler. Later in 1934, Göring acquired another appointment, Master of the Reich Hunt and Forest Office. This became a pet project for him, and he assiduously set about creating wildlife preserves and introducing game laws and forest-management reforms that are still in use in Germany today.

While Göring was an able steward of his nation's natural resources, he did not hesitate to eliminate political enemies. At Hitler's behest, he played a major role in the purge of the SA during the so-called Night of the Long Knives (June 30, 1934), in which potential rivals for power (among them, SA chief Ernst Rohm) were murdered en masse. The next year, as Reichsminister for Air and commander of the *Luftwaffe*, Göring began covertly, in defiance of the Treaty of Versailles, to organize and build what would become the world's most advanced and formidable air force. While this was under way, he assumed power second only to Hitler himself, as director of the four-year plan (1936). This gave him virtually total authority in matters of the German economy, and he reorganized state-owned industries as the Hermann Göring Works during 1937-1941 as he put the nation's economy on a war footing—beginning well in advance of the start of World War II. In 1939, Göring was officially appointed Adolf Hitler's successor, effective upon his resignation or death. In 1940, Göring was given the military title of *Reichsmarschall.*

The opening months of World War II tested the mettle of Göring's *Luftwaffe*, which played a major role in the rapid conquest of Poland during September 1-October 6, 1939. The air arm was integral to the leading German military doctrine of *Blitzkrieg* ("lighting war"), the rapid, overwhelming attack, by ground and air forces, aimed not just at the front lines but, simultaneously, at the rear echelons of supply and reinforcement.

In large part due to the performance of the *Luftwaffe*, Göring rated highly in Hitler's estimation early in the war. During Germany's great success in the Battle of France (May 10-June 25, 1940), his *Luftwaffe* performed well in ground-support operations until it came to interdicting the evacuation of Anglo-French forces from Dunkirk (May 28-June 4). Had the *Luftwaffe* destroyed the BEF and French forces gathered there, either invasion of England or a negotiated peace between Britain and Germany would likely have handed Hitler victory. As great as this missed opportunity was, the *Luftwaffe* suffered a failure of even greater significance in the Battle of Britain (July 10-October 31, 1940). This cannot be laid entirely at the feet of Hermann Göring, who had strategically targeted Royal Air Force (RAF) bases in initial air raids over the British Isles. His priority was to destroy aircraft on the ground and crater runways, thereby degrading if not neutralizing the RAF as a threat. However, he bowed to Hitler's insistence that he bomb major cities. Not only did this fail to break the British will to fight (quite the contrary, it rallied civilian support for the war), it bought time for the RAF to regroup and meet the *Luftwaffe* in the skies above England. Defending their homeland, the RAF pilots proved more than a match for the German pilots. Of 2,550 serviceable German and Italian aircraft used against Britain, 1,977 were destroyed, and nearly 1,700 aircrew killed, wounded, or captured before the *Luftwaffe* ended the air raid campaign. The defeat essentially meant the end of a German invasion threat against Britain.

Toward the close of 1942, Göring made another critical strategic error. When the German Sixth Army was being battered at Stalingrad by both the Russian winter and the Red Army, Göring pledged to resupply the troops with air drops. Hitler counted on this, but the *Luftwaffe* failed to come through during November-December 1942. As a result, the battered Sixth Army surrendered, and the war on the Russian front now turned against Germany. It was following this debacle that Hitler's confidence in Göring crumbled. Worse, Göring no longer made much of a secret about his personal corruption. He freely embezzled from his own government and looted the art treasures of conquered nations. He built a palace and decorated it with the spoils of war. Here he lived a life of dissipation, which disgusted the teetotaling, straitlaced Hitler. As the war turned inexorably against Germany, Göring increased his use of morphine and became increasingly irresponsible in his attitude and actions.

As Göring lost the confidence of Hitler, so he soon lost the faith of the German people. He had publicly pledged to them that Allied bombs would never rain upon the Fatherland. As early as 1940, British bombs began falling on German cities, and by 1943 the raids were becoming regular and intense. From 1944 to the end of the war, urban Germany was being bombed day and night. Göring had once joked that he would change his name to "Meier" (a proverbially common German name) if a single bomb ever fell on Germany. By 1944, Germans regularly referred to him by that epithet.

Göring finally took a step too far at the very end of the war, during April 1945, with the streets of Berlin a battlefield and Hitler cowering in his bunker. He sent a message to the Führer, invoking his order from many years earlier, naming him as his designated successor. He now volunteered to succeed Hitler. His object in this was to negotiate peace with the Allies. Enraged by the message, Hitler summarily stripped Göring of all his offices and charged him with high treason. Knowing that Göring had fled to Obersalzberg, the Alpine complex that included Hitler's own Berchtesgaden residence, the Führer ordered Göring and his staff to be placed under house arrest on April 23. Three days later, Obersalzberg fell under attack by the Allies, and Göring was evacuated to Mauterndorf, his thirteenth-century castle in nearby Salzberg. He was released on May 5 by a Luftwaffe unit that was passing through. They no longer feared retribution from Hitler, who, with his wife of a few hours, Eva Braun, had committed suicide on April 30. Desperate to escape the Russians, Göring surrendered to elements of the U.S. 36th Infantry Division on May 6. He was detained and then transferred in September to Nuremberg for trial by the war crimes tribunal. Found guilty of conspiracy, waging a war of aggression, war crimes, and crimes against humanity, he was sentenced on October 1, 1946, to hang. On October 15, before the sentence could be carried out, he committed suicide by swallowing cyanide.

#16
JOSEPH GOEBBELS

*Sophisticated mastermind of propaganda central to the rise
of Adolf Hitler, the Nazi Party, and the Third Reich*

Joseph Goebbels (foreground) is flanked, on his right, by Adolf Hitler and
Hermann Göring and, on his left, by Rudolf Hess. (credit: *National Archives and
Records Administration*)

In his seminal autobiographical and political manifesto, *Mein Kampf* (1925), Adolf Hitler wrote of the "big lie," calling it a technique of mass persuasion used by "the Jews." He wrote of...

> the principle—which is quite true within itself—that in the big lie there is always a certain force of credibility; because the broad masses of a nation are always more easily corrupted in the deeper strata of their emotional nature than consciously or voluntarily; and thus in the primitive simplicity of their minds they more readily fall victims to the big lie than the small lie, since they themselves often tell small lies in little matters but would be ashamed to resort to large-scale falsehoods.

Years later, in 1941, Joseph Goebbels wrote an article called "From Churchill's Lie Factory," in which he said that the "English leadership secret does not depend on particular intelligence. Rather, it depends on a remarkably stupid thick-headedness. The English follow the principle that when one lies, one should lie big, and stick to it. They keep up their lies, even at the risk of looking ridiculous."

Hitler believed—or may have believed—he was discussing the target of his unparalleled hatred and contempt, "the *Jews*," on whom all of Germany's woes were to be blamed. Goebbels declared that the "big lie" was the secret of *British* leadership. In fact, both men were defining *propaganda* as a big lie essential to gaining control of the broad masses, who are inherently dim-witted. They were laying out the path of their own rise to power. Furthermore, Hitler understood that he needed a master of the big lie, and Joseph Goebbels was his man. Goebbels crafted the ongoing propaganda campaign that was indispensable in the selling of Hitler, the Nazi Party, the Nazi regime, and the Nazi war aims to the German people.

Paul Joseph Goebbels was born in the Rhenish town of Rheydt on October 29, 1897. His father, Fritz, was a factory clerk, his mother, Katharina Odenhausen, a housewife. She was ethnically Dutch, and in 1932 Goebbels felt obliged to publish a pamphlet to refute rumors that his mother's mother, his maternal grandmother, was Jewish. Both Goebbels's parents were, in fact, practicing Catholics, and they harbored the hope that Joseph, the fourth of their six children, would enter the priesthood. Perhaps he became familiar with the Latin phrase the Catholic Church used to describe the all-important mission of "propagation of the faith": *Propagandum Fidei*. Perhaps his early religious training taught him that "propaganda" was, in essence, a propagation of the faith.

He grew up a sickly child, afflicted with chronic inflammation of the lungs, and he had been born with clubfoot, his right foot turned inward and both shorter and thicker than his left. A childhood operation failed to correct the deformity, and, for the rest of his life, he wore a leg brace and corrective shoe and walked with a pronounced limp. A quiet, reclusive, and studious child, he was educated at a parochial Christian *gymnasium*, from which he graduated at the top of his class. But he did not go into the priesthood. Instead, in 1917, his foot and general ill health disqualifying him for military service, he studied literature and history at the universities of Bonn, Würzburg, Freiburg, and Munich (studies financed in part by the Catholic Albert Magnus Society) before earning a doctorate in philology from the University of Heidelberg in 1921.

After graduation, he had both journalistic and literary aspirations. Goebbels wrote a great deal, but he could find no ready market for his journalism or his literary efforts—although the in-house publishing arm of the Nazi Party, Eher-Verlag, did publish his semi-autobiographical novel, *Michael*, in 1929; anti-Semitic in orientation, the novel told the tale of a charismatic natural leader. Rather like the young Adolf Hitler, who was a frustrated artist, Goebbels was in some measure a frustrated author. He made a living with a low-level job on the stock exchange and then as a bank clerk. He also read voraciously—everything from the rightwing racist writings of Houston Stewart Chamberlain (his 1899 *Foundations of the Nineteenth Century* presented concepts of anti-Semitism and Aryan racial superiority) to the leftwing works of Marx, Engels, and Rosa Luxembourg. By 1923, he was drifting toward the emerging German nationalist *"völkisch"* (populist) movement, and the next year he became interested in Adolf Hitler —who had been tried for treason in February, after the failure of the Beer Hall Putsch—and Hitler's nascent Nazi movement. A loner by inclination, Goebbels found friends among a group of early Nazis, who drew him into National Socialist politics, where he became increasingly attracted by Hitler's charisma.

Not surprisingly, the Nazi party was poorly supplied with intellectuals and writers of ability. Although the dark-featured, clubfooted Goebbels hardly fit the "Aryan" Nazi mold, he was a talented public speaker who rose quickly within the party, and in 1926, Hitler appointed him *Gauleiter* (district leader) of Berlin. This was an important assignment, since the party, having established itself in Bavaria, had no real presence in the capital. Goebbels rapidly built up the Nazi organization in Berlin while expanding his journalistic career on behalf of the party by editing a new magazine, *Der Angriff* (*The Assault*). In 1928, Hitler recognized that, in Goebbels, he had both a true-believing loyalist, an able administrator, and a man of unique ability as a communicator. He appointed him propaganda director for the party.

Armed with a background in literature and mythology as well as an understanding of popular religion, Goebbels set to work not merely to promote the Nazi political agenda, but to create around Adolf Hitler himself a powerful cult of personality. He sought to imbue Hitler with the "Führer myth," molding his image into that of a combination savior, messiah, and infallible leader. Goebbels's propaganda program went far beyond the printed page. He developed speeches and radio broadcasts, and he orchestrated and choreographed vast ritualistic party convocations, demonstrations, rallies, and celebrations. It was Goebbels who introduced the universal Nazi salute (which he borrowed from Mussolini's Roman salute) and the salutation, *"Heil Hitler!"* No person other than Adolf Hitler himself was more responsible for the creation of the Führer's public persona.

In his *Mein Kampf*, Hitler wrote: "It was not until the [First World] War that it became evident what immense results could be obtained by a correct application of propaganda. Here again, unfortunately, all our studying had to be done on the enemy side." Joseph Goebbels understood this as well, and he almost certainly was familiar with the work of the Committee on Public Information (CPI), America's own propaganda bureau, which a journalist named George Creel created at the behest of President Woodrow Wilson to whip up popular enthusiasm for U.S. entry into World War I. Edward Bernays, the father of the uniquely American profession of public relations, had worked for the CPI during the Great War, and he wrote two early books on PR in part based on his wartime experience—*Crystallizing Popular Opinion* (1923) and *Propaganda* (1928). In 1933, he hosted a dinner at which Karl von Weigand, U.S. foreign correspondent for the Hearst newspapers, having just returned from Germany, where Hitler had been named chancellor, told stories of having met Goebbels. Weigand told of how he boasted of his plans to consolidate Nazi power and showed him his extensive private library of works relating to propaganda. Turning now to Bernays, Weigand reported that Goebbels specifically mentioned Bernays's own *Crystallizing Public Opinion* "as a basis for his destructive campaign against the Jews of Germany." Bernays, an Austrian-born Jew, nephew of Sigmund Freud, was dumbfounded.

When Hitler rose to the office of chancellor in 1933, one of his first official acts was to formally create a Ministry for Public Enlightenment and Propaganda at the cabinet level, with Joseph Goebbels as its minister. He also named Goebbels president of the Reich Chamber of Culture, which gave him control not only of the print press and radio, but also the stage, cinema, literature, music, and the other fine arts. On his own initiative, Goebbels also enlarged his brief to encompass education, especially at the high school level, which became an important institution for the dissemination of propaganda.

Unlike most other Nazis, Goebbels exercised his extraordinary authority with a sophisticated and light touch. He regulated the various media and arts with a surprisingly liberal hand. He understood that he was, in effect, a salesman and that his wares consisted of Adolf Hitler and National Socialism, and he further understood that nothing dulls the appeal of merchandise like enforced repetition and the feeling that one is being bullied into belief. Nobody likes a pushy salesman. Goebbels therefore integrated propaganda into the stream of general culture and took care to avoid smothering the media and the arts. Moreover, he worked with creative writers, artists, and especially film makers to produce propaganda that was entertaining and even aesthetically appealing. His own youngest sister, Maria, married an important German film director and screenwriter, Max W. Kimmich, who had begun making nationalist-themed movies as early as 1935. In 1938, after he married Maria Goebbels, her brother began working closely with him. The numerous movies he directed or wrote at the behest of Goebbels from 1938 to 1944 made him a wealthy man. Kimmich, like the other filmmakers Goebbels courted—most notably the extraordinary documentarian Leni Riefenstahl (best known for her chronicle of the 1934 Nazi Party Congress at Nuremburg, *Triumph of the Will*)—knew that what he wanted was not to coerce the people into belief, but to seduce them.

❖

Many within the party hierarchy grew increasingly jealous of the power of "Dr. Goebbels," and by the late 1930s his critics were making inroads into his domain, which lessened his influence. Goebbels also allowed his personal life to compromise his political existence when a romantic affair with Lída Baarová, a beautiful Czech-Austrian movie star who was his mistress from 1936 to 1938, became widely known and created a scandal in outwardly prudish Nazi society. Hitler finally intervened on August 16, 1938. He warned Goebbels that, as Germany was about to annex the Czech Sudetenland (which occurred during October 1-10, 1938), he could not tolerate an adulterous affair between one of his top ministers and a Czech actress. Heartbroken, Goebbels broke off the affair and even managed to salvage his career, but his influence during the run-up to World War II was greatly diminished. Indeed, while he had been indispensable to the rise of Hitler and Nazism, he did not believe that starting a great war was wise.

But then the war began, on September 1, 1939, with Hitler's invasion of Poland. Responding to this reality, Goebbels quickly carved out a fresh niche for himself with a program of propaganda directed toward Germany's enemies and aimed at undermining their morale. He developed broadcasts to be beamed to Polish and French soldiers, and he planted rumors concerning fifth column subversion in the Allied nations. He also fashioned for such stand-out generals as Erwin Rommel heroic myths of invincibility, much as he had done for Hitler during the dictator's rise. Among Goebbels's best-known creations were Axis Sally and Lord Haw Haw. Axis Sally was an American named Mildred Gillars, who lived in Germany and whom Goebbels hired to broadcast propaganda to American troops. (After the war, Gillars was convicted of treason and sentenced to twelve years' imprisonment; she was paroled in 1951.) Lord Haw Haw was an American-born Englishman named William Joyce, who joined the British Fascist Party in 1923 and, in 1933, the British Union of Fascists. In 1937, he founded the pro-Nazi British National Socialist League and then fled Britain in 1939 to work in Germany for an English-language radio station. As Lord Haw Haw (a name he appropriated from an earlier German propaganda broadcaster, usually identified as Norman Baillie-Stewart), Joyce broadcast propaganda intended to erode the morale of British as well as American troops. (Although Joyce was naturalized as a German citizen in 1940, a postwar court ruled that his allegiance was still to the Crown because he held a British passport. Found guilty of high treason, he was hanged in 1946.)

Goebbels's efforts at subverting Allied morale did not achieve the success of his earlier propaganda. Both civilians and soldiers saw through the broadcasts. American GIs, in particular, enjoyed listening to both Axis Sally and Lord Haw Haw, who became objects of ridicule. But Goebbels was not finished. As the tide of war turned against Germany, he reemerged as a master of crisis management. As bad news came out of North Africa and the Soviet Union, Goebbels launched his most elaborate and far-reaching propaganda campaigns. He was not merely a censor or a liar, but, rather, a shaper of popular interpretation. He continually presented himself before the German public with a vision of inevitable, predestined victory. The defeats and the setbacks mattered not at all in the face of national destiny.

If his earlier merchandise had been Hitler and the Nazi party, his new product was hope, which he built up by references to historical examples on the one hand and the imminence of future salvation on the other. Goebbels repeatedly invoked the emergence of new *Wunderwaffen* ("wonder weapons"), products of advanced German science, which would surely reverse the fortunes of war yet again. (There was more than a grain of truth in these assertions, as Germany developed and deployed both the V-1 "buzz bomb," an early cruise missile, and the far more advanced V-2, a long-range ballistic missile. Before the end of the war, the Luftwaffe was also deploying remarkably advanced jet aircraft and rocket-propelled aircraft—but too little too late to have a strategic impact on the war.) In dramatic contrast to other highly placed Nazis, who retreated from the public as defeat was piled upon defeat during 1944 and early 1945, Goebbels continually thrust himself into the forefront.

As the perimeter of Nazi conquest shrank in the final months of the war, Goebbels turned his attention to rallying the home front for a final apocalyptic stand, advocating what he called "total war." When the attempted assassination of Hitler failed on July 20, 1944, Goebbels took charge of the situation in Berlin and suppressed the incipient *coup d'etat* there. This earned from Hitler a grandiose appointment as Reich Plenipotentiary for Total War, making Goebbels the third most powerful figure in the Third Reich, behind only Hitler himself and Heinrich Himmler. Yet, of course, by this time, it was an empty appointment. Goebbels remained at Hitler's side to the bitterest of bitter ends. He served as witness to the marriage of Hitler and his long-time mistress Eva Braun on April 29, 1945, in the Führerbunker beneath the garden of the Reich Chancellery. On the next day, before taking his life and that of his bride, Hitler named Goebbels chancellor of the Reich.

It was an office in which Goebbels served barely a day. On May 1, 1945, Goebbels and his wife, Magda, both living now in Hitler's bunker, administered cyanide capsules to each of their six children. It is believed they then walked outside into the ruined Chancellery garden as Soviet soldiers were even then almost in complete possession of Berlin. Goebbels shot his wife at pointblank range and then shot himself.

#17
HEINRICH HIMMLER

*Adolf Hitler's most trusted lieutenant, Himmler headed the
SS and was among those most directly responsible
for the Holocaust*

Heinrich Himmler inspects a prisoner of war camp in a portion of German-
occupied Russia. (credit: *National Archives and Records Administration*)

Born on October 7, 1900, Heinrich Luitpold Himmler was the son of a Roman Catholic schoolmaster, Joseph Gebhard Himmler, and his wife, Anna Maria Heyder. He was the middle child in a family of three boys, and he bore the given name of his godfather, Prince Heinrich of Bavaria, who had been tutored by Himmler's father. Young Himmler attended grammar school in Landshut, where his father served as deputy principal. He was a hard-working student, though awkward and sickly. Determined to build himself up, Himmler engaged in a self-imposed workout regimen and, in 1915, enthusiastically enrolled in the Landshut Cadet Corps. Drawing on his tangential connection with the Bavarian royal house, Joseph obtained a posting for his son as an officer candidate in the reserve battalion of the 11th Bavarian Regiment at the end of 1917. While his older brother, Gebhard, served on the Western Front, earning an Iron Cross and receiving a field promotion to lieutenant, Heinrich was still in training at the time of the November 11, 1918, armistice. He saw no active service in World War I.

Returning to Landshut after his discharge in December 1918, he completed his grammar school education and then enrolled in an agronomy program at *Munich Technische Hochschule* (today the Technical University of Munich), where he studied from 1919 to 1922. An avid fencer, he joined a fencing fraternity, even though it included a number of Jewish members. He also sought to reenter the military, but without success, and he therefore turned to the *Freikorps* paramilitary movement that was active in postwar Germany. He met Ernst Röhm, an early member of the Nazi Party and the cofounder of the *Sturmabteilung* (SA, or Storm Troopers). By this time—and his membership in the fencing fraternity notwithstanding—Himmler was becoming increasingly anti-Semitic. Attracted to Röhm because of his distinguished performance in combat during World War I, he heeded his advice to join the anti-Semitic *Bund Reichskriegsflagge* (Imperial War Flag Society), in which Himmler's anti-Semitism grew into a conviction and a passion.

After receiving a diploma in agriculture, Himmler went to work as a fertilizer salesman and a chicken farmer. He joined the Nazi Party in August 1923 and, in November, participated in the Beer Hall Putsch. The collapse of the Putsch and trial and imprisonment of Adolf Hitler drove Himmler to express anti-Semitic opinions and even anti-Catholic sentiments that alienated his friends and family. While Hitler was in Landsberg Prison, Himmler struggled to keep the Nazi Party from disintegrating. During 1924, he was the deputy of Gregor Strasser, one the party's charter members. In this capacity, Himmler became well known throughout Bavaria as an agitator and speechmaker. Strasser put him in charge of Lower Bavaria, and it was largely thanks to Himmler that the members of the original Nazi Party there were readily reintegrated into the party when Hitler, released from prison, revived it in February 1925.

Himmler's yeoman service did not go unnoticed by Hitler. Himmler was admitted to the *Schutzstaffel* (SS) *as SS-Führer* (SS leader). This put him within Hitler's inner circle, since, at the time, the SS was essentially his personal bodyguard. In 1926, Himmler was promoted to *SS-Gauführer* (district leader) for Lower Bavaria. The following year, Strasser added to this an appointment as propaganda chief. Acting on his own initiative, Himmler began meticulously compiling data on the Jews, Freemasons, and other enemies of the Nazi Party active in his district. He also created an impressive bureaucracy in the administration of the party in Lower Bavaria. In September of 1927, he took his statistics to Hitler and made his case for allowing him to develop the SS independently from the SA, to refashion it into an elite and racially pure cadre of soldiers personally loyal to Hitler and capable of acting against all those opposed to Hitler or the party. Hitler was both impressed and convinced. He immediately appointed him *Reichsführer-SS* (leader) at the rank of *SS-Oberführer*. Himmler began a program of recruitment intended to expand *his* SS to rival and replace the SA, of which it was still technically a part. By the end of 1929, Himmler had expanded the SS from just under three hundred men to more than three thousand, and in 1930, he persuaded Hitler to officially separate it from the SA.

By January 1933, when Hitler had been appointed chancellor of Germany by President Paul von Hindenburg, SS membership was fifty-three thousand, making Himmler a very powerful presence in the Nazi Party and the government. As the new chancellor, Hitler named him chief of the Munich police and, shortly afterward, commander of all German police units outside of Prussia. Combined with his SS leadership, this gave Himmler virtually absolute police powers throughout Germany. In March 1933, three months after Hitler assumed office, Himmler established Dachau, the first of the Nazi concentration camps. Located twelve miles north of Munich, it was intended as a repository for political prisoners, a "correctional" facility for those who dared speak out against Hitler or his regime and, ultimately, for anyone regarded as undesirable. Between its opening in 1933 and the end of the war in May 1945, some 225,000 persons had been inmates at the prison.

Official Nazi records listed 31,950 deaths in the camp—a figure certainly much too low. Eventually, Jews were among those sent here, but the camp was first and foremost for political prisoners, including the former Austrian chancellor Kurt von Schuschnigg, who was confined in it after the *Anschluss* (German annexation of Austria) in March 1938. During its grim career, Dachau would be the scene of atrocities that included so-called medical experiments, the most notorious of which involved deliberately infecting inmate test subjects with malaria and also measuring the effects on the human body of immersion in cold water for long periods. The rationale for the malaria work was to develop vaccines to protect German troops against the disease. The immersion "experiments" were supposedly intended to develop survival methods for Luftwaffe pilots downed in the icy North Atlantic. More likely, however, these atrocities were nothing more or less than acts of sadism.

In April 1934, Himmler proceeded further to consolidate his control over Germany's policing structure when he was appointed assistant chief of the Gestapo (*Geheime Staatspolizei,* Secret State Police) in Prussia. Hermann Göring had formed the Gestapo on April 26, 1933, building it from the political and espionage units of the regular Prussian police. At about the same time, Himmler, in his capacity as SS chief, and his principal lieutenant, Reinhard Heydrich, performed much the same transformation on the Bavarian police and then with the police forces of the other German *Länder* (states). Hitler's appointment of Himmler as assistant Gestapo chief effectively gave him operational control over Göring's creation. Two years later, on June 17, 1936, Hitler named Himmler *Reichsführer* in charge of the state police. In this way, he came to control outright both the SS and the Gestapo.

Himmler assigned day-to-day operational direction of the Gestapo to *Gruppenführer* Heinrich Müller and joined the Gestapo to the *Kriminalpolizei* (Criminal Police) within a newly created organization, the *Sicherheitspolizei* (Sipo, or Security Police). In 1939, the SS was extensively reorganized, and Sipo was combined with the *Sicherheitsdienst* (SD) (Security Service), the SS intelligence department, to create the *Reichssicherheitshauptamt* (Reich Security Central Office) commanded by Heydrich. The consolidation of these various forces did not submerge the Gestapo, which retained a high profile throughout the war years, but it did create confusion, competition, and duplication of effort among the agencies—almost certainly something Himmler wanted, so that one agency would always look over the shoulder of another.

As Himmler designed it, the Gestapo had virtually limitless power, including the authority of preventative arrest. Its actions were outside of the conventional judicial system and could not be appealed through the courts or, indeed, to any authority. Gestapo agents swept up political dissidents, social undesirables, uncooperative clergy, "dangerous" intellectuals, homosexuals, and, of course, Jews. These individuals were customarily "deported" to concentration camps such as Dachau.

During the war, working in conjunction with the SS, the Gestapo was also made responsible for the suppression of resistance and partisan activities outside of Germany, in the occupied territories. Gestapo agents were charged with executing reprisal actions against civilians in the occupied territories as a means of suppressing the resistance. They were also attached to the SS *Einsatzgruppen,* which followed close behind the regular German army in Poland and Russia, their mission to round up and summarily murder Jews as well as others deemed undesirable. Gestapo officer Adolf Eichmann headed Bureau IV B4, which was responsible for the mass deportation of Jews from occupied countries to the death camps of Poland. All of these operations were ultimately under the direction of Heinrich Himmler.

Before the series of actions by which he consolidated his control of "policing" throughout Germany, Himmler saw to the elimination of the only real threat to his power, the SA. It was Himmler who persuaded Hitler that Ernst Röhm—the very man who had enabled Himmler's initial rise within the Nazi Party—and his followers were a danger to Hitler's authority over the party. Having persuaded the Führer of this, Himmler was given the mission of planning and executing the "Night of the Long Knives," the June 30, 1934, purge in which the SA was summarily eliminated and Röhm condemned to death.

The SA purge not only gave Hitler final and complete control of the Nazi Party, it left Himmler's SS as the party's sole armed branch. Under Himmler, the SS became second only to the regular German military (the *Wehrmacht*) as the most powerful armed force in the country. Himmler saw to it that the SS obtained absolute police powers, not only in Germany but, with the commencement of the war, within all the occupied territories. The SS also oversaw security, espionage, and counterespionage activities— although, in these areas, it often conflicted with such agencies as the *Abwehr* (Wehrmacht intelligence service) under Admiral Wilhelm Canaris. No matter, Himmler aggressively built up the SS in three significant ways. In 1931, he created the SS Race and Settlement Office (*SS-Rasse und Siedlungsamt*), in which Nazi anti-Semitism was thoroughly institutionalized and most policies of the Final Solution were initially formulated, as were other aspects of the racial basis of Nazism. In 1939, Himmler established the *Waffen SS*, a complete field army existing parallel to and outside of the control of the *Wehrmacht*. By the end of World War II, the *Waffen SS* alone was 800,000 strong. Although the original conception of the SS was as a force of racially pure Germans, soldiers of the *Waffen SS* came to include many volunteers from occupied countries. It was nevertheless an elite force, often highly effective in military operations and fanatically loyal to Himmler and Hitler.

Finally, during the invasion of the Soviet Union, Hitler assigned Himmler to administer all conquered Soviet territory and to do so with the goal of totally eliminating the Soviet system as well as all Jews within Soviet territory. To accomplish this, Himmler created the *SS Einsatzgruppen* ("deployment groups"), which followed close behind the advancing army and saw to the murder of local Soviet political leaders—directly pursuant to Hitler's *Kommisarbefehl* (Commissar Order) of June 6, 1941—and to the mass murder of Jews.

In addition to organizing the *SS Einsatzgruppen*, Himmler was directly responsible for implementing the Holocaust by establishing a network of concentration and death camps throughout German-occupied Poland. These facilities were not only the instruments and scene of genocide, but were also the sources of slave labor for the German war machine. The SS charged German war industries a fee for each slave worker it provided and thus became a major profit center for the Third Reich, even as it supplied labor for war production.

In 1943, Himmler added to his other duties the titles of Minister of the Interior and Plenipotentiary for Reich Administration. Acting under these titles, he consolidated his absolute control of all German intelligence as well as oversight of the armaments industry. Indeed, having created a massive slave labor operation, Himmler sought to establish a war industries empire solely controlled by his SS. This, however, brought him into direct conflict with Albert Speer, Hitler's designated minister for armaments and war production. Himmler plotted—abortively, as it turned out—the assassination of his rival in February 1944.

As the German war effort became increasingly desperate in 1944, Himmler created and controlled the *Volkssturm* ("People's Storm Troop"), a conscript home guard army consisting of overage men and underage boys. Himmler later added to this the secret Werewolf force, a guerrilla army that would (he hoped) carry on the fight even after Germany's conventional military forces had been defeated. Additionally, at the close of the war, Himmler assumed personal command of Army Group Upper Rhine, which was intended to check the Allied offensives of November 1944 at the Rhine River. Lacking military experience, Himmler failed miserably.

Like Hitler, Himmler descended into profound mental instability as the war became obviously hopeless. During the closing months of the conflict, he was in a perpetual state of nervous collapse, and Hitler, noting this, marginalized him within what little order was left of the Nazi regime. In April 1945, Himmler secretly made overtures through Count Folke Bernadotte of neutral Sweden, representing himself as the provisional leader of Germany and offering surrender terms. He wanted to meet with General Dwight Eisenhower to propose an alliance against the Soviets. On the evening of April 28, 1945, however, the BBC broadcasted a news report about Himmler's peace feelers. Hitler, holed up in the bunker beneath Berlin, heard this over the radio, denounced the man he had used to call "the loyal Heinrich," ordered his arrest for treason, and named Grand Admiral Karl Dönitz to succeed him as head of state. Hearing of this, Himmler met Dönitz in Flensburg and offered to be his second-in-command. Rejected, he tried to find a place to hide. Impersonating a Sergeant Heinrich Hitzinger, he headed south on May 11 but was arrested by British troops on May 21. Under interrogation, he confessed his true identity and was taken to Second British Army headquarters in Lüneburg, where he was examined on May 23 by an army doctor. When the physician attempted to look inside Himmler's mouth, his uncooperative patient suddenly turned his head aside and bit down on a cyanide capsule. Death was almost instantaneous.

#18
REINHARD HEYDRICH

*Convened the Wannsee Conference at which the
"Final Solution" was finalized and the
Holocaust thereby authorized*

Artist Terrence Cuneo painted this dramatic depiction of the May 27, 1942, assassination of Reinhard Heydrich in Prague. Cuneo (1907-1996) was a British painter who specialized in horses, railroads, and military action. (credit: *The National Archives (UK)*)

As chief of the Reich Security Main Office, Reinhard Heydrich came closest to being the central instigator and manager of the Final Solution, by which some six million Jews were murdered. Like the Holocaust itself, Heydrich formed a part of the inner core of the Nazi regime. He was an SS general who headed the Security Service (*Sicherheitsdienst*, or SD) as *Reichsführer-SS* from 1931 until 1942; the Gestapo, from 1934 to 1936; and the German Security Police (*Sicherheitspolizei*, or Sipo), which included the Gestapo and the criminal police detective forces (*Kriminalpolizei*, or Kripo), from 1936 to 1942. In addition, he was chief of the Reich Security Main Office (*Reichssicherheitshauptamt*, the RSHA), which absorbed the SD after September 1939. It was the RSHA that most directly implemented the Final Solution. In 1941, the office of Reich Protector of the Protectorate of Bohemia and Moravia was added to Heydrich's portfolio. It was in this capacity that he came to be called the "Butcher of Prague."

Reinhard Tristan Eugen Heydrich was born on March 7, 1904, in Halle, Germany—not into a military or political family, but a musical one. His father, Bruno, directed a conservatory and was a leading *Heldentenor*—a "heroic tenor" specializing in the operas of Richard Wagner. Reinhard Heydrich was thoroughly educated in classical music and had the skills of a concert violinist. His worship of Richard Wagner's philosophy, anti-Semitism, and music created a bond with Adolf Hitler, whose dedication to the Wagnerian opera was universally known and figured prominently in Nazi mythology. While Heydrich was baptized a Roman Catholic, it was widely believed—and whispered—that he was of Jewish ancestry. (Most modern historians believe these whispers were groundless rumors.)

After World War I, in which he was too young to fight, Heydrich joined the *Freikorps*—the proto-Nazi popular militia—and, after graduating from high school, defied his father's wishes that he pursue a career as a professional violinist and instead entered the German navy in 1922 with a commission as an officer. He served until 1931, when he was dishonorably discharged for misconduct after he refused to marry a shipyard official's daughter with whom he was conducting a sexual affair. Cashiered from the navy, Heydrich joined the *Schutzstaffel* (SS) and greatly impressed SS chief Heinrich Himmler. Seeing in Heydrich both an officer and administrator of great promise, one who was also thoroughly committed to the Nazi world vision, Himmler tasked him with organizing the *Sicherheitsdienst* (SD) as a special security service for the SS. As Heydrich created it, the SD was a highly efficient intelligence and surveillance organization, absolutely loyal to both himself and Himmler.

When Germany's President Paul von Hindenburg, bowing to political pressure, named Adolf Hitler chancellor of German Reich in 1933, Heydrich was named chief of the political department of the Munich police. From this post, he brought together the political departments of all German municipal police forces under the control of the SS and Heinrich Himmler. This brilliant act of administration catapulted Heydrich into the top levels of the SD. With this success, however, the ambitious Heydrich also came to understand that he was very unlikely ever to advance above Himmler. For the present, he worked all the more ruthlessly to amass more power within the SD. In 1934, he became SS chief for Berlin and, two years later, took full operational charge of the SD as well as the criminal police and the Gestapo. Himmler was the titular chief of all German police forces, but it was Heydrich who directed daily operations—and he did so with great zeal. They called him *Der Henker,* "The Hangman." It was a sobriquet he did not discourage.

In 1938, Heydrich was instrumental in Hitler's purge of the German army high command. At the same time, he masterminded an extraordinary program of disinformation to discredit members of the Red Army officer corps, which was one of the incitements to Joseph Stalin's wholesale purge of the Soviet military's high command during the Moscow Trials of 1936-1938. Heydrich's objective had been to weaken the senior command of the Red Army. It is difficult to know how significant a role his disinformation campaign played, but it is beyond question that Stalin's purge put the Red Army at a great disadvantage when Hitler launched Operation Barbarossa, the invasion of the Soviet Union, on June 22, 1941.

It was in his position as chief of the Gestapo, however, that Heydrich most reveled. It gave him essentially unlimited powers of arrest. He also was zealous in the planning of *Kristallnacht*—Crystal Night, November 9-10, 1938—a state-sanctioned anti-Semitic pogrom masquerading as a spontaneous public uprising against Jewish businesses, homes, and places of worship throughout much of Nazi Germany. This event was the prelude to the Holocaust.

In 1939, Heydrich was appointed head of the *Reichssicherheitshauptamt* ("Reich Security Central Office"), which expanded his police administrative authority to encompass all security and secret police in the Third Reich. From this office, Heydrich orchestrated the faked Polish attack on a German radio transmitter at the frontier town of Gleiwitz on the evening of August 31, 1939. A prisoner—his identity unknown to history—was taken from a concentration camp, outfitted in the uniform of a Polish soldier, driven to Gleiwitz on the Polish frontier, and there shot by the Gestapo. In a broadcast the next day, September 1, day one of World War II, Hitler announced that a Polish soldier was shot during a Polish attack on a German radio transmitter in Gleiwitz. This blatant instance of Polish aggression was offered as abundant reason for going to war.

Early in the war begun by the invasion of Poland, Heydrich collaborated with *SS-Obersturmbannführer* (lieutenant colonel) Adolf Eichmann in outlining the Final Solution, the systematic genocide of all European Jewry, beginning with the "deportation" of Jews from Germany and Austria to Polish ghettos and then continuing with the murder of Soviet and Polish Jews by *SS Einsatzgruppen* ("deployment groups"), which Heydrich recruited and deployed to follow close behind the conquering Nazi armies, rounding up Jews in occupied territories and killing them, mainly through mass execution by rifle fire.

Despite the terrible toll taken by the Einsatzgruppen, it is by no means clear that Heydrich began with the intention of "exterminating" all European Jews. His initial objective was apparently to remove Jews completely "from German life"—a life, both he and Hitler believed, that would soon come to encompass the life of all Europe. The ethnic cleansing would be conducted in stages. First would come confinement of Jews to reservations established to contain them. Next, he proposed mass deportation to Madagascar. Both of these plans rapidly appeared unfeasible, leaving, Heydrich determined, only one option: genocide.

On July 31, 1941, Hermann Göring personally authorized Heydrich to carry out the Final Solution. This order occasioned the Wannsee Conference, held at Wannsee, a villa on Lake Wannsee in southwestern Berlin. The purpose of the conference was to secure the cooperation of the SS and key officials of the civilian German government in carrying out the genocidal program. At the conference, policy and plans for mass murder were laid out in detail. Most important, Heydrich was eager to impress on the civilian administrators that the elimination of European Jewry was of the highest priority—a major war aim. Heydrich ensured that complicity in the Holocaust reached virtually all German government agencies.

In addition to a leadership role in the German secret police agencies and as architect of the Final Solution, Heydrich, as of September 1941, served as *Reichsprotektor* (governor) of Bohemia and Moravia, the former Czechoslovakia. He ruled with an iron hand, making extensive use of terror, torture, and mass executions to "pacify" the Czech population and suppress resistance movements. He approached this pacification with his customary zeal, earning a new nickname—the Butcher of Prague.

On May 27, 1942, two resistance operatives, members of the Free Czech movement, hurled a bomb at Heydrich's staff car, following up with gunfire as he was driven through the streets of Prague. It is a measure of Heydrich's arrogance that he assumed his repressive measures had, in fact, extinguished all resistance. He therefore drove in an open car, unaccompanied by armed escorts. Severely wounded in the assault, Heydrich never recovered from his injuries and died on June 4, 1942. The assassination triggered horrific SS reprisals throughout the former Czechoslovakia, including the infamous massacre of Lidice on June 10, 1942, in which 173 men over fifteen years of age were rounded up and summarily executed.

#19
DWIGHT DAVID
EISENHOWER

Supreme Allied Commander, Europe

Dwight David Eisenhower, Supreme Allied Commander in Europe.
(credit: *U.S. Army via Wikimedia Commons*)

Before World War II, West Point-educated "Ike" Eisenhower never fired a shot in anger or even personally heard a shot fired in battle. During his entire military career, which spanned 1915 to 1952, he personally led not one soldier into combat. His only "wound" was a twisted knee suffered while helping to push a jeep out of the Normandy mud. No matter. As Supreme Allied Commander in Europe, General Eisenhower had charge of the greatest, largest, and most consequential military effort in the history of warfare. Millions of American, British and Commonwealth, Free French, and other soldiers and sailors served under him in what he himself called the "crusade in Europe," the victorious effort to defeat Nazi Germany and its allies, thereby liberating the Continent and its occupied dependencies.

Without question, Eisenhower was a desk soldier—though that desk was often very close to the battlefront. Trained as a strategist at the Command and General Staff School and the Army War College, he created little original strategy for the Allies but, rather, evaluated and administered the strategies largely formulated by others and, in the field, carried out by others. Yet no one would deny that Eisenhower was at the heart of the Allied total victory in the European theater of World War II.

Eisenhower quickly emerged as an entirely new kind of military leader—a commander who did not lead men into battle but led those who led the men into battle. Eisenhower was a trans-national commander of commanders. This lofty position simultaneously gave him greater responsibility than any other Allied military commander yet less absolute authority than any. Eisenhower's command consisted of the top commanders of the U.S., British (and Commonwealth), and Free French armies—men who answered most immediately not to Eisenhower, but to their own political leaders, not to mention their own military judgment and instincts. It was by consensus of the Allied heads of state that these commanders agreed to be led by Eisenhower, yet Ike himself was answerable both to them and to the political leaders to which *they* answered. It was a most unenviable position. While the responsibility for the great decisions rested on Eisenhower, he could make no decision unilaterally. Each was the product of compromise and consensus. Empowered by heads of state, Eisenhower's command authority ultimately rested on the consent of those under his command.

❖

In December 1942, when Army Chief of Staff George C. Marshall named him Commanding General, European Theater of Operations, 366 U.S. Army officers were senior to Dwight Eisenhower. What prompted this leap over them? There was nothing in his ancestry that foretold a military career, let alone military greatness. Born on October 14, 1890, in the little town of Denison, Texas, he was the third of seven sons of David Jacob and Ida Elizabeth Stover Eisenhower. His father failed trying to run a hardware business and struggled to support his family as an "engine wiper" (locomotive cleaner) for the Missouri, Kansas & Texas Railway. Before Dwight was a year old, the family moved to Abilene, Kansas, where they had roots in a Mennonite colony, and David Jacob found work in a local creamery.

In school, Ike Eisenhower earned a reputation as a fine athlete but a mediocre student. After graduating from high school in 1909, he worked a series of odd jobs, partly to support his older brother Edgar's studies at the University of Michigan. A former classmate told him stories about the U.S. Naval Academy, where he was a midshipman. Seeking a way out of Abilene, young Ike wrote to his Congressman and his Senator, asking for a nomination to *either* of the service academies, Annapolis or West Point. In the end, he secured a nomination to West Point, and, contrary to his mother's Mennonite pacifist counsel, he enrolled in 1911 as a member of the Class of 1915—which would become known as the "class the stars fell on," because it produced fifty-nine generals out of 164 graduates.

Ike was a middling cadet, whose standout athletic career was cut short by a knee injury suffered in a football game, and he ended up graduating 61st out of 164 cadets. Posted to Fort Sam Houston in San Antonio, Texas, he met Mamie Geneva Doud, daughter of a wealthy Denver meat packer, who had wintered with his family in an exclusive San Antonio neighborhood. The two married in 1916 and had two sons: Doud Dwight, who was born in 1917 and died of scarlet fever just four years later; and John Sheldon Doud, born in 1922. But while Ike loved his family, what he most longed for was battle experience. Woodrow Wilson maintained American neutrality in the "European War" (World War I, 1914-1918), and when he finally took the nation into the war in April 1917, Eisenhower was not sent to France, but instead assigned to a succession of training missions in U.S. installations. He performed so well, however, that he was soon promoted to captain, even though he had not proven himself in combat.

In 1919, after the armistice ending World War I, Ike reported to Camp Meade, Maryland, as a tank officer. There he met another early champion of armored mobile warfare, George S. Patton, Jr. The two men spent long nights discussing their belief that the next war would not be fought in trenches, like those of the Western Front, but would be a fast-moving war of maneuver. In 1919, this was definitely a minority view, which opposed prevailing opinion that any major war would likely be a war of position, a static trench war. Eisenhower and Patton both feared that the American military was determined to equip and train for the wrong war.

At this time, Eisenhower volunteered to be part of a U.S. Army demonstration of long-distance overland military transport. On July 7, 1919, eighty-one military vehicles embarked from Washington, D.C., on a 3,251-mile trek to San Francisco. The convoy arrived sixty-two days after it had left D.C. Because the arrival was "only" five days behind schedule, the army called it a spectacular success. Ike thought differently. Although the experience confirmed his assessment of mobile, mechanized warfare as the future of strategy and doctrine, he also realized that the vehicles had to become far more durable (breakdowns were frequent) and that the United States had an urgent need for good roads to replace the inadequate patchwork of paved and unpaved byways the convoy had struggled over. The roads were essential not only to commerce, he realized, but to the effective defense of the nation. Thirty-seven years later, as president of the United States, Eisenhower would sign into law the Interstate Highway Act of 1956, authorizing construction of the modern Interstate Highway System—which was made eligible for federal funding by deeming it a defense-related project. When he took command of the European theater in World War II, Eisenhower made mobile warfare—both in combat and supply—a top priority.

While Patton would play an important role in Eisenhower's development as a modern military officer, Brigadier General Fox Conner, Ike's commanding officer when he served in the Panama Canal Zone from 1922 to 1924, was even more important to him as a mentor. He introduced Eisenhower to the full range of world history, which profoundly shaped Eisenhower's thinking during World War II. He also facilitated Ike's enrollment at the army's Command and General Staff School at Fort Leavenworth, Kansas, which gave him entrée into staff duty at the senior level. Eisenhower, now a major, graduated first out of the 275-member Class of 1926. This opened the way to the Army War College, the training school for future commanding generals.

After Ike graduated from the War College in 1928, he went to France as part of the American Battle Monuments Commission. In this role, he served on the staff of the army's most senior commander, John J. Pershing, who had led the American Expeditionary Force (AEF) in the Great War. He also toured all the battlefields of western Europe, about which he compiled an official guidebook. This work gave him extraordinary familiarity with the European battlegrounds that would become *his* battlefield. When he returned to the United States in 1929, Eisenhower served in the War Department as assistant executive officer to Brigadier General George Van Horn Moseley, principal adviser to the secretary of war. Assigned to edit General Pershing's wartime memoirs, Ike became a close friend of Lieutenant Colonel George C. Marshall, Pershing's aide-de-camp and one of the army's rising stars. In 1933, Eisenhower came into the orbit of yet another key officer when he was appointed principal aide to Douglas MacArthur, at the time the Army chief of staff.

For a young staff officer, working as MacArthur's aide was a top assignment. MacArthur loaded Eisenhower with work and soon became highly dependent on him. In 1935, he accompanied MacArthur to the Philippines to assist in the organization of the commonwealth's army. While other ambitious officers envied Eisenhower's position, Ike himself longed to leave staff work and command troops in the field. Nevertheless, he absorbed many lessons about command and the exercise of power from MacArthur in the Philippines. Not the least of these was how to build an army from scratch and with few resources.

In 1938, as Hitler threatened war in Europe, Lieutenant Colonel Eisenhower finally acted on his determination to leave MacArthur and the Philippines. Manuel Quezon, the nation's president, pleaded with the "indispensable" aide to remain.

"I'm a soldier," Eisenhower replied. "I'm going home. We're going to go to war and I'm going to be in it." When President Quezon offered him a lofty salary, Ike responded, "Mr. President, no amount of money can make me change my mind."

He left in August 1939. By the time he reached home, World War II had begun in Europe with Hitler's September 1939 invasion of Poland, and Eisenhower was quickly appointed both regimental executive officer and commander of the 1st Battalion, 15th Infantry, 3rd Division, at Fort Lewis, Washington. By January 1940, he was training recruits and commanding troops—in the field. In March of the following year, Eisenhower was promoted to full colonel and in June transferred to Fort Sam Houston, Texas, as chief of staff of the Third Army. With this move came a promotion to temporary brigadier general. He served as one of the principal planners of the mammoth Louisiana Maneuvers of September 1941. The most ambitious war games the U.S. Army had—or has—ever staged, the Maneuvers involved more than a half-million troops, and Eisenhower's high-profile role drew the attention of George Marshall, who was now army chief of staff.

Dwight Eisenhower, who had risen in the army not as a combat leader but as a staff officer, was now ideally positioned for an important post when the Japanese attack on Pearl Harbor, December 7, 1941, drew the United States in World War II. Summoning Eisenhower to Washington, Marshall tersely summed up the catastrophic situation in the Pacific: the fleet at Pearl Harbor smashed, Wake Island under heavy attack, Guam fallen, the possessions of Britain and the Netherlands fallen or falling, and the Philippines under attack and about to be invaded. Ending his grim situation report, Marshall posed to Eisenhower a single question: "What should be our general course of action?"

It was a stunning question, to which Eisenhower calmly replied with a request for a few hours to formulate his response. Before the end of the day, he returned and laid out what he believed was the only immediately viable course: Do everything militarily possible, no matter how little that might be, by establishing a base of operations in Australia. He justified his recommendation by telling Marshall, "The people of China, of the Philippines, of the Dutch East Indies will be watching us. They may excuse failure but they will not excuse abandonment." In this instant, Marshall realized that Dwight Eisenhower was a leader willing and able to provide realistic solutions in apparently hopeless situations. He named him as assistant chief of the Army War Plans Division, a post in which he served through most of June 1942.

In March 1942, Eisenhower was promoted to major general and tasked with preparing strategy for an Allied invasion of Europe. The plan was completed, only to be shelved when British prime minister Winston Churchill persuaded President Franklin D. Roosevelt to fight Germany and Italy first in North Africa, then step off from there to assault Europe by way of mainland Italy and the Mediterranean coast. While his plan was temporarily set aside, Eisenhower was thrust to the forefront of the war in Europe. He was sent to London to evaluate issues related to joint U.S.-British defense, and on June 15, 1942, he jumped over 366 more senior officers to take command of all U.S. troops in the European Theater of Operations (which included North Africa). In July, he was promoted to temporary lieutenant general.

❖

During the run-up to American entry into World War II, Eisenhower had been so obscure an officer that news reports about the Louisiana Maneuvers persistently referred to him as "Lt. Col. D. D. Ersenbeing." Less than a year later, he was the nation's top commander in North Africa and Europe.

What Marshall saw in him was an extraordinary combination of aptitude for strategy, a deep understanding of logistics and organization, and a flair for military politics. He could persuade others of high rank, mediate their disputes, direct their focus, encourage them, and correct them. Personally, he was gifted with an infectious smile that projected humility, amiability, and unsinkable optimism. Those who knew Ike well were quick to point out that he was in fact an impatient man with a sharp temper, who often doubted himself. Yet he invariably managed to suppress these traits, hiding them beneath a convincing surface of geniality and self-confidence.

On November 8, 1942, Eisenhower directed Operation Torch, the Allied invasion of North Africa. Successfully completed in May 1943, Torch was plagued by some serious errors and setbacks. Eisenhower accepted personal responsibility for everything that went wrong while giving to commanders in the field the credit for every success. This built trust and esprit de corps that were vital to the ultimate success of Allied forces facing long odds. Eisenhower also made a controversial decision to work with Admiral Jean-François Darlan, who was the Vichy French (German collaborationist) commander in French North Africa, rather than treat him as an enemy. In this, and against a storm of protest, President Roosevelt supported his general. Eisenhower's decision certainly saved Allied lives and demonstrated Ike's acute understanding of the ambiguities of wartime diplomacy as well as his willingness to make unpopular decisions.

Promoted to temporary four-star general in February 1943, Eisenhower next directed the amphibious assault from North Africa against Sicily (July 1943). This was followed by the Allied invasion of the Italian mainland, launched from Sicily in September 1943. Prime Minister Churchill had believed that fighting in Italy would have a greater chance of rapid success than prematurely attempting an assault on Europe from the west. In fact, the Italian Campaign proved bitter, costly, and would not end until the war in Europe was all but over. Fortunately for his career—and quite probably for the Allied cause—Eisenhower was transferred from the Italian front on December 24, 1943, and sent to England as Supreme Commander of Allied Expeditionary Forces. This entailed his appointment as commander of Operation Overlord, the planned invasion of occupied Europe via a cross-Channel assault from England. It would be the biggest, most dangerous, and most consequential military operation in the history of warfare.

In commanding Overlord, Eisenhower was faced with resolving the myriad details of the European war's make-or-break, all-in operation. He was also responsible for managing the often sharply differing opinions and always jarring egos not only of the top U.S. field commanders, but those of Britain, Canada, and the Free French (under the supremely contentious Brigadier General Charles de Gaulle). The most acutely critical of the decisions that had to be made was the enormous calculated risk of launching the Normandy invasion on June 6, 1944, to exploit a narrow window in which tides, moonlight, and acceptable weather briefly coincided during a period of English Channel storms that were a feature of the most violent weather Europe had suffered in some thirty years. Timing was critical, and the lives of more than 156,000 troops in the initial assault, as well as the viability of the follow-up waves of the invasion, were immediately at stake. In the longer, larger view, also at stake was the outcome of a war between nothing less than the forces of democratic civilization and those of mass-murdering Nazi totalitarianism.

The Order of the Day Ike issued on June 6, 1944 was stirring: "You are about to embark upon the Great Crusade, toward which we have striven these many months. The eyes of the world are upon you. The hopes and prayers of liberty-loving people everywhere march with you.... The tide has turned! The free men of the world are marching together to Victory!" At the same time, Ike wrote a speech to be used in the event of failure:

> Our landings in the Cherbourg-Havre area have failed to gain a satisfactory foothold and I have withdrawn the troops. My decision to attack at this time and place was based upon the best information

available. The troops, the air and the Navy did all that Bravery and devotion to duty could do. If any blame or fault attaches to the attempt it is mine alone.

He placed this speech in his wallet, forgot about it after D-Day was a success, and came across it by accident weeks later. As he was about to throw it away, his aide asked to have it as a souvenir.

The success of the Normandy landings was only the beginning of the "great crusade." Every decision relating to the course of the campaign that followed D-Day ultimately involved Dwight Eisenhower. At every turn, he not only had to confront the Allies' common enemy, Germany, but, often even more urgently, discordant elements among the Allies. Political leaders determined diplomatic policy, but it was up to Eisenhower to implement these policies in ways that advanced rather than hindered the war effort.

Militarily, once the invasion beachheads had been firmly secured and the principal Allied forces had broken through the treacherous *bocage*, or hedgerow country, of Normandy, the invasion of Europe proceeded with remarkable speed, so that, by the end of 1944, Ike faced a new problem. He called it "victory fever," a pervasive sense of invulnerability born of success, which readily leads to complacence.

By the end of 1944, Dwight Eisenhower had been promoted to General of the Army, the newly created five-star rank first awarded to George C. Marshall. He did not let the honor go to his head, especially because he recognized the dangers of victory fever. Indeed, shortly after his five-star promotion, victory fever contributed to American vulnerability in the Forest of the Ardennes, through which the Germans, supposedly beaten, launched a devastating counteroffensive in December dubbed the Battle of the Bulge (December 16, 1944-January 19, 1945). With great reassuring calm, Eisenhower directed the response to the Bulge counteroffensive and then resumed the Allied advance on February 8, crossing the Rhine during March. Allied forces entered Germany during March 28-May 8, 1945. In a controversial political and strategic decision, with which Eisenhower fully concurred, the Western Allies relinquished occupation of eastern Germany and Berlin to the Soviet troops of the Red Army.

Ike was hailed as a hero after V-E Day, but he faced fierce and bitter criticism for Berlin, which had been only partly his decision. The political aspect of this decision was the responsibility of the Allied heads of state (Churchill and Roosevelt promised Berlin to the Soviets at the Yalta

Conference of February 1945), but, militarily, Ike agreed: Berlin was more a "prestige" objective than a military objective, and it was best left to the Russians, who were closer, who had more troops, and, even more important, who were willing to lose large numbers of men in order to capture the Nazi capital. Ike's objective was never to take territory or take a city. Indeed, it was the politicians who had ordered him to liberate Paris on August 25, 1944; he wanted to pass it by so that he could continue pursuing and destroying the enemy army.

A month after VE Day, in June 1945, General Eisenhower returned to the United States on a visit. He announced his intention to retire from the army but delayed doing so when, in November, President Harry S. Truman named him to replace General Marshall as army chief of staff. In February 1948, Ike finally retired from active service, wrote his highly absorbing war memoir, *Crusade in Europe,* and accepted appointment as president of Columbia University in New York City. He worked briefly as military consultant to the nation's first Secretary of Defense, James Forrestal. Beginning in 1949, Eisenhower served informally as chairman of the newly created Joint Chiefs of Staff and, after the Korean War began, accepted on December 18, 1950, at the request of President Harry S. Truman, the position of Supreme Commander of the North Atlantic Treaty Organization (NATO).

In June 1952, Dwight Eisenhower formally retired from the army to campaign as the Republican candidate for president of the United States. He would be elected to two highly successful terms. On completion of his second term in January 1961, Congress ceremonially reinstated the five-star rank Ike had resigned when he assumed the presidency. Dwight Eisenhower died eight years later, on March 28, 1969. Even critics of aspects of his management of the war in Europe acknowledge that Dwight David Eisenhower was one of history's indispensable men. Few historians can imagine another military leader who could have held together so complex and difficult an alliance as that which won World War II.

#20
DOUGLAS MACARTHUR

The "American Caesar" of the Pacific Theater

Douglas MacArthur wears the five stars of a General of the Army on a visit to Manila, Philippines, August 24, 1945, between the Japanese announcement of surrender on August 15 and the surrender ceremony aboard USS *Missouri,* which he presided over on September 2. (credit: *Library of Congress*)

Like any great general, Douglas MacArthur was larger than life. The thing is, he was also larger than the life of almost any other general of World War II—and he knew it, and he felt it, and he expected everyone else, from private to president, to know and feel it as well.

By any measure, he was an extraordinary soldier, his strategic and tactical brilliance matched only by his boundless ego, which sometimes assumed proportions of a Greek tragic hero. Beyond question, one of World War II's most successful generals, he made himself master of the amphibious strategy without which the war in the Pacific would have been a lost cause. Moreover, for all his brashness, egocentrism, and hunger for glory, MacArthur was sincerely concerned for the welfare of his troops. He planned his amphibious operations meticulously and methodically, not only for their effect against the enemy, but with the object of keeping casualties to a minimum. In this, he was highly successful, especially considering the determined, even fanatical nature of the Japanese adversary—whom he opposed fiercely, yet in contrast, say, to George S. Patton's public attitude toward the Germans, never personally demonized. When the war was won, MacArthur administered the military occupation of Japan with great competence, compassion, and always toward the remarkable objective of transforming the conquered nation into a viable democracy.

The son of Lieutenant General Arthur MacArthur Jr., who ended his military career (1861-1909) as the army's senior ranking officer, Douglas MacArthur was born at Little Rock Barracks, Arkansas, on January 26, 1880, when his father was still a captain. His mother, Mary Pinkney Hardy MacArthur, was a redoubtable army wife, her nickname, Pinky, belying her toughness. Yet, from infancy to adulthood, she relentlessly doted on Douglas, the youngest of her three sons. Captain MacArthur had already become a legend in the small world of the nineteenth-century U.S. Army, having inspired his regiment by seizing its flag and planting it on the crest of Missionary Ridge during the Civil War Battle of Missionary Ridge (November 25, 1863). It was an action for which he would later receive the Medal of Honor. By the end of the war, he was breveted to colonel and held the regular rank of lieutenant colonel. He was twenty years old at the time and dubbed The Boy Colonel.

The MacArthurs lived on Army posts throughout the West, Douglas MacArthur later writing that he "learned to ride and shoot before he could read or write—indeed, almost before I could walk and talk." In July 1889, Arthur MacArthur was transferred to Washington, D.C., where Douglas attended public school until 1893, when his father was transferred to San Antonio, Texas. Douglas was enrolled in the West Texas Military Academy, where he earned a gold medal for "scholarship and deportment." He also revealed himself as an all-around athlete, playing on the school tennis team, football team (quarterback), and baseball team (shortstop). Graduating first in his class, he was valedictorian. Both his father and grandfather lobbied both Presidents Grover Cleveland and William McKinley to secure for Douglas an appointment to the U.S. Military Academy at West Point. Failing in this, the young man submitted to a rigorous program of private tutoring, passed the academy entrance exam with a very high score, and received an appointment from Congressman Theobald Otjen. Even as a young man, MacArthur saw the events of his life as lessons intended expressly for him, and he later wrote that the intensive study taught him that "Preparedness is the key to success and victory."

When MacArthur entered West Point in 1899, Pinky moved into a suite at Craney's Hotel, which overlooked the Academy. Southern classmates targeted both MacArthur and Ulysses S. Grant III for especially severe hazing—not so much because they were the sons of celebrated Union officers, but because their mothers lived at Craney's. MacArthur never complained, not even after he was called to testify in 1901 before a Congressional committee investigating the death of Cadet Oscar Booz, who had left West Point after being relentlessly hazed. The cause of his death was tuberculosis, but the inquiry focused on the hazing. MacArthur did not hesitate to testify against the cadets who had hazed Booz but minimized his own experience. Congress passed legislation outlawing hazing—but to little avail. When MacArthur was named superintendent of the Academy in 1919, his list of progressive reforms included more effective curbs on hazing.

Cadet MacArthur excelled at West Point, becoming a company corporal in his second year, a first sergeant in his third year, and First Captain in his fourth. He played left field for the baseball team and graduated with 2424.12 merits out of 2470.00, the third highest score in USMA history. He was first in the ninety-three-man class of 1903 and received a commission in the United States Army Corps of Engineers, the arm to which the most distinguished graduates were assigned.

❖

As a 2nd lieutenant of engineers, MacArthur was sent to the Philippines with the 3rd Battalion of Engineers in October 1903. While supervising construction at Guimaras in November, he was ambushed by two guerillas, whom he shot and killed with his sidearm. Promoted to first lieutenant in 1904, he contracted a severe case of malaria and was sent back to San Francisco, where he was appointed chief engineer of the Division of the Pacific in July 1905. He was assigned in October to accompany his father as aide-de-camp on a military tour of Asia spanning 1905-1906 and including Japan, China, Java, Singapore, India, Siam (Thailand), and French Indo-China (Vietnam). On their return to the States, MacArthur continued as his father's ADC until he was sent to Washington Headquarters, in the capital, to enroll in Engineering School and, at the request of President Theodore Roosevelt, to serve as an aide at official White House functions.

After serving in the engineer district office in Milwaukee, the home of his parents, from August 1907 to April 1908, he was transferred to Fort Leavenworth, Kansas, and assigned command of a company of the 3rd Engineer Battalion. Promotion came rapidly. He became battalion adjutant in 1909, engineer officer of Fort Leavenworth the following year, and captain in February 1911, when he was appointed to head the Military Engineering Department and the Field Engineer School.

Early in 1912, he served in Panama, returning to Milwaukee after the death of his father on September 5, 1912. His mother had fallen ill, and he requested transfer to Washington, where his ailing mother could be near Johns Hopkins Hospital in Baltimore. In response, Secretary of War Henry Stimson arranged for a posting to the Office of the Chief of Staff in 1912. MacArthur served in this post until 1917, also participating in the occupation of Veracruz, Mexico, which President Woodrow Wilson ordered on April 21, 1914. While returning from a mission to secure locomotives at Alvarado, Veracruz, MacArthur had an adventure that at once catapulted him to the legendary status his father enjoyed. He and his party were ambushed by five armed men. They outran their attackers, MacArthur shooting and killing two. Next, fifteen mounted guerrillas attacked but withdrew after MacArthur shot four. Three bullet holes had drilled his uniform, but he escaped unscathed. In a third attack, MacArthur and his men, pumping a railroad handcar, outran all but one of three mounted attackers. MacArthur shot and killed the third, both man and horse. For his performance in the Veracruz episode, MacArthur was recommended for a Medal of Honor—which he very much wanted to win, just as his father had—but the recommendation was turned down because MacArthur had acted against the advice of the local commander.

On his return to Washington and the War Department, MacArthur was promoted to major on December 11, 1915, and was assigned in June 1916 to head the Bureau of Information in the Office of Secretary of War Newton Baker. In effect, MacArthur became the U.S. Army's first press officer. When Woodrow Wilson secured a declaration of war from Congress on April 6, 1917, taking the United States into World War I, MacArthur persuaded the president to activate the National Guard and use it on the Western Front. Partly in his capacity as press officer but mostly out of his natural sense of symbolism and showmanship, MacArthur recommended sending a first division organized from units drawn from all over the nation. Secretary Baker approved, and the initial National Guard formation, which was called the 42nd Division, was nicknamed the "Rainbow Division" because, MacArthur commented, "The 42nd Division stretches like a rainbow from one end of American to the other." The 42nd was assigned to the command of Major General William A. Mann, with MacArthur, now promoted to colonel, as his chief of staff.

The Rainbow Division shipped out to France in October 1917. On February 26, 1918, MacArthur was instrumental in the capture of German prisoners when he was part of a French trench raid. He received the Croix de guerre and, later, a U.S. Silver Star. His participation in U.S. trench raids on March 9 gained him a Distinguished Service Cross. On June 26, MacArthur was promoted to brigadier general and, for action in countering the German Champagne-Marne Offensive, MacArthur received a second, a third, and fourth Silver Star in addition to a second Croix de guerre and elevation to the French Légion d'honneur.

On September 12, 1918, the 42nd Division returned to the line for the Battle of Saint-Mihiel (September 12-15). MacArthur was awarded a fifth Silver Star for his leadership of the 84th Infantry Brigade and a sixth for his command of an extended trench raid on September 25-26. The 42nd

Division was next committed to the Meuse-Argonne Offensive (September 29-November 11, 1918) on October 14. MacArthur commanded his brigade in a counterattack at Châtillon, in which he was lightly wounded. Nominated for the Medal of Honor and recommended for promotion to major general, MacArthur received neither but was awarded a second Distinguished Service Cross. In the final action of the 42nd, during the so-called race to Sedan, MacArthur narrowly avoided becoming the victim of friendly fire, picked up a seventh Silver Star, and on November 10, 1918, the eve of the armistice, was appointed commanding officer of the 42nd Division and awarded the Distinguished Service Medal.

At war's end, MacArthur served with occupation forces in Germany, returning to the United States in April 1919, when he was appointed superintendent of West Point. He introduced reforms that substantially modernized the curriculum of the Academy and that formalized the institution's Code of Honor, thereby substantially improving morale and raising the caliber of the cadets. A major general, he left the Point in 1922 to accept a command in the Philippines, where he remained until January 1925. After an interval in the States, MacArthur returned to the Philippines as commander of the Department of the Philippines from 1928 to 1930.

MacArthur returned to Washington in 1930, this time as chief of staff of the U.S. Army, and served in this high post through 1935. In the summer of 1932, he brought down upon himself and the army a storm of controversy when he personally led a large detachment of troops against the so-called Bonus Army, unemployed World War I veterans, victims of the Great Depression, who demanded early payment of promised government benefits. The Bonus Army was camped in and around Washington, D.C. His patience at an end, President Herbert Hoover ordered MacArthur to move the Bonus marchers out. MacArthur massed troops and tanks against them and managed to clear the campground with tear gas. Tragically, some of the gas canisters ignited fires in the ramshackle camp, killing one Bonus marcher. Because MacArthur had decided to personally lead the operation, he bore the brunt of scathing press coverage. A minority of hardline conservatives praised him for taking a stand against "communist agitators," but most of the public was outraged.

❖

MacArthur's career survived the controversy, and in October 1935, he was sent back to the Philippines to organize its defenses in preparation for its planned independence from the United States. In August 1936, the incoming Philippine Government offered MacArthur an appointment as field marshal of its military forces. In a move that shocked his fellow U.S. Army officers, he accepted the appointment and resigned his commission in the U.S. Army.

World War II had begun in Europe with the German invasion of Poland on September 1, 1939, and American entry into the war seemed more certain with each passing month. MacArthur did not want to leave the Philippines before completing preparations for its defense; however, he accepted recall to U.S. Army service on July 26, 1941, when war with Japan looked imminent. Promoted to lieutenant general, he was assigned overall command of U.S. Army Forces in the Far East (USAFFE) and remained headquartered in Manila.

Like other senior American officers, MacArthur was taken completely by surprise when the Japanese bombed Pearl Harbor on December 7, 1941. He was also unprepared for Japanese air attacks on Clark and Iba airfields in the Philippines the following day. Although hopelessly undermanned and underequipped, he mounted a skillful defense of the Philippines, withdrawing to fortified positions on Bataan during a long fighting retreat (December 23, 1941-January 1, 1942), which he made costly to Japanese ground forces. MacArthur personally commanded the defense of Bataan and the Manila Bay forts until President Franklin D. Roosevelt ordered his evacuation to Australia. While some of the members of the garrisons on Bataan and Corregidor, to which MacArthur moved his combat headquarters, derided their commander as "Dugout Doug," he and a select party, which included his wife and son, made an extremely perilous escape from Corregidor via PT-boat to Mindanao, from which they flew by B-17 bomber to Australia. From an Australian railroad station on March 20, 1942, he broadcast his famous message, "I came through and I shall return." Roosevelt was relieved to learn that MacArthur had survived, but he was appalled by his use of the first-person singular. The White House asked MacArthur to amend the declaration to "We shall return." He never did.

With the American positions in the Philippines surrendered in April (Bataan) and May (Corregidor), U.S. Army Chief of Staff George C. Marshall requested that MacArthur finally be awarded the Medal of Honor—specifically "to offset any propaganda by the enemy directed at his leaving his command," even though (as Marshall's own chief of staff Dwight D. Eisenhower pointed out) he had performed no act of valor.

Acting now as supreme commander in the Southwest Pacific Area, MacArthur commenced the reconquest of New Guinea as a first step in the liberation of the Pacific—and as a means of securing Australia from Japanese invasion. He successfully directed the repulse of a strong Japanese assault on Port Moresby, New Guinea, during July-September 1942, and then seized the initiative with an offensive advance across New Guinea's forbidding Owen Stanley Range during September-November, ultimately assaulting and taking the Japanese-held Buna-Gona fortifications during November 20, 1942-January 22, 1943.

Following this hard-won gain, MacArthur directed execution of the "island-hopping strategy" by which the Allied forces planned to retake the Pacific islands and advance inexorably against mainland Japan. The strategy, which proved key to victory in the theater, was based on the realization that it was unnecessary to capture each and every Japanese-occupied island in serial fashion. Instead, the Allies decided to invade some Japanese positions and use submarine and air attacks to blockade and isolate others, thereby preventing their resupply and reinforcement. As MacArthur said, these Japanese island garrisons, cut off, would simply "wither on the vine." The island-hopping idea was a U.S. Navy initiative proposed by Admiral Chester W. Nimitz and approved by FDR, but it was enthusiastically supported by MacArthur, who just as enthusiastically claimed credit for having originated it. No matter, it was he who chiefly led its execution as Operation Cartwheel, beginning in 1943.

After campaigning along the north coast of New Guinea, he invaded western New Britain during December 15-30, 1943, cutting off the major Japanese base at Rabaul. Next came victories at Hollandia Jayapura and Aitape, which isolated the Japanese Eighteenth Army in April 1944. Moving west along the New Guinea coast, MacArthur took Sansapor on July 30, and then, in September, coordinated a massive offensive with Nimitz in the central Pacific. MacArthur's amphibious forces took Morotai in the Molucca Islands while Nimitz pounded and then invaded the Palau Islands (Carolines).

❖

In July 1944, President Roosevelt summoned MacArthur to a meeting with him and Admiral Nimitz in Hawaii to decide on the next phase of the war against Japan. Nimitz made a strong case for attacking Formosa (Taiwan), thereby opening up a land front on what was effectively the flank of Japanese forces. Strategically, it made eminent sense. MacArthur, however, insisted that his return to liberate the Philippines, which he had left at the start of the war, was a moral imperative and a solemn American obligation. He implied to Roosevelt that he would resign if he were not permitted to proceed. The president agreed, and, on October 20, 1944, MacArthur personally commanded the ground forces invading Leyte, wading ashore with Philippine president Sergio Osmeña in the knee-deep surf, thereby redeeming his pledge to return to the islands. "People of the Philippines," he broadcast, "I have returned.... The hour of your redemption is here.... Rally to me. Let the indomitable spirit of Bataan and Corregidor lead on. As the line of battle rolls forward to bring you within the zone of operations, rise and strike. For future generations of your sons and daughters, strike! In the name of your sacred dead, strike! Let no heart be faint, let every arm be steeled. The guidance of Divine God points the way. Follow in His name to the Holy Grail of righteous victory!"

Critics, both during the war and after it, expressed fear that MacArthur's personal obsession with the Philippines compromised other aspects of the Pacific war effort and lengthened the war. Nevertheless, intent on liberating the islands, MacArthur concentrated on expansion of operations to Mindoro on December 1 and Luzon on January 9, 1945. Following the Luzon campaign (February 3-August 15, 1945), he readily liberated the rest of the Philippines. Simultaneously, on Borneo, MacArthur's forces took the coastal oilfields, cutting off much of the Japanese forces' fuel supply.

In April 1945, MacArthur was named commander of all U.S. ground forces in the Pacific. This put him in overall command of Operation Downfall, the anticipated invasion of Japan. It would have been the crowning achievement of his military career—had the dropping of the atomic bombs on Hiroshima (August 6, 1945) and Nagasaki (August 9) not pushed the Japanese to surrender before the invasion was launched. MacArthur was clearly disappointed, but, promoted to general of the army—five stars— he was accorded the honor of accepting the Japanese surrender on behalf of all the Allied forces. The ceremony took place aboard the United States battleship *Missouri* riding at anchor in Tokyo Bay on September 2, 1945. The commander that biographer William Manchester called the "American Caesar" presided over the surrender with great dignity, grace, wisdom, and—unexpectedly—humility. With a nod toward the unprecedented horrors of World War II and the atomic weapons that had brought it to an end, MacArthur spoke: "Men since the beginning of time have sought peace. Various methods through the ages have attempted to devise an international process to prevent or settle disputes between nations. From the very start workable methods were found insofar as individual citizens were concerned, but the mechanics of an instrumentality of larger international scope have never been successful. Military alliances, balances of power, leagues of nations, all in turn failed, leaving the only path to be by way of the crucible of war. We have had our last chance. If we do not now devise some greater and more equitable system, Armageddon will be at our door."

From 1945 to April 11, 1951, Douglas MacArthur served masterfully as supreme commander of Allied occupation forces in Japan, governing the broken nation with a strong hand tempered by great benevolence and understanding. He administered both the rebuilding and the democratization of Japan. In most quarters throughout the conquered nation, he became a wildly popular figure.

While he was serving in the Japanese occupation, on June 25, 1950, communist North Korean troops invaded South Korea, and MacArthur was named supreme commander of United Nations forces in Korea by a U.N. Security Council resolution on July 8. He set about directing the defense of the Pusan perimeter during August 5-September 15, and then staged perhaps the greatest military operation of his career with the amphibious landing of a force at Inchon on September 15, thereby enveloping the North Koreans and ultimately destroying enemy forces in the South. In October, he secured U.N. and U.S. approval to invade North Korea. He swept through and pushed the communist forces deep into the north, all the way to the Yalu River, the border with China.

During November 25-26, communist Chinese forces suddenly crossed the Yalu into North Korea and entered the war. It was a shocking reversal of fortune for MacArthur and the United Nations forces. The Chinese offensive pushed his armies rapidly southward. MacArthur conducted a fighting withdrawal and settled into a defensive front just south of the South Korean capital of Seoul.

Thus desperately embattled, MacArthur publicly advocated bombing targets in China itself, a move that American politicians, chief among them President Harry S. Truman, feared would trigger a nuclear Third World War. When MacArthur persisted in insubordination by flatly refusing to conduct a limited war, Truman relieved him of command on April 11, 1951, even though he had recaptured Seoul on March 14.

Replaced in Korea by Lieutenant General Matthew B. Ridgway, MacArthur returned to the United States, where he was hailed as a national hero. On April 19, 1951, he delivered a stirring retirement address to Congress—in which he implied his condemnation of Truman by declaring that there is "no substitute for victory" and then announced his retirement from the military, quoting the lyrics of a traditional barracks ballad: "old soldiers never die, they just fade away." Amid much talk of his entering politics at the presidential level, he retired from public life. He died on April 5, 1964, at the age of eighty-four.

#21
GEORGE S. PATTON, JR.

The quintessential, indispensable American commander in the European theater

Comedian, movie star, and indefatigable USO performer Bob Hope shakes hands with George S. Patton in Sicily, August 21, 1943. Among the other USO performers are writer Hal Block (left, with cigar), writer Barney Dean (between Hope and Patton), singer Frances Langford, and jazz guitarist and singer Tony Romano. (credit: *Library of Congress*)

Field Marshal Gerd von Rundstedt, the superb and ruthless German commander who masterminded the Ardennes offensive that stunned the Allies with the Battle of the Bulge (December 16, 1944-January 25, 1945), responded to a postwar request to name the American commander who most impressed him.

"Patton was your best," came the answer.

Even Marshal Joseph Stalin, loath to praise the Western Allies, could not restrain himself from praising Patton. "The Red Army," he declared, "could not have conceived and certainly could not have executed the advance made by the Third Army across France." Patton's own countrymen were less certain. While Lucian Truscott, a gallant cavalry commander who clashed bitterly with his chief during operations in Sicily, called Patton "perhaps the most colorful, as he was certainly the most outstanding battle leader of World War II," some ordinary GIs found him intolerable. One called him "a swaggering bigmouth, a Fascist-minded aristocrat...compared to the dreary run of us, General Patton was quite mad," and the cultural historian Dwight Macdonald pronounced Patton "brutal and hysterical, coarse and affected, violent and empty." The late Andy Rooney, a young war correspondent who went on to become a commentator on CBS Television's *60 Minutes*, confessed that he "detested Patton and everything about the way he was. It was because we had so few soldiers like him that we won the war.... Patton was the kind of officer that our wartime enlisted man was smarter than...."

The fact is that no modern American commander created more vehement controversy than Patton, who combined rule-breaking flamboyance with by-the-book spit-and-polish, who was profoundly religious, a writer of poetry, and a well-read student of history, yet an impulsive, foul-mouthed blasphemer. As a strategist, he fell short—not through lack of brilliance, but because of absence of interest. His genius and his focus lay exclusively in tactics, and his headlong drive through France, Germany, and into Czechoslovakia spanning 1944-1945 was as great a military masterpiece as Hannibal's double envelopment of the Roman Republican army at Cannae (August 2, 216 BC). For many Americans who fought in Europe during World War II, George Smith Patton, Jr. was the quintessential commander, a general who invariably brought victory into the field.

He was born, November 11, 1885, on his father's Los Angeles County ranch and vineyard, sprawling across what is today much of the UCLA campus and extending as far as the city of Pasadena. A rather delicate child, he was pampered by adoring parents but, inspired by his father's stories about his Virginia Civil War ancestors, became determined to build his body and fashion himself into a tough-as-nails soldier.

Afflicted with dyslexia, young Patton struggled through home schooling and a private preparatory school. From here, he decided to enroll in Virginia Military Institute (VMI) for a year to prepare for a hoped-for appointment to West Point. It came in 1904, but his U.S. Military Academy years were marked by intense academic struggle, which included a failing grade in mathematics that sent him back to repeat his entire plebe year. Patton nevertheless not only persevered, but became a standout cadet, a star athlete who earned the coveted rank of cadet adjutant. After graduating in 1909 with a second lieutenant's commission, Patton served in several posts, earning a reputation as a young officer of great energy and initiative. He competed on the U.S. pentathlon team in the 1912 Olympics at Stockholm, Sweden. Although his fifth-place showing failed to win a medal, Patton drew praise from the Swedish press, which commented on his dynamism and prowess as a fencer. In fact, Patton's swordsmanship was exemplary, and the army sent him to the French cavalry school at Saumur, from which he returned to the United States and the Mounted Service School at Fort Riley, Kansas, in 1913. He served as an instructor at Fort Riley from 1914 to 1916 and was appointed Master of the Sword, with responsibility for writing the army's new saber manual. Patton went one step beyond this, working with the Army Ordnance Department to design a new sword for the cavalry. Officially called U.S. Saber, M-1913, it remains known to this day as the "Patton sword." Instead of the curved blade intended for defensive slashing, Patton's new weapon was straight, a saber intended for making offensive thrusts. It embodied the man's aggressive conception of battle.

Teaching, writing manuals, and designing sabers were fine, but Lieutenant Patton yearned for action, and in 1916 he volunteered to serve with Brigadier General John J. "Black Jack" Pershing in a "punitive expedition" against the Mexican revolutionary bandit Pancho Villa, whose men had violently raided the town of Columbus, New Mexico. President Woodrow Wilson dispatched Pershing to pursue and capture or kill Villa. The expedition lasted nearly a year, from March 1916 to February 7, 1917. Patton managed to get into a firefight with some of Villa's men, killing them all, but Villa himself eluded the expedition. Nevertheless, Pershing was impressed with Patton, who was promoted to captain in 1917. For his part, Patton saw in Pershing the ideal U.S. Army officer. He was a model for emulation.

In May, a month after the United States had entered World War I (on April 6, 1917), Patton successfully appealed to Pershing for an assignment to his staff and was sent to France with the very first small contingent of the American Expeditionary Force (AEF). Once he was in Europe and as soon as American troops got into combat, Patton transferred from Pershing's staff to field duty as the first American officer to receive training with a weapon new to warfare, the tank. While many scoffed at these vehicles, which were as yet highly unreliable, Patton saw them as a means of breaking the stalemate of Western Front trench warfare. This was a testament to his military vision. He was trained as a cavalryman and held the archaic title of Master of the Sword, yet he instantly recognized in the ungainly looking machines the future of combat. As soon as he himself had been trained, Patton was assigned in November 1917 to create the AEF Tank School at Langres. He personally trained the very first generation of American armored soldiers and, promoted to temporary lieutenant colonel, organized and led the 1st Provisional Tank Brigade in the first offensive operation the AEF fought independently of the French and British, the reduction of the Saint-Mihiel Salient (September 12-15, 1918). This was followed by his command of tanks in the massive Meuse-Argonne Offensive, the culminating Allied offensive of World War I (September 26-November 11). Patton was seriously wounded in combat on the very first day of the Meuse-Argonne operation, after having led his tanks and the infantry troops they supported in an advance of some five miles. He repeatedly waved off rescue and evacuation as he continued to conduct operations from the shelter of a shell hole. After this battle, Patton was promoted to temporary colonel in the Tank Corps and received the Distinguished Service Medal (as well as a Purple Heart, awarded retroactively in 1932, immediately after the decoration was created). The wound sidelined him for the rest of the war.

On his return to the United States in 1919, Patton reverted to his permanent rank of captain but was very rapidly promoted to major and given command of the successor to the 1st Provisional Tank Brigade, the 304th Tank Brigade, at Fort Meade, Maryland (1919-1921). Here he met another rising young officer with an interest in armor, Dwight David Eisenhower, and the two had long discussions on how mobile warfare was destined to be the future of ground-level combat. Those in the upper echelons of command were not of like belief, however, and, perceiving that, for now at least, armored service was a career dead end, Patton returned to the cavalry as soon as he was offered a coveted posting at Fort Myer, Virginia, a relatively luxurious installation close to heart of American military leadership in nearby Washington, D.C. He served here only until 1922, when he eagerly enrolled in the Command and General Staff School, stepping stone to higher rank and responsibility. Graduating with honors in 1923, Patton was appointed to the general staff, on which he served until 1928, when he was made chief of cavalry.

In 1932, Patton was admitted to the Army War College, the institution that educated the army's top commanders. He was promoted to lieutenant colonel (1934) and then colonel (1937). After commanding cavalry for a time, Patton returned to armor—now a much more firmly established arm—and was given command of the 2nd Armored Brigade in 1940. As war clouds thickened, the pace of Patton's promotions accelerated. He was soon jumped to temporary brigadier general and then to temporary major general, with command of the 2nd Armored Division in April 1941.

In June 1941, major military maneuvers (war games) took place in Tennessee, and during July through September, even larger maneuvers—to this day, the largest ever conducted—were played out across parts of Louisiana and Texas. These were followed by exercises in the Carolinas during October and November. The standout in all of these was George S. Patton, whose innovative approach to tactics (at one point, he even purchased fuel for his tanks at local filling stations, using money out of his own pocket) defeated all comers.

Thanks to his performance in the maneuvers during the run-up to December 7, 1941, and American entry into World War II, the eyes of army high command were fixed on Patton. Yet his spectacular showing did not prompt his superiors to send him where he wanted to be—in the theaters of combat. Instead, Patton was assigned to create the Desert Training Center in the Mojave and Sonoran deserts of Southern California and Western

Arizona. At this time, military planners understood that, per the wishes of Churchill and the agreement of Roosevelt, the U.S. Army would not get into the European fight directly, but via a contest with the German Afrika Korps and a variety of Italian forces in North Africa. After this region had been cleared of the enemy, they would jump off for an invasion of Sicily, followed by a campaign up the Italian mainland. The immediate problem was that the United States Army had absolutely no experience fighting a large-scale battle—especially with tanks—in the desert. From March 26 to July 30, 1942, Patton swallowed his disappointment and turned to the task of training a first generation of desert fighters.

He proved himself to be a superb trainer of troops as he formulated the doctrine and tactics of desert warfare. His soldiers emerged from the desert center as highly skilled desert warriors. This assignment completed, Patton was summoned in August to participate in the planning of Operation Torch, the American amphibious assault on North Africa. Now at last he received his first major combat command as field commander of the Western Task Force in the Torch landings, which took place on November 8, 1942. These were successful, and in March of 1942, he was urgently called on to replace Major General Lloyd R. Fredendall as commanding officer of II Corps, which had suffered a stunning and humiliating defeat at Kasserine Pass, Tunisia (February 19-24, 1943). The crisis that this loss had created was very grave. Abject defeat in the first contest between German and American troops was a major blow to army morale and to confidence on the U.S. home front. Patton quickly analyzed the problem as an issue of discipline. The II Corps Fredendall had created was unsoldierly, more rabble than army. Patton, whose oft-repeated mantra was "The soldier is the army," instituted the kind of strict spit-and-polish regime that outraged many but succeeded in converting civilians into soldiers. "The only discipline," Patton declared, "is perfect discipline," and he began rigorously enforcing regulations governing uniforms, including the wearing of neckties, leggings, and helmets. Omar N. Bradley, who entered World War II as Patton's subordinate and was destined to end the war as a five-star general—one more star than Patton wore—immediately understood what Patton was up to. "Each time a soldier knotted his necktie, threaded his leggings, and buckled on his heavy steel helmet, he was forcibly reminded that Patton had come to command the II Corps, that the pre-Kasserine days had ended, and that a tough new era had begun."

Patton wanted the men of II Corps at all times to look and feel like soldiers so that they would act like soldiers. The success of his approach to creating discipline was measured in the record of victory II Corps soon established.

Also established, however, was the difficult nature of Patton's extreme warrior persona. Friction with other commanders was frequent, especially with the British—and his rivalry with the most famous of all British military leaders, Bernard Law Montgomery, became the stuff of legend. Some of the friction was relieved by the transfer of Patton from command of II Corps to command of I Armored Corps, which soon grew into the Seventh Army. From July 10 through August 17, Patton led the Seventh Army through a difficult but triumphant invasion of Sicily, which culminated in his race to beat Montgomery's British Eighth Army to Messina, intended as the jumping-off point from the Sicily campaign to the campaign for the capture of mainland Italy. Along the way, Patton liberated the Sicilian capital city of Palermo (July 22, 1943) and on the night of August 16, his forces arrived in Messina—before Montgomery.

The Sicilian campaign was not an unqualified success. Although Patton took pride in his conquests, he failed to prevent the evacuation of most of the German and Italian forces to the mainland. They would live to fight the Allies on the Italian peninsula. Worse—for Patton—came a pair of incidents that nearly destroyed his reputation and ended his career.

On August 3, 1943, Patton stopped by the 15th Evacuation Hospital to visit with wounded troops. Among the patients, most of them very badly injured, was one Private First Class Charles H. Kuhl. Unlike the others, he was not in bed, and he bore no visible wounds. He had been diagnosed with "exhaustion"—battle fatigue—although it was also later discovered that he suffered from malarial parasites. To Patton, he looked like nothing more or less than a malingerer. The general asked him what his problem was.

"I guess I can't take it."

Patton responded by calling Kuhl a coward and ordering him out of the hospital tent. When Kuhl did not move, Patton slapped him across the chin with his gloves and then forcibly lifted him to his feet by his shirt collar, sending him out of the tent with a kick in the rear.

This would have been the end of an ugly incident, but on August 10, when he was visiting another evac hospital, Patton encountered another case of battle fatigue.

"It's my nerves," Private First Class Paul G. Bennett told the general.

"What did you say?"

"It's my nerves. I can't stand the shelling anymore."

"Your nerves, Hell, you are just a goddamned coward.... I ought to shoot you myself right now."

Patton slapped him across the face twice, sending his helmet liner flying into the next tent. "You're going back to the front lines," Patton bellowed, "and you may get shot and killed, but you're going to fight. If you don't, I'll stand you up against a wall and have a firing squad kill you on purpose." With this, Patton reached for his ivory-handled Colt revolver, a Patton trademark. With his hand hovering above the ivory handle, he barked, "In fact, I ought to shoot you myself, you Goddamned whimpering coward."

He did not pull the weapon but turned around and stalked out of the tent, shouting to stunned doctors and nurses: "Send that yellow son of a bitch back to the front line!"

The physician in charge wrote a report that found its way to the desk of General Eisenhower himself. Even worse, it was leaked to the press. Eisenhower contemplated relieving Patton but instead ordered him to apologize for the incident. On his own, Patton also apologized personally to Kuhl and Bennett—who accepted the gesture as sincere. Although Patton was not sent home, he was idled, kept out of the action until January 1944. At that time, he was sent to England, where he was assigned to command the Third Army, which was in the process of being formed. Aware that the Germans would never believe that Patton—the American army's most illustrious general—was being kept on ice as punishment for lashing out at two soldiers, Eisenhower pressed him into service as a decoy intended to deceive the enemy into concluding that he was going to lead the long-anticipated invasion of France and to do so not with landings on the beaches of Normandy, but from England to northern France via the Pas de Calais.

It was, in fact, a brilliant deception, but it was also profoundly demoralizing to Patton, who was given no role at all in the D-Day landings of June 6, 1944. Only after the initial assault did Patton and the Third Army sail piecemeal to France during July. But once he arrived across the Channel, Patton came into his own. He led the southern flank of a great breakout from Normandy that tore across France and created the true-life legend of this extraordinary general.

The achievement of the Third Army is set down succinctly in the official record, *The Third Army's After Action Report.* "In nine months and eight days of campaigning," the report begins, "Third U.S. Army compiled a record of offensive operations that could only be measured in superlatives, for not only did the Army's achievements astonish the world but its deeds in terms of figures challenged the imagination." Under Patton, the army liberated or gained 81,522 square miles in France, 1,010 in Luxembourg, 156 in Belgium, 29,940 square miles in Germany, 3,485 in Czechoslovakia, and 2,103 in Austria. An estimated twelve thousand cities, towns, and villages were liberated or captured, twenty-seven of which contained more than fifty thousand people. The Third Army captured 1,280,688 prisoners of war from August 1, 1944 to May 13, 1945. The enemy lost 47,500 killed and 115,700 wounded—a total of 1,443,888 casualties—to the Third Army, which incurred 160,692 casualties, including 27,104 killed, 86,267 wounded, 18,957 injured, and 28,237 missing (most of whom were later reported captured and eventually repatriated). Under Patton, the Third Army advanced farther and faster than any other Allied army in the European theater. Some believe the fighting advance was the most rapid and productive in the history of modern warfare.

As if this achievement were not sufficient to assure Patton's place in military history, he responded to the Ardennes Offensive—the Battle of the Bulge—by turning his nearly half-million-man army on a dime. Diverting them from their relentless eastward advance, Patton pointed his troops north and set them on a forced march some 90 miles to Bastogne, Belgium, where they mounted a counteroffensive against the German offensive, in the process relieving the 101st Airborne Division, which had been enveloped.

In January, following the Battle of the Bulge, in which his Third Army broke the back of the remnant of the German army, Patton resumed his eastward advance, crossing the Rhine in March and pushing into central Germany and northern Bavaria. By V-E Day, the German surrender on May 8, 1945, Patton's Third Army had penetrated as far as Linz, Austria, and Pilsen, Czechoslovakia.

With the war in Europe won, Patton looked forward to a command in the Pacific theater, hoping to play a role in the culmination of the war against Japan. He realized, however, that the supreme commander in that theater, General Douglas MacArthur, would never tolerate his star-power competition. Indeed, with his usefulness as a tactician essentially ended, Eisenhower and George C. Marshall gave Patton the job of military governor of Bavaria. It was a post for which this warrior was temperamentally unsuited. He became a diplomatic nightmare, publicly denigrating the Soviet allies—while privately advising higher command to prevail on America's political leaders to employ the U.S. Army *against* the Soviets, who, he believed, were as great a menace as Hitler had been. He caused additional outrage by refusing orders to "de-Nazify" Germany's postwar civil administration. Pointing out that the only qualified administrators had all been members of the Nazi Party—essentially a requirement to hold office—he put them in administrative positions in the provisional Bavarian government. As the public outcry increased in volume, Patton was relieved as Third Army commander in October 1945 and assigned to the newly created Fifteenth Army, a skeleton administrative organization, whose only assignment was to compile a history of the war in Europe.

Depressed as he was by this, Patton carried out his mission diligently—until December 9, 1945. He was being chauffeured with another officer to a marsh near Mannheim for some duck hunting. The Cadillac staff car collided at slow speed with a turning truck. It was a trivial accident—yet it caused Patton to slide off the back seat. In this action, he snapped a vertebra in his neck. Paralyzed from the neck down, he was hospitalized and put in traction with the hope that this might promote some restoration of the injured nerves. By all reports, he was a cheerful and courteous patient. Pulmonary edema and congestive heart failure developed, however, and Patton—who had remarked immediately after his injury that is was "a hell of a way to die"—died on December 21, 1945. He was buried alongside many of his Third Army soldiers at the Luxembourg American Cemetery and Memorial in the Hamm district of Luxembourg City.

#22
GEORGE C. MARSHALL

Driver of American mobilization and strategy;
architect of peace and recovery

The United States Military Academy commissioned the Welsh-American artist
Thomas Edgar Stephens to paint this portrait of General George C. Marshall
toward the end of World War II. Marshall wears the five stars of a general of the
army. (credit: *Google Art Project*)

Geeorge Catlett Marshall, who would rise to the highest level of the United States military, serving as U.S. Army chief of staff and top military advisor to President Franklin D. Roosevelt, was not a graduate of the United States Military Academy at West Point. Born in Uniontown, Pennsylvania, he graduated from Virginia Military Institute in 1901. He was commissioned a second lieutenant of Infantry on February 3, 1902, and was posted to Mindoro in the Philippines during the closing months of the Philippine-American War. He served on the island with the 30th Infantry Regiment during 1902-1903. Back in the States, he attended Infantry and Cavalry School at Fort Leavenworth, graduating at the very top of the class of 1907 and continuing his professional education at the Staff College during 1907-1908. Promoted to first lieutenant in 1907, he was assigned as an instructor at both the Infantry and Cavalry School and the Staff College from 1908 to 1910.

Following a series of miscellaneous assignments during 1910-1913, Marshall was once against dispatched to the Philippines, where, for the next three years, he served as aide-de-camp to Brigadier General Hunter Liggett. During his second tour in the Philippines, Marshall was promoted to captain in 1916 and returned to the United States as aide-de-camp to Major General J. Franklin Bell, first in the Western Department and then, in 1917, the Eastern Department. Bell had direct command of the Officers' Training Camps that had been created as part of a preparedness program in anticipation of U.S. entry into World War I. Marshall had the unenviable task of doing battle with the U.S. Army supply system in what was a perpetual struggle to secure all that was needed to feed, house, and clothe the rapid influx of volunteers. He proved himself so efficient in this thankless role that, in June 1917—less than three months after United States entry into the world war—he was sent to France as a staff officer with the U.S. 1st Division.

Marshall was assigned as 1st Division operations officer and thus became one of the principal planners of the American attack in the Battle of Cantigny (May 28-31, 1918), the first U.S. offensive victory in the war. Promoted to temporary colonel in July, Marshall was assigned the following month to General Headquarters at Chaumont, working directly for General John J. Pershing, commander of the American Expeditionary Force (AEF). He became the lead member of the team that planned the first offensive the AEF conducted independently of the French and English allies. This was the reduction of the large German salient at Saint-Mihiel during September 12-16, 1918. Marshall capped this success by planning and overseeing the movement of the entire U.S. First Army from Saint-Mihiel to the starting position for its role in the massive Meuse-Argonne offensive. During a two-week period, Marshall directed the movement of more than 820,000 men, together with tanks, field artillery, and even heavy artillery, over just three bad roads, always under cover of darkness to preserve secrecy. While some 600,000 Americans of the First Army entered the Meuse-Argonne sector, 220,000 French and Italian troops were simultaneously transported out. Marshall managed this complex transfer without any major complication, an achievement that earned him universal praise as a logistician and prompted Pershing to appoint him chief of operations for the U.S. First Army in October. The next month, he was made chief of staff of VIII Corps.

After serving occupation duty in Germany, Marshall returned to the United States in September 1919. Although he reverted to his prewar rank of captain, he was appointed aide to General Pershing, who was now Army chief of staff. In his capacity as Pershing's aide through 1924, Marshall collaborated with the general on many aspects of the National Defense Act. He was also instrumental in writing Pershing's reports on the AEF in the war. Promoted to major in July 1920 and lieutenant colonel three years later, Marshall, after leaving Pershing's staff, served in Tientsin, China, as executive officer of the 15th Infantry. On his return to the United States in 1927, he became assistant commandant of the Infantry School at Fort Benning, serving there through 1932. Promoted to colonel, he worked with the Depression-era Civilian Conservation Corps (CCC) in 1933 and then became senior instructor to the Illinois National Guard from 1933 to 1936, when he was promoted to brigadier general and assigned command of 5th Infantry Brigade at Vancouver Barracks, Washington. He left this assignment in 1938 and came to Washington, D.C., as head of the War Plans Division of the Army General Staff.

Promoted to major general in July, Marshall was named deputy chief of staff. On July 1, 1939, with the retirement of General Malin Craig, Marshall was named acting chief of staff. Three months later, on September 1, he was promoted to temporary general and appointed chief of staff. From this position, Marshall launched the rapid expansion of the army preparatory to war. He would preside over an increase from the regular army's prewar strength of 200,000 to eight million soldiers before World War II ended.

Shortly after Pearl Harbor propelled the United States into the war, Marshall reorganized the General Staff and, by March 1942, restructured the army itself into three major commands: Army Ground Forces, Army

Service Forces, and Army Air Forces. As army chief of staff, Marshall served on the Joint Chiefs of Staff and was one of President Franklin D. Roosevelt's principal military advisors. He had a seat at all the great Allied conferences of the war, during the administrations of both Roosevelt and President Harry S. Truman. Both presidents relied on Marshall to function as one of the key architects of U.S. and Allied military strategy. He was also consulted on American political strategy bearing directly on the war.

It is a measure of the man that virtually everyone who worked with him, from his staff to the American presidents and the leaders of other Allied nations, used a virtually identical phrase to describe him: "the greatest man I ever met." Nevertheless, after the war ended, Marshall was faulted by a congressional Joint Committee on the Investigation of the Pearl Harbor Attack for having delayed sending General Walter Short, the U.S. Army commander in Hawaii, information obtained from intercepted Japanese diplomatic communications. Additionally, the congressional report criticized Marshall's lack of knowledge concerning the poor state of readiness of the Hawaiian Command during November and December 1941. Yet the report refrained from censuring Marshall, instead putting the blame on key subordinates for failing to pass on important information to their superiors, Marshall among them. A secret document, the Clausen Report, commissioned by Secretary of War Henry Stimson, definitively vindicated Marshall by showing that Colonel Rufus S. Bratton, an intelligence officer who received all intercepted Japanese communications, including a diplomatic message announcing Japan's sudden severance of diplomatic relations with the United States, had lied to Congress. He falsely testified that he had been unable to get in touch with Marshall on December 7, 1941, during the Pearl Harbor attack. In fact, Bratton had arrived at his office that Sunday later than he told Congress.

Marshall survived incipient scandal related to Pearl Harbor and was a key figure in planning the "D-Day" invasion of the European continent. He called for the invasion—Operation Overlord—to take place on April 1, 1943, but was blocked by Winston Churchill, who argued that the Allies were not yet ready to attempt a cross-Channel invasion and instead advocated for Operation Husky, the invasion of Italy, as a follow-on to Operation Torch, the invasion of North Africa, which spanned November 8-16, 1942. Most historians believe that Churchill's caution was well-founded, that the Allied military was not sufficiently prepared in 1943. Nevertheless, significant voices argue that, had Roosevelt backed Marshall, the war might have ended a year earlier than it did. In any case, it was universally assumed that Marshall would be given overall direct command of Overlord. Roosevelt instead chose Dwight David Eisenhower, not because he believed Marshall was not equal to the task, but because he did not want to relinquish his presence in the United States.

On December 16, 1944, Marshall became the first U.S. Army general to be promoted to the newly created five-star rank of General of the Army. No less a figure than Winston Churchill, who had opposed Marshall in 1943, pronounced him the "organizer of Allied victory."

Marshall stepped down as army chief of staff on November 20, 1945. Five days later, President Truman sent him to China as his special envoy. For the next year, Marshall engaged in the heartbreaking work of attempting to mediate peace between Nationalist leader Chiang Kai-shek and Communist leader Mao Zedong. The effort was a failure. Nevertheless, on Marshall's return to the United States, President Truman named him secretary of state. He took office in January 1947.

Six years of war had leveled cities, crushed industry, left millions homeless, and drained national treasuries. The two most acute threats to life itself were the shortage of food and the shortage of coal for heating. In 1946-1947, the nutritional intake of the average German was a mere 1,800 calories, below-subsistence level. Citing this, U.S. state department official William Clayton observed: "millions of people are slowly starving." And they were freezing even faster, with many Germans dying in their unheated homes during the historically severe European winters of 1945, 1946, and 1947. The United States began sending aid to Europe long before the war ended—nine billion dollars in relief by early 1947—and it was hoped that Britain and France would recover on their own. This hope soon proved vain, however, for the war had not just shattered lives and infrastructure, it had profoundly disrupted the very mechanisms of trade. Farmers could still produce food, but urbanites had no way to pay for it. Industrial plants could be rebuilt, but neither farmers nor city folk had money to pay for the goods produced. The vital exchange cycle of Europe's economy was stalled. It needed nothing less than a massive injection of capital to restart.

Various American officials proposed a variety of plans. President Truman's secretary of state James F. Byrnes proposed an aid plan in a speech at the Stuttgart Opera House in Germany on September 6, 1946, and General Lucius D. Clay began to draw up a plan for the reindustrialization of Germany. At about the same time, Undersecretary of State Dean Acheson and Vice President Alben W. Barkley outlined their own relief plans. Working against all these, however, was a plan introduced back in 1944 by Secretary of the Treasury Henry Morgenthau, Jr. The so-called Morgenthau Plan required Germany to finance most of the rebuilding of Europe by paying massive war reparations, which were also meant to disenable Germany from ever rebuilding itself as an industrial power. Morgenthau wanted Germany reduced to a pre-industrial agricultural state—permanently deprived of the capacity to make war.

Initially, President Roosevelt endorsed the Morgenthau Plan, but President Truman saw in it a tragic repetition of the punitive reparations imposed by the Allies after World War I, measures that created fertile soil for the growth of Adolf Hitler and his Nazi regime. Truman was determined, as a popular postwar saying put it, not to have won the war only to lose the peace.

In January 1947, George C. Marshall succeeded Byrnes as secretary of state. Like Truman, he was keenly aware of how the punitive terms of the Treaty of Versailles ending World War I had made World War II inevitable. He also grasped that because Germany had been the most powerful industrial force in Europe before World War II, its devastation held back the postwar economic recovery of the entire continent. Together, Marshall and Truman decided that a bold plan was required not only to save lives in Europe, but to compel its shattered, jarring nations to at long last act in harmony with one another.

Saving lives, restoring lives, rebuilding Germany as Europe's economic engine, and otherwise jump-starting the European economy, all were compelling motives for taking the bold action that would be known as the Marshall Plan. There was yet another motive.

Hailed as a heroic ally of the West during the war, the Soviet Union immediately emerged as an ideological rival to the Western democracies after the war. In February 1946, George F. Kennan, an American diplomat stationed in Moscow, sent a long cablegram to Washington. It was a detailed warning of how the Soviets intended to aggressively expand their power and influence into Europe. To oppose this expansion without touching off a new world war, Kennan advocated a policy of what he called "containment." He advised confronting and foiling the Soviets wherever and whenever they attempted to interfere in the affairs of another nation. Seizing on Kennan's analysis, Marshall saw an American-financed plan of aid as a powerful means of containing Soviet expansionism. American aid would check Soviet influence—and it would do so without firing a bullet or dropping a bomb.

Indeed, Marshall even dared hope that, to build goodwill, Stalin might be nudged into cooperating with the plan. The Foreign Ministers' Conference held in Moscow from March 10 to April 24, 1947, dashed that hope, as Marshall discovered that the United States and the USSR could agree on nothing. Indeed, it became apparent that the Soviet intention was to do everything it could to stall and retard reconstruction. The continued disintegration of European economies and governments would be an ideal vacuum into which Soviet communism could expand.

Marshall's "disillusionment" at the Moscow Conference "proved conclusively that the Soviet Union...could not be induced to cooperate in achieving European recovery." It therefore drove Marshall to urgently propose an unprecedented and vast program of U.S.-funded European aid. Kennan and another State Department staffer, William L. Clayton, drew up the details of the plan, as Marshall took steps to win acceptance for it. His first decision was to make it entirely an American initiative. He would thus have to sell the plan to a single entity, the United States Congress, not to an array of foreign parliaments, prime ministers, and presidents. Yet, Marshall decided, once Congress had authorized the needed appropriations, the plan would leave it to *Europe* to propose precisely how the funds would be used. No funds would be released until all the nations of Europe that wanted to receive aid had agreed on a unified plan for all.

With the plan laid out, Marshall decided to "spring it" (his phrase) on the nation—and on Congress—by mentioning it in his Harvard commencement speech, describing it as an American proposal "aimed at hunger, poverty, and chaos and not against any group" or ideology. He assiduously avoided giving any details. Indeed, he did not supply a single dollar figure or hint at any other number in the speech. Essentially, he called on Europeans to meet and create their own plan for European recovery, which the United States would fund. That was the whole thing. Truman and Marshall believed the plan would not be received enthusiastically by most Americans, so no journalists were contacted to attend the Harvard ceremony. In fact, the president called a press conference devoted to other topics at the same time that Marshall was giving the speech. Through Undersecretary of State Dean Acheson, Truman did make certain that the speech would be intensively covered by *European* journalists. Truman's goal was to make a promise to the people of Europe, which U.S. politicians dared not retract. And, importantly, Marshall and Truman ensured that the promise was made directly to European citizens—not to their governments. Marshall did not discuss the plan with any government in advance of announcing it. No sooner did Marshall make his Harvard speech than he embarked on a nationwide speaking tour, as if he were running for office.

The Marshall Plan was indeed largely *Marshall's* plan—but it was also a collaboration between him and the president. When Truman's young aide Clark Clifford suggested to his boss that the "European Recovery Plan" be dubbed the "Truman Plan," the president roared back: "Are you crazy? If we sent it up to that Republican Congress with my name on it, they'd tear it apart. We're going to call it the Marshall Plan."

In the end, it was the Marshall "brand" that sold the plan, both to the people of Europe and to those of the United States. Prime Minister Winston Churchill, who was as surprised by the plan as every other member of a European government, hailed it as "the most unsordid political act in history." And so it was. Not only did it save countless lives, it kindled the economic recovery of Europe, and, as Marshall believed it would, it proved the most powerful weapon in the struggle between America, representing "the free world," and Soviet communism. It was the opening salvo of a conflict that marked the first fifty years of the post-World War II period: the Cold War.

#23
CURTIS E. LEMAY

The general who deployed the bombs that ended the Pacific war and began the Atomic Age

Colonel (later General) Curtis E. LeMay congratulates a 306th Bomb Group B-17 crew on June 2, 1943. The photo is captioned: "One Flying Fortress Destroyed Eleven F.W.190's…On right, Col. Curtis LeMay…is seen congratulating… Sergeants Adrian, Buchanan, Warminski, Gray, Lieutenants Barberis, McCallum and Smith…. They shot these enemy planes down before being shot down themselves after a raid on Germany and were rescued from the sea by a British Ship after thirty hours on the water." (credit: *Imperial War Museums, London*)

Brash and notoriously intolerant of those who did not see matters his way, Curtis Emerson LeMay was one of the key architects of precision bombing and the air war over Japan. He is best known, of course, as the commanding officer of the 20th U.S. Army Air Force, two of whose B-29s and crews dropped atomic bombs on Hiroshima and Nagasaki. LeMay's influence over the conduct and course of World War II, however, began when he arrived in Britain and set about perfecting the precision bombing tactics that distinguished the American strategic daylight bombing mission from the nighttime carpet-bombing approach of the British. He greatly increased the effectiveness of strategic air raids in Europe by adopting what, on the face of it, seemed the extremely risky tactic of abandoning evasive maneuvering over targets and by also introducing meticulous target studies prior to missions. By these means, LeMay doubled the number of bombs placed on target. In addition to being the first (and so far only) commander to direct a strategic nuclear mission, LeMay deserves to be regarded as the father of precision strategic bombing in World War II and, indeed, in modern warfare.

He was Born in Columbus, Ohio, on November 15, 1906, into a struggling working-class family. LeMay came to grips with disappointment early in his life when, hoping that a military career would lift him out of poverty, he sought an appointment to the United States Military Academy at West Point. Failing to obtain the appointment, he enrolled in Ohio State University and began working his way through college. After completing the university's ROTC program, LeMay entered the U.S. Army in September 1928 as a cadet in the Air Corps Flying School. He earned his wings on October 12, 1929 and was commissioned a second lieutenant in the Air Corps Reserve at that time, receiving a regular commission in the U.S. Army Air Corps in January 1930. He took advanced flight training at Norton Field in Columbus, Ohio, during 1931-1932 while he completed his civil engineering degree at OSU. Although he was on active duty with the 27th Pursuit Squadron, LeMay was seconded to the Depression-era CCC (Civilian Conservation Corps), a vast public works relief program, where his civil engineering expertise would be of value. After this, he was assigned to fly as part of a program instituted by President Franklin Roosevelt in 1934 by which Army Air Corps pilots were assigned to carry airmail. This was demanding, notoriously hazardous flying, and the program was soon discontinued because of a combination of a political patronage scandal and a high rate of accidents; nevertheless, flying the mail in all weather conditions allowed LeMay to hone his skills and his nerve as a pilot.

Promoted to first lieutenant in June 1935, LeMay attended an over-water navigation school in Hawaii Territory before transitioning in 1937 from flying pursuit (fighter) aircraft in the 27th Pursuit Squadron to flying bombers in the 305th Bombardment Group stationed at Langley Field, Virginia. Here LeMay put his over-water training to use by conducting exercises designed to demonstrate the ability of aircraft to find—and attack—ships at sea. During this period, LeMay also became one of the very first army pilots to fly the new Boeing B-17 bombers, the Flying Fortress, which, with the Consolidated B-24 Liberator and (later in the war) the Boeing B-29 Superfortress, would become one of the three great U.S. heavy bombers of World War II. LeMay was chosen to lead a flight of B-17s on a goodwill tour to Latin America during 1937-1938, when President Roosevelt was promoting his "Good Neighbor Policy" with the nations south of the border in a bid to improve hemispheric solidarity as a new European war loomed. When LeMay returned from the tour, he attended the Air Corps Tactical School (1938-1939) and, in January 1940, was promoted to captain and given command of a squadron in 34th Bomb group.

As war approached, Curtis LeMay was clearly on a fast track. He combined great natural and acquired skills as an aviator and was equally at home in fighter aircraft as in heavy bombers. His engineering background gave him a strong grounding in aeronautical theory, and he proved to be a highly effective commander as well as manager of resources. While he encouraged innovative thinking among those he commanded, he also enforced fierce discipline, which did not sit well with all fliers. He earned the distinctly unflattering nickname of "Ironpants."

Promoted early in 1941 to major, he was a lieutenant colonel by January 1942 and, three months later, a full colonel. At this time, in April 1942, he assumed command of the 305th Bombardment Group in California and brought that unit to Britain as part of the Eighth U.S. Air Force. Once his unit was in place overseas, LeMay went to work perfecting precision bombing tactics. He proposed testing a highly controversial theory that the accuracy and effectiveness of bombing would be improved by ceasing to employ evasive maneuvers over targets. While everyone agreed that flying straight and level during a bombing run would certainly result in more accurate bombing, the objection was that far more aircraft would be shot down, especially by ground-based antiaircraft fire. LeMay argued that most bombers were intercepted by enemy fighters long before they even arrived over their targets, within range of ground-based antiaircraft artillery. He pointed out that all daylight strategic bombing missions were inherently high risk and high cost and that flying straight and level over targets would make the missions more effective and therefore better justify those inherent risks. Indeed, by reducing mission effectiveness, evasive maneuvers over targets reduced ratio of reward to risk. LeMay proposed to further add to mission effectiveness by introducing the practice of conducting careful target studies prior to each bombing sortie. It is a measure of LeMay's leadership that he prevailed in gaining adoption of his controversial tactics. The gamble paid off, since LeMay's approach more than doubled the on-target rate of the bombers under his command.

In June 1943, LeMay was assigned command of the 3rd Bombardment Division, which he led on the Schweinfurt-Regensburg mission of August 17, 1943. This was another big, bold experiment, called a "shuttle raid" because it required flying from the airbase to bomb a distant target, continuing to a remote location for refueling and rearming, and then bombing a second target on the way back to the home airbase. LeMay led 376 bombers in sixteen bomb groups against German heavy manufacturing plants, including the plants at Schweinfurt that produced most of the ball bearings for the German war effort. While the Regensburg target was very heavily damaged, the Schweinfurt raid was largely a failure and, because the targets were so far from the bombers' home base, the absence of fighter escort protection meant very heavy casualties. Sixty bombers were lost. Many of the others that returned had been damaged beyond cost-effective repair.

LeMay was less chagrined by the losses than by the fact that Eighth Air Force command vetoed his bid to follow up immediately with a second attack. He argued that the follow-on attack could finish the job on Schweinfurt but was overruled by higher authority, which countered that the Eighth had simply taken too many losses to fly out again so soon.

Despite the failure of the Schweinfurt raid, LeMay was promoted the following month to temporary brigadier general and then, in March 1944, to temporary major general. Holding this rank, he was transferred from the European theater to China to lead the 20th Bomber Command against the Japanese. In January 1945, he was transferred to the 21st Bomber Command, based on Guam. The great problem that confronted him here was the disappointing results of bombing missions executed by the new B-29 Superfortress high-altitude bombers. As usual, LeMay's solution, based on careful study, was unconventional and controversial. The B-29s were designed to fly at very high altitudes—they were the Army Air Forces' first pressurized bomber aircraft—and they featured four remotely controlled turrets, each with twin .50-caliber machine guns. LeMay modified the aircraft by ditching most of these defensive guns. This saved weight by eliminating the heavy weapons and their ammunition and by leaving gun crews behind. The weight savings allowed the aircraft to carry much heavier bomb loads.

Even more controversial were LeMay's orders to fly against targets singly, rather than in formation. It was a strict article of strategic bombing to maintain tight formations to better defend against attack by enemy fighters. That LeMay abandoned this time-tested approach was bad enough, but he also ordered his crews to fly in and bomb at low level—a mere five thousand feet instead of the thirty thousand-foot altitude for which it was designed. The risk of falling prey to ground-based antiaircraft was thus apparently multiplied. LeMay countered that the heavier bomb loads would make each mission far more effective; that Japanese fighter defenses were rapidly dwindling, so that defensive guns were no longer worth their weight as an asset; and that flying low would increase the on-target rate tremendously while decreasing time over targets.

It is a testament to his command presence and his power to persuade that his crews swallowed their skepticism. After the very first mission, it became apparent that LeMay was correct. In the end, the greater apparent risk yielded a dramatic improvement in effectiveness—without (as LeMay had predicted) significantly increasing casualties among air crews.

Curtis LeMay soon earned an unparalleled reputation for performance. His 21st Bomber Command annihilated four major Japanese cities with incendiary bombs in a campaign of destruction that was, in fact, far more devastating than the subsequent atomic bombing of Hiroshima and Nagasaki. Like General Patton in the European ground campaign, LeMay, in the air, earned a reputation as an uncompromising leader who demanded maximum effort from his men but who produced outstanding results. Far from feeling exploited or demoralized, the members of his command were proud of their achievements.

As the war in the Pacific theater entered its late phase, LeMay was named to command the entire Twentieth Air Force (consisting of the 20th and 21st Bomber Commands) in July 1945. He was also made the army's deputy chief of staff for research and development—a post he would hold through 1947. The assignment to drop the world's first two atomic weapons was entrusted to him, partly because of his record as a combat commander, but also because of his sophistication in engineering and science. Pilots and crews under his command dropped "Little Boy," a fifteen-kiloton nuclear weapon, over Hiroshima on August 6, 1945 and, three days later, "Fat Man," a twenty-one-kiloton device, over Nagasaki. These two missions were war-winning and war-ending. Asked about any moral qualms he might have had concerning the Hiroshima and Nagasaki missions, LeMay was coolly unsentimental:

> As far as casualties were concerned I think there were more casualties in the first attack on Tokyo with [conventional] incendiaries than there were with the first use of the atomic bomb on Hiroshima. The fact that it's done instantaneously, maybe that's more humane than incendiary attacks, if you can call any war act humane. I don't, particularly, so to me there wasn't much difference. A weapon is a weapon and it really doesn't make much difference how you kill a man. If you have to kill him, well, that's the evil to start with and how you do it becomes pretty secondary. I think your choice should be which weapon is the most efficient and most likely to get the whole mess over with as early as possible.

Curtis LeMay's influence on U.S. military affairs, earned by his performance in World War II, made him the most powerful man in the Cold War U.S. air arm. In 1947, he was promoted to temporary lieutenant general in an air force just made independent from the army by the Defense Act of 1947. He was assigned to command U.S. Air Forces in Europe on October 1, 1947 and, in this capacity, was a key planner of the spectacular Berlin Airlift of 1948-1949, the archetypal Cold War air mission. It was yet another high-risk, highly demanding mission of monumental proportions. In an effort to block the creation of an independent, democratic West Germany with a capital, West Berlin, deep within Soviet-controlled East Germany, the Soviet Union blockaded West Berlin. Fearing that the loss of West Berlin would ultimately mean the loss of all Germany to the Soviets, President Harry S. Truman ordered the new USAF to overfly the blockade by supplying the people of West Berlin by air. No city had ever been supplied exclusively from the air before, but over the course of 321 days, LeMay directed more than 272,000 flights over Soviet-occupied territory to provide West Berlin with thousands of tons of supplies each day. Failure would have meant a Soviet triumph—and failure always loomed as a real possibility. LeMay's aircraft were flying round the clock in all weather, over potentially hostile territory. Nevertheless, on May 12, 1949, the Soviets were forced to concede that the blockade had failed, and they reopened West Berlin to Western traffic. East and West Germany were formally created as separate nations later in the month.

The Air Force recognized LeMay as a leader who achieved both the difficult and the nearly impossible and always on a grand scale. Accordingly, in October 1948, he was recalled to the United States as head of the newly created Strategic Air Command (SAC), which, until the development of land-based and submarine-based ICBM (intercontinental ballistic missile) systems, functioned as the United States' sole delivery system for nuclear and thermonuclear weapons. Always an innovator, LeMay recognized that the Air Force's inventory of B-29s was inadequate to serve as the nation's primary atomic-age bomber. He led the Air Force into the jet age with the hybrid Convair B-36 Peacemaker (it combined six "conventional" piston engines with four jet engines), followed by the fully jet-driven Boeing B-47 Stratojet and B-52 Stratofortress bombers. LeMay also pioneered the development of midair refueling, using large jet tanker aircraft (KC-135s). This not only greatly extended the bombers' range, it allowed bomber patrols to fly twenty-four hours a day, seven days a week. LeMay pioneered the tactics of continual high readiness, in which nuclear-armed aircraft were always in flight, prepared to retaliate against attack.

Despite being a consummate pilot himself, LeMay was not sentimental about manned aircraft. Many officers resisted the introduction of unmanned missiles, fearing that they would replace pilots and planes. By the 1950s, LeMay oversaw the introduction of ICBM weapons into the Air Force's inventory of nuclear and thermonuclear delivery systems.

Curtis LeMay was promoted to general in October 1951, the youngest four-star general since Ulysses S. Grant. In 1957, he was named vice chief of staff of the Air Force and became chief of staff in 1961. During the 1960s, his hard-nosed, unyielding, and at times frankly racist conservatism brought him into conflict with the liberal administrations of Presidents John F. Kennedy and Lyndon Johnson. His relations with Secretary of Defense Robert S. McNamara were particularly strained and even bitter. As he met with increasing resistance, LeMay became increasingly irascible, extreme, and outspoken. On February 1, 1965, he retired from the Air Force, and as his political conservatism hardened during the turbulent late 1960s, he decided to become the running mate of the notorious segregationist former Alabama governor George Wallace in his failed 1968 third party bid for the presidency.

The association with Wallace, unfortunately, tarnished the image of this uncompromising commander, who demanded "maximum effort" from his air crews and from their aircraft, and who shaped the modern Air Force as the most strategic of the "triad" of services. No one, except for those directly involved in the Manhattan Project, had greater influence in ushering the world into the nuclear age than Curtis E. LeMay.

#24
ARTHUR "BOMBER" HARRIS

British air marshal who championed the controversial tactic of strategic area bombing, deliberately targeting civilian urban populations

The original caption reads: "Air Marshal Sir Arthur Harris (left) observes as Wing Commander Guy Gibson's crew is debriefed after No. 617 Squadron's raid on the Ruhr Dams, 17 May 1943." (credit: *Imperial War Museums, London*)

The British press called him "Bomber Harris," and many within the Royal Air Force (RAF) called him "Butcher" Harris. He was officially Marshal of the Royal Air Force Sir Arthur Travers, 1ˢᵗ Baronet Harris, who, as Air Officer Commanding-in-Chief (AOC) of RAF Bomber Command embraced the Cabinet's authorization of a strategic bombing campaign against the cities of Nazi Germany. He directed the RAF to fly by night and to employ the tactic of "area bombing" or, as some called it, "carpet bombing." Unwilling to endure the heavy losses suffered by flying precision bombing mission by daylight, carefully targeting factories and military installations, RAF and political leadership decided to confine strategic bombing missions to night hours. The problem was that, at night, precision bombing was virtually impossible. Prompted by the Cabinet, Harris advocated dropping massive bomb loads on urban centers with the objective of disrupting military and production facilities, to be sure, but, even more, in the words of the *Area Bombing Directive* the Churchill Cabinet issued to Harris, "To focus attacks on the morale of the enemy civil population and in particular the industrial workers." The policy created, at least for a time, a moral dilemma within the British government. Ultimately, it signified Allied recognition that, in World War II, weapons were pointed at civilians as well as at military targets.

Arthur Harris was born on April 13, 1892, at Cheltenham, Gloucestershire, where his parents were living while his father, George Steel Travers Harris, was on leave from the Indian Civil Service. Harris grew up in England, away from his father, who returned to India, and was cared for much of the time by the family of the Reverend C. E. Graham-Jones. Arthur's two older brothers were educated at Sherborne and Eton, whereas Arthur, the youngest, was sent to the less costly and considerably less prestigious Allhallows School in Devon. By chance, while Harris was still in school, he saw a theatrical play in which a Rhodesian farmer returns to England to marry, only to be disillusioned by the pompous propriety of his fiancée. He ends up marrying her down-to-earth housemaid instead. This performance stuck in the young man's mind and seemed to him a comment on the influence of class versus merit in England. The young man announced that he wanted to emigrate to Southern Rhodesia, where merit seemed to reign supreme, rather than return to Allhallows. Surprisingly, his father agreed and, in 1910, eighteen-year-old Harris settled in Umtali in Manicaland, where he worked in mining, coach-driving, and farming, finally managing a farm for an Irish colonist. He was on the verge of starting his own farm when World War I began in Europe. He joined the 1st Rhodesia Regiment as a bugler—bugling being a skill he had learned at school—and, in 1915, was on the receiving end of a German air attack, which dropped artillery shells on his regiment's advancing column (without effect).

When the South-West African Campaign ended in July 1915, Harris was discharged and returned to England as one of three hundred Southern Rhodesian volunteers. After arriving in London in October, he was turned down by the cavalry and the Royal Artillery, so he settled for his third choice, the Royal Flying Corps. After flight training at Brooklands late in 1915, he was commissioned a flying officer on January 29, 1916, and served in France as a flight commander and then commanding officer of No. 45 Squadron throughout 1917. He was then sent back to England, to command No. 44 Squadron on Home Defence duties. During his service, he was credited with five aerial victories and was awarded the Air Force Cross (AFC), ending the war with the rank of major. After the war, in 1919, he transferred to service in India and the Middle East, serving in foreign posts until 1936, when he was appointed to the RAF planning staff and recalled to England.

At the outbreak of World War II on September 1, 1939, Harris was commanding officer of Bomber Group 5. Within less than a year, he was named deputy chief of the Air Staff, serving in this capacity from 1940 to 1941, being promoted to acting air marshal on June 1 of that year.

On August 18, 1941, the *Butt Report,* commissioned to assess the poor on-target performance of RAF Bomber Command, was published, indicating that no more than a third of bomber aircraft flying at night even reached their assigned targets. In response to the scathing report, Harris was named Commander-in-Chief of Bomber Command in February 1942 and was charged with improving performance. He read a Cabinet paper written by Churchill's friend and scientific adviser, Professor Frederick Lindemann (who was later created Lord Cherwell), which advocated area bombing rather than precision bombing of German cities in a "strategic bombing" campaign. By "strategic," Lindemann meant the bombing of railways, harbors, industrial plants, and worker housing, rather than restricting bombing to specific "tactical" military targets, such as fortresses and troop formations. After considerable debate in the Cabinet, the recommendation was accepted—and was especially welcomed by Harris, who embraced it as a declaration of total war on Germany and appropriate retribution for the German Blitz against London and other cities.

Acting on the orders of the Cabinet, Harris formulated programs of night-time aerial bombing. When the U.S. Eighth Air Force became an active partner of the RAF, the Americans were sent on missions of precision daylight bombing, while Harris, by the summer of 1943, confined the RAF bombers to area bombing by night, targeting major industrial areas with high explosive and incendiary bomb loads. Generally, the high explosive ordnance was dropped first, to create rubble, and the incendiaries followed. The rubble acted as kindling, multiplying the effectiveness of the incendiary ordnance. Indeed, the heaviest raids sometimes spawned horrific firestorms, with conflagrations so intense that they created their own micro weather systems, generating whirlwinds that whipped up the fires beyond control.

Harris staunchly advocated nighttime bombing, arguing that area bombing did not require daylight and that the night sky offered considerable protection from fighters and ground-based antiaircraft fire. Since American doctrine favored daytime bombing, the RAF strategy made for better coordination with the U.S. effort. In this way, weather permitting, Germany and German-held targets were bombed round-the-clock.

In contrast to Churchill, who endorsed the doctrine of strategic "carpet" bombing only grudgingly, worrying that it tended to reduce righteous British warriors to the brute level of the enemy, Harris made no apologies and delighted his subordinates by exhibiting enthusiasm for the aggressiveness of both the strategic area bombing doctrine and the crews that carried it out.

His men admired him, but some politicians criticized two aspects of his strategic bombing doctrine. First, they protested that area bombing created a great deal of collateral damage, which amounted to deliberate terrorism waged against civilian populations. Second, they claimed that strategic bombing, whether carried out indiscriminately by night as area bombing or by day as precision bombing, was having surprisingly little effect on crippling German industry. There was truth in this—much German war manufacturing having moved to hardened facilities, mainly underground. This was especially the case with aircraft production. Moreover, much of the labor in the munitions factories was provided by slaves drawn from concentration camps. Their lives, as far as the Germans were concerned, were eminently expendable. Between the underground sheltering of factories and the endless supply of expendable forced labor, German war industries kept humming.

The greatest criticism followed the massive Allied (combined U.S. and RAF) air raid on the medieval German city of Dresden during February 13/14, 1945. To this day, some historians continue to condemn it as nothing more or less than an act of wanton and vengeful destruction, a mission without defined military purpose. The ancient capital of Saxony, Dresden was a city of beautiful medieval architecture. Its major industry was the creation of fine china, and it harbored little heavy industry, even during the war. Indeed, considered of negligible strategic importance throughout most of the war, it had been bypassed by Allied bombers, except for a minor American raid in October 1944.

In January 1945, Harris oversaw plans for Operation Thunderclap to attack Berlin and other major population centers as the Soviet Red Army was closing in rapidly from the east. The objective of these raids was to impede German defense against the Soviet advance while disrupting the flow of westward-bound refugees from that advance. It was also intended as a demonstration of support from the Western Allies for the Soviet effort.

The first Thunderclap missions were flown over Berlin and Magdeburg on February 3 and over Magdeburg and Chemnitz on February 6. On February 9, Magdeburg was targeted a third time. Harris had intended to put Dresden at the top of the Thunderclap list, but adverse weather repeatedly delayed raids. When February 13 looked good for a night raid, RAF Bomber Command sent 796 Avro Lancaster heavy bombers and 9 Mosquito fighter-bombers over Dresden. Together, they dropped 1,478 tons of high explosive bombs and another 1,182 tons of incendiaries. As planned, the combination of rubble created by the high explosive drops and the intensive incendiary bombing created firestorms, which quickly engulfed the city. As if this were not destructive enough, the U.S. Eighth Air Force followed up with a daylight raid on February 14, using its B-17 Flying Fortresses to multiply the already devastating destruction. Together, the two raids killed more than fifty thousand civilians, including westward-bound refugees. Dresden, a former jewel, lay in ruins.

War correspondents and others began questioning the purpose, utility, and morality of the Dresden operation. The raids even reawakened Churchill's moral qualms—though (as he acknowledged) he had personally endorsed Operation Thunderclap. "Bomber" Harris, however, was unmoved. He explained that he considered the destruction of cities perfectly, if unfortunately, legitimate in a total war, especially when the enemy had not only targeted Allied cities, but was waging genocide against its own people.

After the war, Harris was lavished with British and foreign decorations and honors. He was promoted to Marshal of the Royal Air Force on January 1, 1946, and even the United States Army Air Forces presented him with the Distinguished Service Medal. The Labor government in postwar Britain continued to harbor misgivings. After his retirement on September 15, 1946, Harris wrote a war memoir in which he acknowledged the controversy created by "the destruction of so large and splendid a city at this late stage of the war," but he pointed out that "the attack on Dresden was at the time considered a military necessity by much more important people than myself." When Bomber Command crews were denied a separate campaign medal for their achievement, Harris declined, in protest, the offer of a peerage in 1946. This made him the only British commander-in-chief of World War II not to be created a peer of the realm. Harris returned to Africa—not Rhodesia, but South Africa, where he worked as an executive of the South African Marine Corporation (Safmarine) from 1946 to 1953. When Winston Churchill was returned as prime minister in February 1953, Harris acceded to Churchill's personal entreaty that he accept a baronetcy. Harris returned to the UK and spent the rest of his life in the Ferry House, Goring-on-Thames. He died there on April 5, 1984, aged ninety-one.

#25
BERNARD LAW MONTGOMERY

The British army's leading general in World War II, victorious over the legendary Erwin Rommel and given command of all Allied ground forces during Operation Overlord, from the D-Day landings until the conclusion of the Battle of Normandy

A classic image of Bernard Law Montgomery, in command as his tanks move up against Rommel's Afrika Korps, November 1942.

(credit: *Imperial War Museums, London*)

Dwight D. Eisenhower, Supreme Allied Commander in Europe, wrote of Bernard Law Montgomery that he had...

no superior in two most important characteristics. He quickly develops among British enlisted men an intense devotion and admiration—the greatest personal asset a commander can possess. Montgomery's other outstanding characteristic is his tactical ability in what might be called the "prepared" battle. In the study of enemy positions and situations and in the combining of his own armor, artillery, air and infantry to secure tactical success against the enemy he is careful, meticulous, and certain.

Eisenhower, of course, was celebrated as a masterful diplomat among military commanders. Other American generals, most notably George S. Patton—who was anything but diplomatic—thought Montgomery unimaginative and overcautious. Monty's displays of egotistical self-congratulation, some believed, disguised the intense self-doubt of a military perfectionist who was perpetually on the verge of cracking under the strain of responsibility. The point, however, is that he did not crack, and, in a British army that was often plagued by mediocre leadership at the top, he inspired the confidence and affection of his troops and of the English people. Imperfect and frustrating, he was also an inspiration and an icon of a valiant British army locked in a struggle to save civilization.

Bernard Law Montgomery was born to the Reverend Henry Montgomery (minister in the Ulster-Scots Church of Ireland) and his wife, Maud (Farrar) Montgomery, on November 17, 1887, in Kensington, Surrey, the fourth in what became a family of nine children. He grew up in Tasmania (today an island state of Australia, but in 1880s a colony of the UK), to which his father was assigned as Anglican bishop. Bernard's early education was administered by tutors brought from England, and in 1897, when the family returned to London for an Anglican conference, he attended a term at The King's School, Canterbury. Later, he was sent to St. Paul's School and, in 1906, enrolled at the Royal Military College, Sandhurst. Something of a hellion, young Montgomery came close to being expelled for rowdiness and outright violence, but he managed to graduate in 1908 with a commission as second lieutenant in the 1st Battalion, Royal Warwickshire Regiment. Before the year was out, he and his regiment were sent to India.

Montgomery thrived in the military service, achieving promotion to lieutenant in 1910 and becoming 1st Battalion adjutant in 1912. With the outbreak of World War I in August 1914, his battalion fought at the Battle of Le Cateau (August 26) and then at the First Battle of Ypres (October 19-November 22), in which he distinguished himself for "conspicuous gallantry," by "turning the enemy out of their trenches with the bayonet" and was awarded the Distinguished Service Order (DSO). During the fight, he was shot through the right lung by a sniper and also hit in the knee.

Montgomery's wounds were serious enough to merit a return to England, where he was assigned to training duties during 1915. He returned to the front in France at the beginning of 1916 and served as brigade major in the 104th Brigade at the Somme from June 24 to November 13. He was promoted to staff duty for the 33rd Division at Arras during April 9-15, 1917, and then for IX Corps at Passchendaele from July 31 to November 10. By the end of the war, Montgomery was a staff officer for the 47th Division. He served briefly in the Allied army of occupation after the armistice before being sent to the staff college at Camberley in 1921. After serving in various posts in Britain, Montgomery was appointed an instructor at Camberley in 1926, and in 1929 was assigned to revise the army's *Infantry Training Manual.*

In 1930, Montgomery was posted for three years in the Middle East and India. Promoted to lieutenant colonel in 1931, he became commanding officer of 1st Battalion, Royal Warwickshire Regiment and served with the regiment in Palestine and British India until 1934, when he was appointed chief instructor at Quetta Staff College in what is today Pakistan. He returned to England in 1937 to take command of the 9th Infantry Brigade at Portsmouth, with the temporary rank of brigadier general. The next year, he staged an amphibious combined operations landing exercise that so impressed Sir Archibald Percival Wavell, commander in charge of Southern Command, that he was promoted to major general on October 14, 1938, and sent to command the 8th Infantry Division in Palestine. Montgomery was instrumental in suppressing an Arab revolt before returning to England in July 1939 to command the 3rd "Iron" Infantry Division.

❖

When Britain declared war on Germany on September 3, 1939, Montgomery, as commanding officer of 3rd Division in II Corps of British Expeditionary Force (BEF), fought in Belgium as part of the failed offensive in Flanders. During the Battle of France (May 10-June 25, 1940), his 3rd Division advanced to the River Dijle but was forced to withdraw to Dunkirk in the face of the German offensive. In contrast to other French and British units, however, his division made an effective fighting withdrawal with great discipline, entering the defensive perimeter of Dunkirk via a remarkable night-time march. This positioned the division on the left flank of the BEF, which had been entirely exposed when Belgian forces surrendered. Montgomery held the flank, thereby saving the bulk of the BEF that was huddled at Dunkirk, its back to the English Channel. Montgomery assumed command of the entire II Corps during Operation Dynamo, the evacuation of some 330,000 BEF and French troops from Dunkirk to England by an ad hoc fleet of naval, commercial, and private vessels. Thanks to his skillful tactical leadership, the 3rd Division suffered minimal casualties, and Montgomery won high distinction for his management of the retreat and rearguard action during May-June 1940.

Knighted for his services in Belgium and in Operation Dynamo, Sir Bernard Law Montgomery was named to replace Sir Claude Auchinleck as commander of V Corps in July 1940. In April 1941, he was transferred to the command of XII Corps, and by November, having been promoted to temporary lieutenant general, he commanded the entire Southeastern Army. He played a key role in planning a raid on Dieppe, a German-occupied French port, which, after a postponement, was launched on August 19, 1942. Ambitious for a major success—a victory in the midst of defeat—Montgomery expanded the proposed raid into a full-scale frontal assault on Dieppe, but his plan failed to include preliminary aerial bombardment, which would have softened German defenses.

Because Canada had requested to be given a bigger part in the war, the Dieppe operation was executed primarily by Canadian troops of the 2nd Canadian Division, commanded by Major General J. H. Roberts. When adverse weather on July 7, 1942, postponed the raid, Montgomery reconsidered the entire enterprise and ended up recommending that it be abandoned altogether. Thus, Dieppe might never have happened, but for the fact that

Montgomery, now opposed to the operation he himself had planned, was transferred to command of the Eighth British Army in North Africa.

In Montgomery's absence, Vice Admiral Lord Louis Mountbatten, chief of Combined Operations, decided to revive the raid as Operation Jubilee. Having been planned and cancelled, the operation was no longer secret, and its prospects for success, always dim, were now totally extinguished. The operation was launched nevertheless but soon aborted, with all forces ordered to withdraw from the landing beaches. Of 4,963 Canadians committed to battle, 3,367 were killed, wounded, or taken prisoner. British ground casualties were 275, and the Royal Navy lost a destroyer and thirty-three landing craft, suffering 550 casualties, killed or wounded. The Royal Air Force (RAF) suffered a staggering loss of 106 aircraft.

Prime Minister Winston Churchill, who had been among those prematurely demanding offensive action in the war, nearly became a political casualty of Dieppe, and Mountbatten endured much well-justified criticism. Montgomery, on record as having recommended abandoning the operation, escaped blame. He had taken command of the Eighth Army on August 13, 1942, and went about reorganizing the force and working to lift the morale of its men, appearing before his troops as often as possible. He and his army found themselves immediately under attack by the German "Desert Fox," Erwin Rommel. Montgomery's predecessor, General Claude John Ayre Auchinleck, had staged a successful defense against Rommel during July 1-4. Rommel, who wanted to seize the Suez Canal, was determined to strike the British Eighth Army again. In September 1942, he attacked at Alam Halfa. This time, it was Montgomery who beat back the August 31-September 7 offensive.

Seizing the initiative, Montgomery next launched a counteroffensive during October 23-November 4, 1942, at El Alamein, a small Egyptian settlement along the railroad that followed the coastline of the Mediterranean Sea. He saw an opportunity to take advantage of the fact that Rommel had temporarily assumed a defensive position west of El Alamein because he was short of fuel and other supplies. On the move, Montgomery conceded, "The Desert Fox" was practically unbeatable, but in a situation of static defense, the British general believed, he was just as vulnerable as any other commander. Unknown to Montgomery, Rommel, who had fallen ill, left his 15th Panzer Division to go on sick leave and would not return until October 25, two days after the Second Battle of El Alamein had begun. Before he left, however, he prepared very strong defenses, the most important of which was a dense minefield consisting of some half-million antitank devices. Interspersed among what the British called a "Devil's Garden" were many more antipersonnel mines. Rommel gave great thought to the deployment of his assets, dividing his troops and tanks into six groups ideally placed to detect and repulse attacks from virtually any direction.

Formidable as Rommel had made his position, Montgomery enjoyed significant superiority of numbers: 195,000 troops versus 104,000 (of which slightly more than half were Italians, notorious for their poor performance); 1,029 medium tanks versus 496; 1,451 antitank guns versus 800; 908 pieces of mobile artillery versus 500; 530 aircraft versus 350 (although an additional 150 were available to Rommel from some distance away). Working meticulously as always, Montgomery devised Operation Lightfoot to pierce Rommel's defenses from the north using four infantry divisions deployed across a ten-mile front. These units would also clear a route through the minefield to accommodate the next wave, the armored divisions of X Corps. This unit was to assume a defensive position at a place called Kidney Ridge, directly facing the Panzers. Here the British tanks were to halt and hold their positions to fend off any German counterattack while the infantry pressed the offensive forward. Montgomery called this a "crumbling" process. Only after the infantry had prevailed would X Corps be ordered to assume full offensive operations.

The brilliance of Montgomery's plan was that his attack fell precisely where it was least expected: against the most strongly defended German sector. To reinforce this element of surprise, Montgomery employed smaller units to make diversionary attacks in the more obvious sectors. He conceived the battle as a three-stage contest, beginning with what he called a break-in, followed by a "dogfight," and then a break-out. He anticipated that the break-in, benefitting from surprise, would be quickly over, but that the dogfight would consume at least a bloody week of "crumbling."

Surprise was in fact achieved, but the break-in attack, beginning on the night of October 23-24, was slowed by the sheer depth of Rommel's defenses. As a result, X Corps armor did not pass beyond "Oxalic," the code name for the initial line of infantry advance, which was well short of the Kidney Ridge objective. Nevertheless, supporting units, including the 9th Australian Division and the 1st Armored Division, made excellent headway, the 1st Armored flanking the Kidney Ridge position. Rommel responded with intensive counterattacks, which were, at significant cost, contained.

The grim and protracted process of infantry "crumbling" unfolded, supported by ceaseless Allied aerial and artillery bombardment. This relentless action was coordinated with the more mobile advance of the Australians, who continually drew off Rommel's best forces, leaving the weaker Italian units exposed and finally opening up a weak spot against which Montgomery launched a second attack, code-named Supercharge, during the night of November 1-2, north of Kidney Ridge, using the New Zealand Division and other infantry units. These forces quickly penetrated the weakened sector, Rommel's elite troops having had to engage the Australians. Now Montgomery unleashed the full fury of his armored units, in the face of which Rommel, realizing he was defeated, sent a coded message to Adolf Hitler on November 2 announcing his intention to withdraw and save his force. Hitler responded with a demand that he hold his ground at all costs. But Rommel could not, and Montgomery chased him across the Libyan desert, claiming in the process some thirty thousand prisoners. The vaunted "Panzer Army Africa" was badly beaten and emerged barely intact. The Italians were totally shattered. This was the turning point in the Western Desert Campaign. Seeing that the Axis forces had been beaten, the Vichy French Government in North Africa was persuaded to begin cooperating with the Allies.

Promoted to general later in November, Montgomery dogged Rommel's Afrika Korps to the border of Tunisia from November 5, 1942, to January 1943. The Desert Fox counterattacked at Medenine on March 6, 1943, and at Mareth on March 20, but Montgomery outflanked the German position during March 27-April 7. He continued to lead the Eighth Army through the balance of the Tunisian campaign, which ended on May 13.

From Africa, the Anglo-American armies launched an invasion of Sicily, which would be a jumping-off point for an invasion of the Italian mainland. Montgomery's Eighth Army began the campaign by pushing the Germans out of their positions around Mount Etna during July 9-August 17, 1943. From here, Montgomery captured the airfields at Foggia during September 3-27, only to get bogged down at the Sangro River by the end of the year. At this point of great frustration, he was relieved to be recalled to Britain, where he was assigned command of the Twenty-First Army Group in preparation for the invasion of France.

Montgomery was given overall command of ground forces during the Normandy invasion, which, after several postponements, commenced with the "D-Day" landings on June 6, 1944. While the landings succeeded—despite intense resistance on Omaha Beach, in the American sector—the breakout from Normandy eastward soon fell behind schedule, and Montgomery came under heavy criticism from his American counterparts, particularly George S. Patton, who commanded the Third U.S. Army in the southern portion of the advance. As planned, Montgomery relinquished overall command of ground forces to the supreme Allied commander, Dwight D. Eisenhower, on September 1, the very day he was promoted to field marshal, retaining command of the Twenty-First Army Group in the northern sector of the invasion.

While Patton and his Third Army advanced rapidly at the southern end of the invasion, Montgomery devised what he intended as a breakthrough to Germany in the north. He conceived Operation Market-Garden in a bid to push the war to a speedy conclusion by outflanking the "West Wall" German defensive line and establishing a bridgehead across the lower Rhine at Arnhem, Netherlands. This would put the Allied armies at the doorstep of the Ruhr River Valley, thereby gaining early and expeditious entry into the German industrial heartland. Over the protest of Patton and, to some extent, U.S. General Omar N. Bradley, Supreme Allied Commander Dwight Eisenhower approved Market-Garden on September 10, adding to Montgomery's Twenty-first Army Group the First Allied Airborne Army and then diverting to the operation much-needed supplies from both Bradley and Patton.

Under the tactical command of British Lieutenant General Frederick Browning, Market-Garden was a twofold operation. The "Market" portion was an airborne assault aimed at capturing bridges across eight key waterways; "Garden" was the ground advance of the British XXX Corps (under Lieutenant General Brian Horrocks) across those bridges. The combined operations depended wholly on speed, and this was both the great boldness and terrible vulnerability of the plan. XXX Corps was expected to advance nearly sixty miles in three days, from the Meuse-Escaut Canal to Arnhem. The Dutch government-in-exile, broadcasting from London, called for a railway strike to impede the Germans' ability to resist this movement. The strike was effective in interdicting the flow of German military supplies, but it also triggered reprisals in the form of a German stoppage of all canal traffic, which created acute food shortages that brought on a winter famine throughout the Netherlands.

Operation Market-Garden was launched on September 17, 1944, when the U.S. 101st Airborne Division landed between Eindhoven and Veghel, the U.S. 82nd Airborne Division landed around Grave and Groesbeek, and the British 1st Airborne Division parachuted near Arnhem. The first drops, 16,500 paratroopers and 3,500 glider troops, were accomplished with great accuracy, and the two American divisions landed quite near their bridgehead objectives. The British airborne troops, however, did not land near enough to Arnhem to take the vital bridges there—and on this failure turned the failure of the entire operation. Portions of two SS Panzer Divisions, the 9th and 10th, were being refitted near Arnhem. During the four hours it took the British troopers to reach the Arnhem bridges on foot, German resistance was built up in the area. The Germans quickly blew up the railway bridge and pinned down the British paratroops. Reinforcements from the Polish Parachute Brigade might have enabled a breakout, but a siege of bad weather delayed their arrival, then forced them to drop too far away, at Driel, where the Germans bottled them up.

In the meantime, gathering German resistance slowed the land assault as well. British XXX Corps was late linking up with 101st Airborne Division near Eindhoven. The delay was compounded by the necessity of erecting a temporary Bailey bridge at Zon to replace the bridge the Germans had destroyed. This put General Horrocks nearly a day and a half behind schedule. The delay menaced the 101st Airborne, which was exposed to flank attacks that succeeded in cutting the Eindhoven-Nijmegen road so frequently that the troopers dubbed it "Hell's Highway." At first, the 82nd Airborne Division fared better, taking the Groesbeek Bridge, thereby blocking German counterattacks. On September 20, after elements of the British corps finally began arriving, a battalion of the 82nd embarked across the Waal River in assault boats and took both Nijmegen bridges. After this, however, like the 101st, the 82nd was forced to await the arrival of the main body of XXX Corps, which was unable to commence its march to Arnhem for twenty-four hours after the 82nd had secured the bridges. This final delay proved fatal to Operation Market-Garden.

By the time the main body of XXX Corps was on the move, the Germans had driven the British airborne troops from the Arnhem bridgehead. German artillery then crossed the bridge and checked the advance of XXX Corps at Ressen. Despite last-minute maneuvering, it was no longer possible to organize sufficient strength to overcome the German defenses, and on September

25, a retreat was ordered. Nearly 2,300 British and Polish paratroops were able to withdraw from the Arnhem area, but more than six thousand were captured—about half of them wounded. The U.S. 101st and 82nd airborne divisions, loath to relinquish ground gained, remained in contact with the enemy for another two months and suffered a combined total of 3,532 casualties, killed and wounded. This action allowed the Allies to hold onto a salient from which a later advance into Germany (Operation Veritable) was launched in February 1945. In all other respects, however, Operation Market-Garden was a costly and heartbreaking failure, which seriously tarnished Montgomery's reputation, prompting Eisenhower to temporarily shift Montgomery to a secondary role in what was turning out to be the final months of the war in Europe.

Montgomery partially redeemed himself when he took command of the northern end of the American line during the Battle of the Bulge (December 16, 1944-January 15, 1945), in which a surprise German offensive pushed back the American position, resulting in the heaviest casualties US forces suffered on the Western Front. At the time, Montgomery's intervention was not welcomed by the American commanders. Nevertheless, it was Montgomery who was tasked with planning and leading the British crossing of the Rhine at Wesel on March 23, 1945. From here, he pushed into northern Germany and accepted the surrender of German forces in the Netherlands, Denmark, and, on May 4, northwestern Germany.

After Germany capitulated on May 8, 1945, Montgomery was named to command British occupation forces and was created Viscount Montgomery of Alamein in January of the following year. In June 1946, he became successor to Lord Alanbrooke as chief of the Imperial General Staff but was never popular in this role among his colleagues. He was the opposite of Eisenhower when it came to the practice of military diplomacy, and he never hesitated to belittle those who disagreed with or questioned him. He soon left the Imperial General Staff to become chairman of the Western European Union Commanders in Chief in 1948. This evolved into the military arm of NATO and led to Montgomery's appointment as the first commander of NATO forces in Europe and as Eisenhower's deputy supreme commander in Europe. Montgomery fared better in the NATO post, serving in it from March 1951 until his retirement from the army in September 1958.

Bernard Law Montgomery's wartime memoirs, published in 1958, touched off a minor scandal for their harsh criticism of his former comrades in arms. Eisenhower let the opprobrium roll of his back, but Auchinleck threatened a lawsuit for libel. In the 1960s, Montgomery created a further uproar with his support for the South African policy of apartheid (racial segregation), his praise for the Communist leadership of China, and his outspoken objections to the decriminalization of homosexuality in Britain. He denounced the Sexual Offences Act of 1967 as a "charter for buggery," which prompted at least one biographer to assert that Montgomery was likely a repressed homosexual. Montgomery was an outspoken critic of U.S. strategy in the Vietnam War, and he also bluntly told officers of the Egyptian Army in 1967 that they would be defeated in any war they launched against Israel. (They were.)

Montgomery died on March 25, 1976, at his home in Islington, Hampshire, at the age of eighty-eight. The cause of death has never been specified.

#26
CHESTER W. NIMITZ

Assembled and led the United States Navy Pacific Fleet of two million sailors and one thousand ships that won victory at sea against Japan

"Admiral Chester W. Nimitz, USN, Commander-in-Chief, Pacific Fleet, pins the Navy Cross on Doris Miller, Steward's Mate 1/c, USN, at a ceremony on board a U.S. Navy warship in Pearl Harbor, T.H., May 27, 1942," reads the original caption. Miller was Ship's Cook Third Class aboard the USS *West Virginia* at Pearl Harbor on December 7, 1941. While the battleship was strafed and bombed, Miller "assisted in moving his Captain, who had been mortally wounded, to a place of greater safety and later manned and operated a machine gun until ordered to leave the bridge." (credit: *Library of Congress*)

The Japanese attack on Pearl Harbor was devastating but not defeating, thanks in no small measure to the leadership of Admiral Chester W. Nimitz. His predecessor, Admiral Husband E. Kimmel, commander in chief of the United States Fleet and the U.S. Pacific Fleet on December 7, 1941, was forever associated with that Sunday of defeat, on which America saw its navy and its nation humbled. Ten days later, President Franklin D. Roosevelt promoted Nimitz to command the Pacific Fleet with the rank of admiral. The ceremony transferring command took place, on December 31, on the deck of a submarine—all the battleships at Pearl having been sunk or damaged. His mission was as simple as it was daunting: defeat Japan. His first task was to halt the Japanese advance across the Pacific and to do so despite the loss, either temporary or permanent, of all eight Pacific Fleet battleships (four sunk, four severely damaged), three cruisers (sunk or damaged), three destroyers, and many lesser vessels. One hundred eighty-eight aircraft had been destroyed at Pearl Harbor, most of them on the ground, and 2,403 Americans had been killed, another 1,178 wounded.

Nimitz had not only to restore but to expand the fleet, repairing and building vessels and rebuilding morale while creating total confidence in victory. His enemies were the massive Japanese fleet as well as time itself. No United States naval leader was ever handed a more challenging mission.

Chester William Nimitz was born on February 24, 1885, in the small town of Fredericksburg in the middle of Texas and very far from either the Atlantic or the Pacific oceans. Like most area residents, his family was of German lineage—the town was the epicenter of *Texasdeutsch*, "Texas German," a distinct German dialect spoken nowhere else. Chester was a half-orphan, his father, Chester Bernhard Nimitz, having died of a rheumatic ailment six months before his birth. His mother, Anna Josephine (Henke) Nimitz, was aided in her son's upbringing by his German-born paternal grandfather, Charles Henry Nimitz, who had sailed with the German Merchant Marine and, after immigrating to Texas, became a Texas Ranger in the Texas Mounted Volunteers in 1851. During the Civil War, he was commissioned captain of the Gillespie Rifles Company in the Confederate States Army. As an adult, Nimitz never forgot his grandfather's advice about the sea, which he called a "stern taskmaster," explaining that it was like life itself: "The best way to get along with either is to learn all you can, then do your best and don't worry—especially about things over which you have no control." It was advice Nimitz would use in the weeks and months after Pearl Harbor.

Young Nimitz wanted a military career and applied to West Point. When his congressman, James L. Slayden, told him that no more appointments to the military academy were available but that he could give him a chance at an appointment to the United States Naval Academy at Annapolis, Nimitz, seeking mainly an opportunity for an expenses-paid education, studied diligently and won the appointment. He enrolled in 1901 and graduated in 1905, seventh in a class of 114 midshipmen. At the time, academy graduates were obliged to serve two years at sea as a warrant officer before receiving an ensign's commission. He was therefore dispatched to San Francisco, where he joined the crew of the newly commissioned (October 4, 1904) battleship *Ohio* (BB-12), cruised with her to the Far East and, in September 1906, transferred to the much older cruiser *Baltimore* (C-3) on January 31, 1907, aboard which he was commissioned an ensign. While in what was then called the "China Station," he saw service aboard the gunboat *Panay*, the destroyer *Decatur* (DD-5), and the cruiser *Denver* (CL-16). He was in command of the *Decatur* when the ship ran aground in the Philippines on July 7, 1908. It was safely towed off a mud bank; however, a court-martial found the young ensign guilty of neglect of duty. It could well have been a career-ending conviction, but he was only issued a letter of reprimand and went on to serve briefly aboard the *Denver* before returning to the United States on USS *Ranger* (IX-18), a gunboat with full-rig sail that was in use as a school ship.

In January 1908, Nimitz began submarine instruction in the First Submarine Flotilla and, in May, was assigned to command the flotilla as well as the submarine USS *Plunger* (SS-2), commissioned in 1903 as one of the U.S. Navy's first subs. In 1910, promoted to lieutenant, he was assigned to command USS *Snapper* (SS-16) upon its commissioning that year, followed by command of the USS *Narwhal* (SS-17) in November 1910. He was named to command the 3rd Submarine Division Atlantic Torpedo

Fleet in October 1911 and, the next month, assisted in the fitting out of USS *Skipjack* (SS-24), of which he assumed command in 1912 while also commanding the Atlantic Submarine Flotilla.

The navy assigned Nimitz to supervise the building of diesel engines for a new oil tanker, the USS *Maumee* (AO-2), and then sent Nimitz, who spoke fluent German, to study diesel engine technology in Germany and Belgium. In 1916, he was promoted to lieutenant commander and, in the fall, assigned as executive officer of the *Maumee*. After the United States entered World War I on April 6, 1917, Nimitz served as *Maumee's* chief engineer when the vessel was used for underway refueling of navy destroyers crossing the Atlantic. Nimitz pioneered the procedures for underway refueling, which he further refined during World War II. Underway refueling and replenishment would prove vital to operations of the Pacific Fleet during 1942-1945. On August 10, 1917, Nimitz was appointed aide to Rear Admiral Samuel S. Robison, Commander, Submarine Force, U.S. Atlantic Fleet, and on February 6, 1918, became chief of Robison's staff. In September of that year, he was transferred to the office of the Chief of Naval Operations in Washington and, on October 25, days before the armistice of November 11, 1918, he was given additional duty as a senior member of the Board of Submarine Design.

Between the world wars, Nimitz served as executive officer on the battleship *South Carolina* (BB-26), as captain of the cruiser *Chicago* (an aging ship launched in 1885), while also commanding Submarine Division 14 out of Pearl Harbor. Promoted to commander in 1921, he attended the Naval War College during 1922-1923 and from 1923 to 1925 was attached to the staff of the commander in chief, Battle Fleet. During 1925-1926, he served as aide to the commander in chief, U.S. Fleet. Following this assignment, he organized the first training division for naval reserve officers at the University of California, Berkeley, and headed this program from 1926 to 1929. During this period, he was promoted to captain (1927) and, in 1929, was assigned command of Submarine Division 20, serving in this capacity through 1931. He was assigned to command the cruiser USS *Augusta* (CA-31) in 1933, sailing as her skipper until 1935, when he was named assistant chief of the Bureau of Navigation, the navy bureau at the time responsible for personnel management. In 1938, promoted to rear admiral, Nimitz left his desk to command a cruiser division and then a battleship division, returning to the Bureau of Navigation in June 1939 as its chief.

When Nimitz was promoted to admiral and named to replace Admiral Kimmel ten days after Pearl Harbor, he wasted no time in reorganizing all defenses in the Hawaiian Islands and directing the rebuilding of the partially shattered Pacific fleet. On March 30, 1942, he was given unified command of all U.S. naval, sea, and air forces in the Pacific Ocean Area.

Admiral Nimitz devoted a great deal of attention to developing naval intelligence operations throughout the Pacific, making use of a network of civilian observers who lived on or near the Japanese-occupied islands. He made superb use of such intelligence in his efforts to check Japanese operations against Port Moresby, New Guinea, at the Battle of the Coral Sea on May 4-8, 1942. Outnumbered and outgunned, Nimitz suffered a tactical defeat, but he scored a major strategic victory by repelling a Japanese invasion that menaced Australia. The battle is especially significant in the history of naval warfare as the first in which aircraft carriers engaged with one another, so that much of the action took place "over the horizon," without the surface ships visible to one another.

Coral Sea was the first battle in the Pacific theater in which the Japanese were denied advance. While the U.S. Navy lost one of its precious aircraft carriers, the *Lexington,* the Japanese lost two, which Admiral Isoroku Yamamoto intended to use in the Battle of Midway. Yamamoto planned to lure the U.S. Pacific Fleet to its destruction, thereby forcing the United States to seek a negotiated peace in the Pacific theater.

Midway Island, just one thousand miles west of Hawaii, was a strategically located position from which either side could launch major attacks against the other. Believing that he could corner the U.S. fleet here and administer a *coup de grâce*, Yamamoto sent a diversionary force to the Aleutian Islands, U.S. Territory, in the northern Pacific, while Admiral Chuichi Nagumo, the very man who had led the attack on Pearl Harbor, led a four-carrier striking force followed by an invasion fleet—a total of about eighty-eight ships—to Midway. Thanks to ULTRA decrypts (top-secret intercepts of Japanese communications), Nimitz was able to divine and anticipate Yamamoto's motives and moves. Boldly, he decided to oblige the Japanese admiral by providing the decisive battle he wanted. He intended to give him, however, a very different outcome: an American victory.

Nimitz rushed to assemble two task forces east of Midway: Number 16, under Admiral Raymond Spruance, and Number 18, commanded by Admiral Frank Fletcher. In addition to the aircraft launched from the fleet carriers *Enterprise*, *Hornet*, and *Yorktown*, land-based planes would operate from fields on Midway itself.

Midway-based planes attacked a portion of the Japanese fleet more than five hundred miles west of the island on June 3, 1942. The attack was hardly an auspicious beginning. It failed to do significant damage, and American losses were heavy. On the morning of June 4, the Japanese seized the initiative, sending 108 planes against Midway, causing heavy damage, including the loss on the ground of fifteen of the twenty-five Marine Corps fighter planes defending the island. At the same time, U.S. torpedo bombers made a second air attack against the Japanese fleet—once again with profoundly discouraging results. The bombers hit no enemy ships, and the force lost seven aircraft. In a second strike on this day, eight of twenty-seven Marine dive bombers were lost, again without having inflicted damage on the enemy. Next, fifteen heavy B-17 bombers, flying out of Midway, attacked, but again, the Japanese carriers escaped unscathed.

Finally, U.S. Navy torpedo bombers launched from all three American carriers made yet another attack on the Japanese fleet. They inflicted little damage, and, worst of all, thirty-five of the forty-one bombers engaged were shot down. However, this costly attack forced the Japanese carriers to launch all of their aircraft to intercept the torpedo bombers, leaving the carriers wide open to a counterattack. As the Japanese crews were still preparing their aircraft, which had just returned from defending against the latest torpedo bomber attacks, fifty-four dive bombers from the USS *Enterprise* and USS *Yorktown* (the USS *Hornet*'s planes failed to find their targets) descended on three of the great Japanese carriers—*Akagi*, *Kaga*, and *Soryu*. All were loaded with just-recovered aircraft not yet ready to take off. In a mere five minutes, all three carriers were sent to the bottom, along with crews, aircraft, and pilots. A fourth carrier, *Hiryu*, was sunk in a second attack later in the afternoon—although not before the *Hiryu's* planes had savaged the *Yorktown*, ultimately sinking it.

The Battle of Midway exacted a heavy cost in American pilots and sailors, but it was fatal to the Japanese. Losing four aircraft carriers in a single engagement, along with many aircraft, and—perhaps worst of all—many of its most highly skilled pilots, the Japanese fleet withdrew on June 5. The U.S. forces in the area were themselves too battered to give chase—although they did subsequently sink a heavy cruiser, the *Mikuma*, on June 6. Without question, the Battle of Midway turned the tide of the Pacific war. Up to this point, Japan had been on the offensive, a veritable juggernaut. After Midway, it could fight only a defensive war, and its hold on the vast Pacific was steadily eroded. Nimitz understood the cost of this momentous strategic triumph: 150 planes, 307 men, a destroyer, and the carrier *Yorktown*. Japanese losses, however, were 275 planes, four carriers, a heavy cruiser, and nearly five thousand sailors and airmen—the latter an irreplaceable loss.

Following the victory at Midway, Nimitz promoted his "island-hopping" strategy with the army's Pacific commander, General Douglas MacArthur. It was the overall plan for the conduct of the amphibious war in the Pacific theater and consisted of developing a series of assaults on selected Japanese island fortresses while either entirely skipping over others or subjecting some islands to air attack only and to submarine attack on ships attempting to resupply and reinforce the islands. What Nimitz recognized and MacArthur acknowledged (although he later claimed originating credit for the strategy) was that isolating some Japanese forces was as effective as attacking and destroying them—and, of course, was far less costly. While the Japanese had control of many islands early in the war, the far-flung deployment of occupying forces rendered each of those forces vulnerable if communication with other occupied islands were severed.

As developed, the island-hopping campaign consisted of two prongs, a northern prong and a southern prong. The northern prong was projected from Midway into the central Pacific, reaching Iwo Jima in February 1945. The southern prong originated from Guadalcanal and moved out to the Solomon Islands and, finally, the Philippines in early 1945.

Nimitz personally directed the campaign in the Gilbert Islands (November 20-23, 1943) and in the Marshalls (January 31-February 23, 1944), but he was superbly skilled in delegating specific tactical authority to key subordinates, with whom he worked brilliantly and whom he was always able to inspire. He oversaw the advance into the Marianas during June 14-August 10, 1944, and then into the Palaus during September 15-November 25.

Nimitz advocated attacking the Japanese in China via a major operation to take Formosa (Taiwan) and, in this, sharply disagreed with MacArthur's demand that amphibious operations instead be devoted to the liberation of the Philippines, which MacArthur had been forced to abandon as Bataan and Corregidor were about to fall to the Japanese in 1942. Nevertheless, when President Roosevelt chose to execute MacArthur's plan, Nimitz gave the invasion of Leyte in the Philippines his full cooperation. With MacArthur's forces operating from New Guinea, Nimitz coordinated the Leyte landings and invasion of Leyte in the promised U.S. return to the Philippines on October 20, 1944.

Nimitz was promoted to the newly created rank of fleet admiral—the naval equivalent of five-star general of the army—on December 15, 1944. He then went on to direct the capture of Iwo Jima during February 19-March 24, 1945. Iwo Jima was strategically critical because it was the best available air base between Saipan (some seven hundred miles to the south, which U.S. forces had already taken) and Tokyo. With the capture of Iwo Jima, United States forces were clearly closing in on the Japanese home-land. Next came the campaign to take Okinawa (April 1-June 21, 1945), which was followed by operations against Japan itself during January 1945 to the end of the war, when the Japanese surrendered aboard Nimitz's flagship, USS *Missouri,* on September 2, 1945.

Following the war, Nimitz served as chief of naval operations (CNO) from December 15, 1945 to December 15, 1947 and was then appointed special assistant to the Secretary of the Navy during 1948-1949. The man who had been a pioneer in the submarine service and had been instrumental in implementing conversion of much of the surface fleet to diesel propulsion and the submarine fleet from gasoline to diesel (when operating on the surface) also played a key postwar role in securing approval for building the world's first nuclear-powered submarine, USS *Nautilus* (SSN-571), commissioned in 1954. Nimitz served as United Nations commissioner for Kashmir from 1949 to 1951 and wrote (with E. B. Potter) an important history of warfare at sea, *Sea Power: A Naval History,* published in 1960. In 1965, he suffered a stroke, which was complicated by pneumonia. He died, at eighty, on February 20, 1966.

#27
HEINZ GUDERIAN

*Innovator of "Blitzkrieg," the distinguishing military tactic
of World War II in Europe*

Heinz Guderian (right) is pictured in 1929 while overseeing the covert creation
of a German *Panzer* (tank) corps in direct violation of the terms of the Treaty of
Versailles. (credit: *Armémuseum, Stockholm, Sweden*)

After its first full month, August 1914, as the German army swung like a scythe through Belgium and northern France, executing the Schlieffen Plan intended to bring quick victory, the Western Front of World War I congealed into stubbornly static warfare along an all but unmoving line of trenches that extended through France from the English Channel in the north to the Swiss border in the south. From the late autumn of 1914 to the late autumn of 1918, there was a stalemate of slaughter. Most of the military minds in the years following the armistice of 1918 believed the next war, when it came, would be much the same, a trench war of static attrition. They trained accordingly.

A few dissenting voices were heard. In the United States, such generals as George S. Patton and Dwight D. Eisenhower lobbied their superiors to prepare for a mobile war, a war of maneuver, in which armor (tanks and highly mobile artillery) and aircraft would play leading roles. They argued that, in the 1914-1918 war, development of the weapons of defense, the heavy machine gun and heavy artillery, had outstripped weapons of offense. This imbalance in weapons technology ensured that the fighting would be static. Since then, however, the development of offensive weapons had made great strides, in the air and on the ground. With these, the next world war would not be fought along trench lines. It would be fought on the march.

In the United States, victorious in World War I, the army was a remarkably hidebound institution. Patton, Ike, and the other apostles of mobile war faced an uphill climb. In Germany, however, defeat had brought the draconian provisions of the Treaty of Versailles, which included disbanding the army, except for a small body of 100,000 officers and men. Between the wars, German militarists shaped this core into an elite force, which would serve as the kernel around which a much larger army could be quickly formed when needed. Precisely because it was elite, the officer corps of the core army tended to be forward thinking. They were receptive to ideas of maneuver, and, therefore, Heinz Guderian, an apostle of armor, author of a prescient 1937 book on the application of mechanized warfare, *Achtung! Panzer* (*Beware the Tank!*), found an eager audience for a doctrine and set of tactics that would come to be called *Blitzkrieg,* "lightning war." No approach to combat had greater effect on the nature of World War II.

Heinz Guderian was born on January 17, 1888, in Kulm, West Prussia (today Chelmno, Poland), the son of a Prussian army officer, Freidrich Guderian, and Clara (Kirchoff) Guderian. Heinz was destined from birth for a military career and attended the cadet school in Karlsruhe from September 1900 to April 1903. From here, he enrolled in the main cadet school at Gross Lichteffelde, from which he graduated in December 1907, entering the 10th Hanoverian Jager Battalion on January 27, 1908, as a second lieutenant. A promising officer, he was selected to attend the *Kriegsakademie* (War College), which he did, on the eve of World War I, during 1913-1914.

When war broke out in July 1914, Guderian was serving as a signals officer in the 5th Cavalry Division, in command of a wireless (radio) station. By April 1915, he was serving as assistant signals officer for the entire Fourth Army, holding this post through April 1917, when he moved through a variety of staff positions, culminating in an appointment to the General Staff Corps in February 1918. He served in this role until the armistice of November 11. Thus, Guderian saw little combat in the 1914-1918 war, but he had been in an excellent position to view the big picture. Like many German citizens and most career military officers, he opposed the signing of the Treaty of Versailles, and he believed that liberal elements had betrayed the German Empire into surrender and dissolution.

Like many others, he refused to give up the fight. Guderian joined the *Freikorps* ("Free Corps"), a name applied to several non-government paramilitary groups that sprang into existence throughout Germany beginning in December 1918. Initially, the *Freikorps* consisted of recently discharged veterans, both enlisted men and officers, as well as an admixture of unemployed and discontented civilian youths. They shared an intense nationalism and reactionary conservatism and took it upon themselves, often with unofficial sanction from elements within the post-Versailles Weimar government, to put down left-wing demonstrations and uprisings in Berlin, Bremen, Brunswick, Hamburg, Halle, Leipzig, Silesia, Thuringia, and the Ruhr. Guderian participated in *Freikorps* operations in Latvia during March-July 1919 as chief of staff of the Iron Division, defending the German eastern border against communist incursions during the Russian Civil War.

Late in 1919, Guderian left the *Freikorps* when he was selected as one of the four thousand officers to remain as part of the *Reichswehr*, the

100,000-man German rump army permitted by the Treaty of Versailles. In January 1922, he was assigned to the Inspectorate of Transport Troops in the *Truppenamt* ("Troop Office"), which was the cover designation for what had been the General Staff, a body officially banned by the Versailles treaty. Guderian served in a transport battalion in Munich until 1924 and was then appointed an instructor in tactics and military history on the staff of 2nd Division during 1924-1927. He returned to General Staff duty from October 1927 to February 1930. It was during this assignment that he was briefly attached to a Swedish tank battalion as an observer. After this experience, he was given command of a motor transport battalion, which he reorganized as a provisional armored reconnaissance battalion during 1930-1931. This was a covert step designed to deceive Allied officials charged with overseeing Treaty of Versailles compliance. Guderian was actually creating the kernel of a *Panzer* (armored) force, a tank corps. After Guderian was appointed chief of staff to the inspector of Transport Troops in October 1931, he began work in earnest on plans for the creation of German army tank forces.

As Adolf Hitler and the Nazi Party rose to prominence within and then to control of the German government, the pretense of abiding by the restrictions in the Treaty of Versailles increasingly fell away. In October 1935, Guderian left his staff post as inspector of Transport Troops to assume command of what was now openly called the 2nd Panzer Division at Würzburg. The following year, he was promoted from colonel to major general and, in 1937, gained wide attention with his *Achtung! Panzer*. In it, he digested his theories of mechanized warfare, which embodied the doctrine and set of tactics that would be informally but universally called *Blitzkrieg*—"lightning war." (The term was not invented by the German military but was likely the coinage of a journalist. It was not discouraged by the military, however, and its use was widespread both inside and outside of Germany.)

As presented in *Achtung! Panzer*, the tactics later called *Blitzkrieg* were intended to overawe defenders with rapid, violent, and, above all, highly mobile action coordinated among armor, mechanized infantry, massed firepower, and air power, with special forces units acting to disrupt the defenders' communication and supply lines, thereby increasing confusion during the onslaught. While always advancing, the simultaneous object of *Blitzkrieg* is to disable and paralyze the enemy's capacity to coordinate defenses effectively. If defenses are *disabled*, the attacker need not be delayed by a costly campaign aimed at *destroying* defenses, and thus the attack may be accelerated with maximum penetration.

The *Blitzkrieg* concepts Guderian set forth in *Achtung! Panzer* may be traced to two pre-World War II German commanders. In World War I, General Oskar von Hutier (1857-1934) executed newly formulated German infiltration tactics (developed largely from earlier British and French models) in the capture of Riga (in what is today Latvia) on September 3, 1917. Violent, highly coordinated, and swift, the attack on Riga demoralized and overwhelmed the defenders. This approach to combat was dubbed "Hutier tactics." During the interwar period, Hans von Seeckt (1866-1936), head of the *Reichswehr*, used the precedent of Hutier tactics to further develop the tactics Guderian subsequently elaborated on in his book and in his tactical thinking as a Panzer commander.

From 1937 to 1938, Guderian commanded XVI Corps, comprising three Panzer divisions. During the *Anschluss* (the annexation of Austria to Germany), Guderian led the 2nd Panzer Division through Linz to Vienna (March 12-13, 1938). In the invasion of Poland that opened World War II, he led XIX Panzer Corps throughout the entire Polish campaign (September 1-October 5, 1939), demonstrating the role of armor in the *Blitzkrieg* by advancing with great speed from Pomerania and across the Polish Corridor on September 4. As executed by Guderian and other German field commanders in the invasion, *Blitzkrieg* was aimed at thrusting through a relatively narrow front using armor, motorized artillery, and aircraft, especially the Junkers Ju 87 "Stuka" dive bomber. This concentrated breakthrough created a point of attack, which Guderian and others called the *Schwerpunkt* ("strong point"), a gap in which defenders were fatally weakened. Before this gap could be repaired and reinforced by the defenders, wide, rapid sweeps by massed tanks followed, along with mechanized infantry (mainly specially trained "shock troops" transported by vehicle). This further disrupted the enemy's lines of defense, creating areas in which defenders were trapped, immobilized, and cut off from one another. Their only option at this point was surrender. Although *Blitzkrieg* depended on extreme violence, its speed, which neutralized rather than destroyed a defender, often spared casualties on both sides. "You are the cavalry," Guderian told his tank commanders and their crews. "Your job is to break through and keep going."

Guderian proved himself a talented field commander. While he was guided by the principles he himself had laid down in *Achtung! Panzer,* he was not a slave to them. Leading his corps in the Battle of Wizna (September 7, 1939) and the Battle of Kobryn (September 14-18), he temporarily abandoned *Blitzkrieg's* rapid maneuver and relentless advance, instead using his tanks to transport a company of sappers (engineer troops), who used explosives to destroy most of the Polish defensive bunkers at Wizna. In the case of Kobryn, he held back the advance, letting the Red Army (at the time, Stalin was allied with Hitler) assume the initiative.

After the campaign in Poland was concluded, Guderian participated in planning the invasion of France. He supported the change to the original plan that had been drawn up by Germany's chief of the Army High Command (OKH), Franz Halder, and embraced the so-called Manstein Plan devised largely by Lieutenant General Erich von Manstein. Whereas Halder had called for a massive invasion through the Low Countries, Manstein shifted the *Schwerpunkt* to the Ardennes, a densely forested area on the eastern border of France, which was weakly defended. French military planners believed that the terrain of the Ardennes was a natural defense.

Guderian led his *Panzer* corps as the spearhead of the invasion drive in May 1940 and succeeded in penetrating the Ardennes and advancing across the Meuse River in just three days. He then led an attack that shattered the French lines at Sedan, which precipitated a chaotic collapse of the French defenses. Once he had broken through, "Der schnelle Heinz" (Speedy Heinz), as he was admiringly nicknamed, took off on a "race to the sea," cleaving the British Expeditionary Force (BEF) from the French army in Northern France and Belgium. His advance cut off both forces from their supply lines, depriving them of ammunition, food, and reinforcements.

Guderian's *Panzers* were at the tip of the spear before which the Allies in the north fell back on Dunkirk, where their backs were to the English Channel. Guderian favored a relentless armored advance, confident that he and his tanks could defeat the Allies at Dunkirk, forcing the mass surrender of those they did not kill. Adolf Hitler, fearful that Guderian, whose tanks were far in advance of the main portion of the invading army, would be cut off, ordered him to halt and await the arrival of reinforcements. Guderian responded by continuing the advance, which he now deceptively called a "reconnaissance in force." Convinced that the *Luftwaffe* could prevent the evacuation of the BEF by air attacks alone, Hitler reasserted his authority on May 24 and repeated his order to halt. Reluctantly, Guderian stopped. The result was that 330,000 BEF and French troops were evacuated from Dunkirk by a ragtag flotilla of British navy and civilian vessels. The total and decisive victory that Germany might have won here had been squandered, and Guderian lost all faith in Hitler's strategic acumen.

France capitulated on June 25, 1940, by which time XIX Corps was on the Swiss frontier near Basel. By November 1940, the unit was expanded into 2nd Panzer Group and was transferred to the east to participate in Field Marshal Fedor von Bock's Army Group Center during Operation Barbarossa (June 22-December 5, 1941), the German invasion of the Soviet Union, which commenced on June 22, 1941.

Guderian's 2nd Panzers, along with the 3rd Panzer Group, encircled Soviet forces at Minsk on July 10 and went on to surround Smolensk and capture Roslavl during July 12-August 8, 1941. From here, Guderian and his *Panzers* were dispatched south to coordinate operations with the 4th Panzer Group of Field Marshal Gerd von Rundstedt's Army Group South in a massive maneuver to encircle 600,000 Red Army troops in the "Kiev pocket" during August 21-September 6.

Guderian's offensive push toward the Soviet capital of Moscow was stalled by a combination of brutally cold weather and unflaggingly fierce Soviet resistance during October 23-November 7, 1941. In an increasingly desperate situation, Guderian made repeated requests to Hitler for permission to withdraw from exposed positions around Tula during December 5-26. At length, by way of final response, Hitler relieved him of command and sent General Gunther von Kluge to take his place on December 26, 1941. Following this, Guderian fell ill. In September 1942, when Erwin Rommel was himself recuperating from a severe illness, the "Desert Fox" recommended that Guderian be called on to replace him in Africa. High Command (OKW) replied tersely: "Guderian is not accepted." Clearly, Adolf Hitler would not brook defiance from his generals.

In the end, Guderian did not recover his health until 1943, and was re-called to duty as Inspector General of Panzer Troops in February of that year. By this time, the *Panzer* forces had been badly mauled at the Battle of Stalingrad (August 23, 1942-February 2, 1943), the epic turning-point engagement on the Russian front. Guderian set about rebuilding German armor, working closely with Armaments Minister Albert Speer to step up and improve tank production.

Some historians believe that Guderian had information about the July 20, 1944, assassination plot against Hitler. Despite his many conflicts with the Führer, he did not participate in the plot—but (assuming he was indeed aware of it) he made no attempt to warn Hitler or blow the whistle on the plotters. Clearly, however, Hitler did not suspect Guderian of any complicity. After the July 20 Plot failed, Guderian emerged as one of the few military leaders Hitler felt he could trust. He appointed him on July 21, 1943, to replace General Kurt Zeitzler as army chief of staff. In this position, he focused on defending the Eastern Front. Predictably, the increasingly delusional Hitler often argued with Guderian and countermanded his orders. By March 1945, a frustrated Guderian was openly opposing Hitler in meetings. With the noose tightening on Berlin, Hitler ordered Guderian to take six weeks' sick leave. With his family, Guderian went to Munich, where he was treated for a cardiac ailment. He knew that Germany had been defeated, and he waited in Munich to be captured by advancing American forces. He surrendered to them on May 10, 1945.

Guderian was held by the Americans until June 17, 1948, when he was cleared of complicity in any war crimes. The British especially regarded him as one of the "good Germans"—like Rommel, a professional soldier just doing his job. He was invited to discuss strategy and tactics before various British veterans' organizations and in the early 1950s, during the Cold War, was formally called upon by the Western allies to assist in organizing the *Bundeswehr,* West Germany's defense force. He died on May 14, 1945, aged sixty-five.

#28
CHIANG KAI-SHEK

Generalissimo against Japan

Chiang Kai-shek attends the Cairo Conference, November 25, 1943, with
Franklin Roosevelt and Winston Churchill.
(credit: *National Archives and Records Administration*)

No ally of the powers opposing the Axis—Japan, Germany, and Italy—was more controversial than Chiang Kai-shek, leader of the Republic of China from 1928 to 1975. During the last twenty-six years of this period, following the defeat of Chiang and the Nationalists in the Chinese Civil War (1927-1936 and 1946-1950), his Republic was a rump portion of the nation confined to Taiwan.

Chiang's stand against the Japanese, in the Second Sino-Japanese War, which began on July 7, 1937 and continued as a theater of World War II through September 9, 1945, made him an ally of necessity of the United States and Britain, as did his opposition to the communist leader Mao Zedong. Yet Chiang came with a great deal of baggage. Although he was opposed to Communism, he was no democrat and was not even pro-Western, but favored traditional Chinese culture under his authoritarian, even dictatorial, rule. He was associated with Shanghai's criminal syndicate (known as the Green Gang), and he worked with the Comintern when it suited him (and against Communism when it no longer suited him). In 1927, he purged dissidents and suspected Communists in Shanghai, carrying out mass killings in what was known as the White Terror. In Shanghai alone, under his direction, his Kuomintang (KMT) Nationalist organization killed some twelve thousand, and by early 1928, about 300,000 Communists and suspected Communists were executed by the KMT nationwide. In all, historians estimate that Chiang and the Nationalists were responsible for between 6 and 18.5 million Chinese deaths before, during, and after World War II—some killed outright, others succumbing to starvation, privation, and disease due to government confiscation of food and other aspects of a scorched-earth "defensive" strategy. In 1938, during the Sino-Japanese War prior to World War II, Chiang opened up dikes on the Yellow River near Zhenzhou with the objective of stopping the Japanese advance. The resulting floods killed between 440,000 and 893,000 Chinese civilians.

While none of Chiang's actions were secret, most people in the West, including Americans and British, were unaware of them. The Roosevelt and Churchill governments sought to keep it that way and chose to portray Chiang as a brilliant commander, courageous fighter against tyranny, and a selfless apostle of Chinese liberation and self-determination. In this propaganda effort, Chiang's wife, Soon Mei-ling, better known in the West as Madame Chiang Kai-Shek, was an invaluable asset. Unlike her husband, she was fluent and even eloquent in English. She was, moreover, a woman of considerable intelligence, beauty, and charisma, who not only personally rallied the Chinese people against the Japanese but, in a 1942 speaking tour throughout the United States, gained much support for China's fight against the Japanese invasion. A remarkable figure, she lived across three centuries. Born in 1898, she did not die until 2003, at the age of 105.

❖

Chiang Kai-shek was born to a prosperous family in rural Chekiang on October 31, 1887. His father died when Chiang was young, and he was raised by his mother, who sent him to good schools, where he obtained a classical Chinese education. Chiang seemed destined for a career in the civil government, but when the civil service examination system was suspended in 1905, during a period of roiling revolution, he enrolled in the Baoding Military Academy in northern China in 1906. He was determined to pursue a military career, which, he thought, would be of value in freeing China from the corruption of the moribund Qing dynasty as well as the rapacity of the Western powers. In 1907, he moved to Japan and enrolled in the Tokyo Shinbu Gakko, a preparatory school for the prestigious Imperial Japanese Military Academy, which catered to the education of Chinese officers for Imperial Japanese Army Service. Here he came into contact with members of the Tongmenghui, a leading Chinese revolutionary society of the era, which he secretly joined. After his graduation from the military academy in 1909, he served with the Imperial Japanese Army until 1911, when he deserted to return to China. He reached Wuhan on October 11 of that year, after the Qing dynasty had already been toppled.

Serving as an artillery officer in the revolutionary forces, Chiang, under the command of Green Gang boss Chien Qimei, led a regiment in fighting in Shanghai. He became a founding member of the KMT. After General Yuan Shikai took over the new republican government, Chiang participated during July 12 through September 1913 in a failed attempt to overthrow him. Like many other KMT members, he evaded arrest by fleeing to Japan, but returned late in 1915, to take part in in the so-called Third Revolution, which blocked Yuan's bid to become emperor. When Yuan's agents assassinated Chen Qimei, Chiang succeeded him as leader of KMT (at the time having been briefly renamed the Chinese Revolutionary Party) in Shanghai. From this point until 1918, Chiang lived in Shanghai, in some obscurity, despite his leadership of the party. He was most active during 1916-1917 in the Green Gang, which was devoted to manipulating the volatile Chinese currency.

At last, in 1918, Chiang Kai-shek resumed his association with Sun Yat-sen, who would be recognized as the founder of the Republic of China. Sun had briefly joined forces with Chen Jiongming, a revolutionary and military governor of Guangdong, before he devoted himself to building up the KMT—with aid from Soviet Russia. In 1923, Chiang held the rank of major general in the KMT army and the next year was made commandant of the party's Whampoa Military Academy, which was designed to train the party's elite and most capable military forces. When Sun died in 1925, Chiang's prestige and power in the KMT rose rapidly. Having worked to consolidate KMT power in southern China during 1923-1925, Chiang led the "Northern Expedition" during July 1926 through May 1928, a campaign against the warlords, who had filled the power vacuum left by the collapse of the Qing dynasty. Chiang enjoyed considerable military success against the warlords, and he bolstered these gains by securing support from the Shanghai business community—a move modeled on fascism as it emerged in both Europe and Japan. This involved violently suppressing the labor movement, breaking with the Soviet Union, purging the KMT of all Communist influence, and then launching a military campaign against the Communists at Nanching and Hunan during August and September 1927. Once he had ousted the Russian military advisors, Chiang recruited many of China's competing warlords for the KMT—including those he had just fought.

Despite Chiang Kai-shek's progress, he was a figure as divisive as he was unifying. He voluntarily—and strategically—stepped down from leadership of the party for a brief period in 1927 in the hope of reducing the factional disputes he himself had kindled. In December of that year, he married Soong Mei-ling, the daughter of a wealthy businessman (and former Methodist missionary), who had studied in the United States, at Wesleyan, Wellesley, and elsewhere. She graduated from Wellesley in 1917, with a major in English and a minor in philosophy. Her American sojourn made her an especially valuable diplomatic asset to Chiang, and she would come into her own as a popular and influential leader.

On January 6, 1928, Chiang Kai-shek returned to the KMT as military commander in chief and as chairman of the party's Central Executive Council. He took up the Northern Campaign once again, capturing Peking (Beijing) on June 4. With this, China was now unified under the Nationalist Party—at least in principle. The fact was that warlords (those who had not been coopted and ushered into the KMT) and Communists still held sway over many large areas. From December 1930 to September 1934, Chiang led five so-called Bandit Suppression Campaigns in southern China, directed primarily against the Communists. Except for the last campaign, which was carried out with assistance from Germany, these proved largely fruitless, as did Chiang's attempt to counter the Japanese occupation of Manchuria in 1931.

As chairman of the KMT executive council from 1935 to 1945, Chiang was the closest thing China had to a single, widely recognized political leader during this period. While he was head of state of a new republic, sovereignty was always a highly relative matter. Chiang was compelled to tread a razor-thin line between two threatening, but rival, powers. Both the Japanese and the Russian-allied Communists vied for domination of China. Indeed, prior to 1937, Chiang tended to favor the Japanese and deemed the Communists the graver threat. Then, in December 1936, he was kidnapped by his own KMT subordinates Zhang Xueliang and Yang Hucheng, who were determined to force him away from Japanese affiliation and toward the Communists. This "Xi'an Incident," as the detention was called, compelled Chiang to create a united front with Mao Zedong and the Communists against the Japanese. Shortly after this alliance was created, on July 7, 1937, Japan invaded China, thereby starting the Second Sino-Japanese War.

Chiang, as commander in chief, commenced a losing battle against the Japanese invaders, progressively retreating with his command post southwest. In August 1937, he dispatched 600,000 of his finest soldiers to the defense of Shanghai. The Japanese killed, wounded, or captured more than 200,000 of them, doing irreparable damage to the nation's military. On the other hand, the battle for Shanghai proved that Japan would have a hard and costly fight to conquer China. More important, Chiang's stand showed the

Western powers that the Chinese would not simply yield to Japan and would persist in resistance against invasion.

Nevertheless, the news on all fronts was bad for Chiang Kai-shek. By December 1937, Nanjing fell to the Japanese, who perpetrated the infamous Nanking Massacre, the mass murder and mass rape of the capital city of the Republic of China. Chiang took his government into exile, first to Wuhan and then to Chongqing. The invaders claimed most of the country's major economic and industrial areas as Chiang withdrew his military forces deeper into the rural reaches of inland China. As Chiang hoped it would, the Imperial Japanese army pursued, getting drawn farther and farther into the interior, stretching lines of supply and communication to the breaking point. Like the Russians during Napoleon's invasion of 1812, Chiang employed a harsh scorched earth policy, purposely destroying crop lands, food supplies, and other sources of sustenance and shelter to deprive the invaders of their use. The price of this was mass starvation and privation among the Chinese civilian population. The most cataclysmic action of the scorched earth policy was the cataclysmic Yellow River flood, mentioned earlier in this chapter.

By the fall of 1938, the Japanese had taken and occupied Wuhan, forcing the Nationalists farther inland, to Chongqing. Along the route of the retreat, Chiang ordered his forces to burn down Changsha, capital of Hunan province, starting a fire that killed twenty thousand Chinese outright and made some hundreds of thousands homeless. KMT commanders had failed—accidentally or deliberately—to warn residents in advance of the arson. Of all the scorched earth tactics, it was the Changsha fire that cost Chiang Kai-shek most heavily. It lost him much of his support throughout China. Chiang therefore looked beyond the nation's borders for support and sent, in 1939, the Muslim leaders Isa Yusuf Alptekin and Ma Fuliang to Egypt, Turkey, and Syria to rally Muslim support against the Japanese invasion. Chinese Muslim military leaders proved to be of great value to Chiang Kai-shek, and he relied on them in 1942 to put down a Tibetan bid for independence. But by this time, the Japanese had coopted Wang Jingwei, a left-leaning KMT member and rival of Chiang Kai-shek. The invaders set Wang up as the puppet ruler of Manchuria, which the Japanese transformed into a puppet state called Manchukuo.

Like Winston Churchill in Europe, Chiang Kai-shek had high hopes for an alliance with the United States, as soon as it was propelled into World War II by the Japanese attack on Pearl Harbor. In 1942, he sent his American-educated wife, Soong Mei-ling, on a tour of the United States, where she was better known as Madame Chiang Kai-shek. She proved to be an extraordinarily persuasive speaker and political lobbyist. With her Western manners, Madame Chiang implied to many American political leaders the possibility that China could be refashioned into a Christian democracy after the war. In any event, President Roosevelt named Chiang Kai-shek Supreme Commander of Allied forces in the China war zone, and Britain's King George VI created Chiang a Knight Grand Cross of the Order of the Bath.

U.S. Army general Joseph "Vinegar Joe" Stilwell was assigned as the U.S. military adviser to Chiang and liaison with him and his commanders. He was, however, both outraged and discouraged by what he judged to be the gross incompetence and shameless corruption of the Chinese military leadership. U.S. funds dedicated to building Chinese airbases as platforms for launching bombing raids on Japan were openly embezzled by Chiang's commanders and KMT party officials. Stilwell blew the whistle but was powerless to interfere with the kleptocracy over which Chiang presided.

Indeed, in many ways, the relationship between China and the United States during World War II was less an alliance than a contest, as Chiang continually played the Soviets and Americans against one another. Chiang welcomed the Americans into talks between China and the Soviets, only to secretly inform the Soviets that he had no intention of listening to the advice of the Americans, much less yielding to their demands. At the same time, Chiang used U.S. military support not just against the Japanese, but also as a threat against the Soviets. This may indeed have discouraged Soviet interference in China during World War II.

Yet, in the end, Chiang needed the United States more than America needed him. His forces stayed in the fight and exacted a heavy toll against the Japanese. Nevertheless, China was losing the war, and as morale among the Nationalist forces dissolved, corruption only increased. Chiang soon found himself increasingly reliant on U.S. aid, both material and military. He reduced his own capacity to fight by stubbornly holding back forces from coordination with the American military because he believed he needed to have a sufficient reserve to fight the Communists after the war.

❖

Despite the losing battle, the KMT Executive Council named Chiang Kai-shek president of China in October 1943. In the United States, he was named *Time* magazine's "Man of the Year." That same year, Madame Chiang became the first Chinese national and only the second woman to address both houses of the U.S. Congress. While doubts about Chiang persisted at the highest levels of the Allied military and political leadership, it was clear that the appearance of a united front had to be maintained. Even if the Chinese military was corrupt and its leadership less than fully competent, the forces loyal to Chiang and those under the command of the Communist Chinese leader, Mao Zedong, were cooperating reasonably well against the mutual Japanese enemy. If Chiang was conducting mostly a retreat, it was always a fighting retreat. The Japanese "conquerors" were suffering casualties, so that action in the Chinese theater was reducing the effectiveness of Japan in prosecuting the war elsewhere in the Asian and Pacific theaters. The American war effort in the Pacific was greatly benefitting from this reduction. On balance, therefore, Chiang Kai-shek was proving indispensable in the victory that was being slowly achieved against Japan. If Chinese forces retreated in China, Japanese forces were retreating everywhere else.

The Japanese surrender in September 1945 ended both the Sino-Japanese War and World War II, of which it had become a part. But, for Chiang, there was little opportunity to rejoice. As he had predicted when he withheld from the Americans a reserve among his forces, the Chinese Civil War between the Nationalists and the Communists immediately resumed once the Japanese threat had ended. Despite his military resources, however, Chiang now paid the price for the KMT's corruption and for the popular support his scorched-earth tactics had cost him. The Nationalists steadily lost ground until, on December 7, 1949, Chiang Kai-shek himself was forced to withdraw to the island of Taiwan with the remnant of his Nationalist Party and Nationalist forces. Here he set up a government in exile, in defiance of Mao Zedong's People's Republic of China, which now controlled the vast mainland. The United States supported its old ally, less out of loyalty than as a token of continued resistance against the inexorable expansion of Communism in Asia. Chiang presided over the Taiwanese government until his death on April 5, 1975.

#29
HAILE SELASSIE

Lion against the Fascists

Haile Selassie, emperor of Ethiopia, is pictured in the study of his palace in Addis Ababa, about 1942. (credit: *Library of Congress*)

Holding the official title "By the Conquering Lion of the Tribe of Judah, His Imperial Majesty Haile Selassie I, King of Kings of Ethiopia, Elect of God," Haile Selassie, emperor of Ethiopia from 1930 to 1974, was an autocrat and, at times, an outright tyrant with limited regard for human rights. Nevertheless, he is most widely remembered today, at least in the West, for the enlightened reforms he brought to the people of Ethiopia and for his valiant defense of the nation against fascism and Italian invasion. In the run-up to World War II, he became an icon of noble nationalist resistance to the rapacity of imperialist fascism under Benito Mussolini. For many throughout the world, who had never before given remote places like Ethiopia a thought, Selassie's intensely dignified stand against Mussolini's 1935 invasion of his country defined the moral stakes of the looming conflict, and the "Lion of Judah's" stand against the forces of fascism (and, by implication, Nazism) was seized on as both a warning and a beacon of defiance. Although he was head of state of small African nation, Haile Selassie became one of the great symbolic figures of the World War II era, exerting an influence on world opinion that far exceeded his nation's negligible military and economic power.

Hailie Selassie was born Tafari Makonnen Woldemikael (and was known in childhood as Lij—"Child"—Tafari Makonnen) on July 23, 1892, the cousin of Emperor Menelik II (1889-1913). In 1906, he assumed the titular office of governor of Selale, a minor realm, and the following year became governor over an entire province, Sidamo. When he was next elevated to governor of the major province of Harar in 1910 or 1911, he assumed the name Ras Tafari Makonnen—"Ras" signifying "head" or "prince." On December 12, 1913, Menelik II died and was succeeded by his grandson Lij Iyasu (1895-1935), who had been converted to Islam and was now a zealous Muslim. A movement to depose Iyasu (who reigned as Iyasu V) developed, and Tafari gained its support. On September 27, 1916, Iyasu was deposed on grounds of his conversion to Islam and his subsequent attempt to change the state religion of Ethiopia from Coptic Christianity to that faith. Forces loyal to Iyasu were defeated at the Battle of Segale (October 27), and Tafari promoted the coronation of his aunt as Empress Zewditu while he himself assumed the regency under the name Ras Tafari. The regency was not absolute, however, since Zewditu retained (and wielded) authority as a final arbiter of the claims of competing factions in the empire. Nevertheless, Ras Tafari declared himself heir to the throne and, as regent, exercised most of the actual governing power.

The period of the Ras Tafari's regency was roiled by intrigue against the regent and heir by conservative supporters of Empress Zewditu. The intrigue came to a head in September 1928, in an armed clash in Addis Ababa between the Zewditu's supporters and a company of troops personally led by Tafari. His forces prevailed in a standoff *inside* Menelik's mausoleum. The support of the people—and, just as important, the support of the police—ensured that Tafari's victory would hold. On October 7, 1928, Empress Zewditu personally crowned Tafari as Negus ("King") of Ethiopia. The coronation of Tafari as king created conflict with Empress Zewditu's absolute rule over overlapping Ethiopian territory. In effect, Ethiopia now had two sovereigns, and a rebellion led by Ras Gugsa Welle, Zewditu's estranged husband, broke out.

Gugsa Wella raised an army and, on March 31, 1930, led it in a march on Addis Ababa. His forces were defeated outside of the city in a clash that took the life of Gugsa Welle. Astoundingly, just two days later, Empress Zewditu also died. Rumor spread that she had been poisoned as soon as word reached the capital that her husband had fallen in battle. The rumors persisted for many years, but the modern consensus among historians is that she died of natural causes, an acute fever complicated by a long-standing diabetic condition.

Whatever the cause of the empress's death, Ras Tafari was proclaimed Emperor Haile Selassie I (his throne name) and crowned on November 2, 1930, at the Coptic Cathedral of St. George in Addis Ababa. Ras Tafari—now Haile Selassie—was already well known among European leaders and other prominent figures in Europe because he had toured the continent in the 1920s. His coronation drew to Addis Ababa the likes of the Duke of Gloucester (son of Britain's George V), Marshal Louis Franchet d'Esperey of France, and the Prince of Udine representing the King of Italy. The United States sent diplomatic officials, as did Egypt, Turkey, Sweden, Belgium, and Japan. American moviegoers even saw newsreel coverage of the ceremony. Many Western political and religious leaders were especially impressed and pleased by the installation of a Christian monarch in this African nation.

Haile Selassie quickly introduced two dramatic reforms in the Ethiopian government. Number one was the nation's first written constitution (July 16, 1931) and second was what that constitution provided: a representative bicameral legislature. Although the constitution pointed the way toward a transition to increasing levels of democracy, it also guaranteed that ultimate governing power would remain in the hands of the nobility and that, furthermore, succession to the throne would be limited to descendants of Haile Selassie. Yet many in the West overlooked these autocratic elements and focused on the hints of democracy, including the dramatic unconditional abolition of slavery.

In 1894-1896, Italy and Ethiopia fought the First Italo-Abyssinian War, which resulted in a humiliating Italian defeat. In the 1930s, Benito Mussolini sought to avenge that loss by launching a new war of colonial conquest and annexation. Italy already held a portion of Eritrea and Somaliland as colonial possessions, and Ethiopia would provide a bridge connecting them, thereby greatly enlarging Italy's contiguous African holdings. Even more important, Mussolini envisioned an easy conquest that would lay the cornerstone of an imperial fascist empire.

On December 5, 1934, Italian armed forces invaded Ethiopia at Walwal, Ogeden Province. Ethiopia, like Italy, was a member of the League of Nations, which opposed the invasion on the grounds of its violating "collective security." Yet the league failed to achieve the necessary unanimous vote to take military action against Italy. There was even worse for Ethiopia. In December of 1935, it was revealed that British Foreign Secretary Samuel Hoare and French Prime Minister Pierre Laval had secretly agreed to intervene in what was then being called the Second Italo-Abyssinian War (1935-1939) by offering to partition Ethiopia and essentially give much of it to Mussolini as a colony. The objective of this secret agreement was to "appease" the fascist dictator and avert a larger—European—war, which would likely involve both Italy and Nazi Germany. British and French public and politicians denounced the pact as a cowardly and infamous promotion of the causes of fascism and Nazism.

In the meantime, Haile Selassie joined his northern armies and commanded them from a headquarters at Desse in Wollo province. He ordered full military mobilization on October 3, 1935. Although he stirred the nation to a valiant resistance, the Ethiopians had a relatively primitive army— no aircraft, no tanks, no significant artillery—whereas the Italians wielded a modern European military, a veteran force from the Great War, which included a large, powerful, and modern air force. The Italians also made extensive use of chemical weapons, which they used indiscriminately against civilians as well as Red Cross field hospitals. Much of the world, though outraged, did nothing.

For all Italy's military advantages, the invasion, which began in early October, bogged down in November as Haile Selassie's northern armies mounted a surprisingly effective counteroffensive during Christmas of 1935. Mussolini responded by sending in more resources, and, at the beginning of 1936, effectively turned back the Ethiopian counteroffensive at the First Battle of Tembien (January 20-24, 1936). This was followed by the Battle of Amba Aradam (February 10-19, 1936), the Second Battle of Tembien (February 27-29, 1936), and the Battle of Shire (February 29-March 2, 1936), which, collectively, destroyed Haile Selassie's northern forces.

The "Lion of Judah" now put himself at the head of his last remaining intact army on the northern front. On March 31, 1936, he personally led a counterattack, only to be defeated at the Battle of Maychew in southern Tigray. Mussolini's air force strafed and bombed all along the route of Ethiopian retreat and then sent Raya and Azebo tribal warriors against the soldiers. Learning they were in rebellion against Haile Selassie, Mussolini paid and armed them. Total Ethiopian casualties were about eleven thousand killed or wounded, whereas the Italians suffered four hundred casualties (out of forty thousand engaged) and the Eritreans, in an Italian colonial force, lost 873 men killed or wounded. In desperation following this terribly one-sided defeat, the emperor made a pilgrimage to the ancient churches of Lalibela, where he fasted and prayed, before returning to Addis Ababa. The government resolved to evacuate to the south, and the emperor's family withdrew to exile in French Somaliland, from which they intended to journey to more permanent refuge in Jerusalem. After much argument and debate, Haile Selassie, who wanted to remain in Ethiopia, at last left with his family into exile. From Jerusalem, he traveled to Europe to plead Ethiopia's case before the League of Nations in Geneva, Switzerland. In his absence, Italian Marshal Pietro Badoglio marched his troops into Addis Ababa on May 5, 1936, whereupon Mussolini declared Ethiopia an Italian province, and the Italian king, Victor Emanuel III, was proclaimed emperor of Ethiopia.

Immediately after the League extended an invitation to Haile Selassie to present his case, Benito Mussolini withdrew the Italian delegation from membership in that body on May 12, 1936. The next month, the emperor walked into the hall of the League in Geneva, where he was greeted by the jeers and whistles of Italian newspaper reporters, who had been issued tin whistles by Count Galeazzo Ciano, Mussolini's son-in-law. In a gesture that became instantly famous, the Romanian delegate, Nicolae Titulescu, leaped to his feet and called out, "Show the savages the door!" With that, the hecklers were ejected, and the emperor, after waiting for the hall to settle, began a speech of such dignity and eloquence that it moved the world. He pleaded for aid from member nations, including those who were already materially aiding Italy. He declared that the Italian forces were using chemical weapons against soldiers and civilians alike. These chemicals, the emperor explained, were being deployed from airborne sprayers by fleets of aircraft in formation to create a lethal aerosol rain that poisoned all on whom it fell. Pointing out that Ethiopia had but "12 million inhabitants, without arms, without resources" whereas Italy, with a population of forty-two million, was heavily armed, Haile Selassie argued that the agonizing fate Ethiopia was suffering now would soon befall small, vulnerable states the world over if the League failed to act. "God and history," he warned, "will remember your judgment."

The speech instantly elevated the Ethiopian emperor to the status of cause célèbre for anti-fascists the world over. Yet, in the end, the League of Nations did nothing more than vote up a few weak, vaguely symbolic sanctions. Ultimately a mere half-dozen nations declined to recognize Italy's occupation: China, New Zealand, the Soviet Union, the Republic of Spain, Mexico and the United States—which was not a League of Nations member.

Impressive, regal, dignified, and firm in his resolve, Haile Selassie made a moving contrast to the brutal, bellicose, bullying figures of both Mussolini and Hitler. He lived in exile in a manor house in Bath, England, from 1936 to 1941, devoting himself to countering Italian propaganda, which claimed that Ethiopia was happy and prosperous as an Italian colony. He made—in vain—repeated appeals for material intervention by the League of Nations. While his pleas were met with sympathy, Ethiopia received no military aid until Italy allied itself with Germany in June 1940. With Italy now in the fold of Hitler, the British expert in unconventional warfare, Colonel Orde Wingate, organized the "Gideon Force," consisting largely of

Ethiopian-supported African and South African colonial troops, and began a counter-invasion of Ethiopia. Haile Selassie joined the Gideon Force's advance across the Sudanese-Ethiopian border on January 18, 1941, and raised the flag of the Lion of Judah over the Ethiopian border village of Um Iddla. The Gideon Force and other soldiers of the British Commonwealth nations, Free France, Free Belgium, and the Ethiopian resistance united to defeat the Italian occupiers. On May 5, 1941, Haile Selassie reentered Addis Ababa and resumed the throne.

He introduced many of his major reforms during the war years, most notably the abolition of slavery, but his record of governance in Ethiopia both during and after World War II can be characterized most generously as *enlightened* despotism, but despotism nonetheless. He personally refused to relinquish any authority, even as he formulated and put into operation long-range plans to modernize his nation, including a gradual program to incrementally introduce democracy. He moved slowly, and, in the postwar years, as Ethiopia emerged more fully into the modern world and the family of nations, his own people became impatient. Organized resistance against the emperor's autocracy grew, and during the 1960s, several attempted *coups d'etat* were launched against his rule. He responded to each attempt with redoubled despotism. At last, aging and ill, Haile Selassie was deposed in a military coup on September 12, 1974. Stripped of his authority, he was subsequently held under the indignity of house arrest. He died in this captivity on August 27, 1975. The official cause was ascribed to complications from a prostate examination and operation. His own doctor refused to accept this explanation, and, while he made no accusations, many believed Selassie had been assassinated. Today, most historians conclude that he did, in fact, fall ill and, while he was not murdered, he was given little or no aid and thus permitted to die.

#30
JOSIP BROZ TITO

*As marshal of Yugoslavia, Tito led the Partisans, the most
brilliantly effective resistance movement against German
occupation in Europe.*

Tito the Partisan leader, his arm in a sling, is pictured with fellow Partisan Ivan
Ribar on June 13, 1943, during the Battle of Sutjeska in German-occupied
Yugoslavia (today southeastern Bosnia). (credit: *Wikimedia*)

Born Josip Broz in the Croatian village of Kumrovec, near Zagreb, on May 7, 1892, Tito—it was a pen name he began using in 1934 in his writing for Communist Party journals—was one of fifteen children in a peasant family. His father, Franjo Broz, was a Croat, and his mother, Marija Javeršek, a Slovene. Both the regions known as Croatia and Slovenia were, at the time, part of the Austro-Hungarian Empire. The family's farm was not successful, and Josip spent his preschool years mainly in the care of his maternal grandparents. He began school at the age of eight but completed only four grades—repeating the second grade—before leaving school in 1905 when he was thirteen. He moved about sixty miles north, to the town of Sisak, where he worked briefly in a restaurant before apprenticing himself to a locksmith. The Czech who owned the shop, Nikola Karas, encouraged his young apprentice to celebrate May Day and to read a socialist newspaper, *Free Word*. Broz not only read it, he began selling it.

Broz completed his three-year apprenticeship in 1910 and found work in Zagreb, where he joined the Metalworkers Union and became a labor activist and a member of the Social-Democratic Party of Croatia and Slavonia. After returning briefly to his hometown, he traveled about central Europe as a metalworker and sometimes organized labor actions at major factories, including the Skoda Works in Pilsen, Bohemia, and the Benz auto factory in Mannheim. In October 1912, he lived for a time in Vienna, staying with his older brother, before going to work for Daimler at Wiener Neustadt. Here he gained considerable experience with automotive technology, and he became a notable fencer—as well as a dancer. More important, he expanded his cultural outlook, learning both German and Czech.

Broz was conscripted into the Austro-Hungarian Army in the spring of 1913 and was granted permission to serve with a unit of the Croatian Home Guard, garrisoned in Zagreb. The army sent him to learn to ski during the winter of 1913-1914, at which he became skilled, and he was sent for training at a school for non-commissioned officers in Budapest. He was promoted to sergeant-major of his regiment, the youngest soldier to achieve that rank in the history of the regiment. He further distinguished himself by winning fencing championships in Budapest in the spring of 1914.

The outbreak of World War I in 1914 interrupted his socialist activism, and he accompanied his regiment in a march to the Serbian border—to fight Serbia, against which the Austro-Hungarian Empire had declared war. While on the march in August, Broz was arrested on charges of sedition for disseminating antiwar propaganda. He was imprisoned in the Petrovardian

Fortress at Novi Sad but was released in January 1915 when the charges were dropped. The details of this incident are unclear, since Broz, in later life, told three distinct versions: he had threatened to desert to the Russians, he was overheard expressing the hope that the Empire would be defeated, he was the victim of a simple clerical error.

He was sent back to his regiment on the Carpathian front and then to the Bukovina front, where his regiment saw heavy action. He showed talent and initiative in action behind enemy lines when he led a scout platoon that captured eighty Russian soldiers. But on March 25, 1915, he was severely wounded by a Circassian cavalryman's lance, which penetrated his back. Captured, he was held in various Russian POW camps after spending thirteen months in a makeshift hospital in a monastery at Sviyazhsk on the Volga. He survived his wound as well as pneumonia and typhus, and he took the opportunity to learn Russian with the help of two schoolgirls, who had volunteered to nurse the wounded.

Broz was at hard labor in a camp near Perm, working on the Trans-Siberian Railway, and was put in charge of his fellow POWs. When he discovered that Red Cross parcels sent to the camp were being stolen by the Russian staff, he protested, was brutally beaten, and put in a separate prison. At this point, the February Revolution (March 8-March 16, 1917) broke out, and an insurgent mob liberated Broz and returned him to the labor camp. There he met a Bolshevik, who helped him to escape to Petrograd (today St. Petersburg). Later, as Tito, Broz explained that he wanted to join the communist revolution, which he regarded as also a revolution against Austro-Hungarian domination of Croatia. Some historians claim, however, that Broz was simply looking to sit out the war. He did join in the July Days uprising against the Russian Provisional Government that followed the overthrow of the Czar Nicholas II, after which he attempted to escape to Finland, from which he planned to make his way to the United States. Apprehended by agents of the Provisional Government, he was imprisoned in Petrograd and then sent back to the labor camp near Perm but escaped at Ekaterinburg and made his way, by train, to Omsk in Siberia, which he reached on November 8, 1917. Police questioned him there but were deceived by his flawless Russian accent. He joined the Bolsheviks and fought in the Red Guard during the Russian Civil War (1917-1922) before making his way back home in 1920.

The Croatia to which Josip Broz returned was now part of Yugoslavia, the independent nation created by the 1919 Treaty of Versailles, which ended World War I. He identified himself as a confirmed Communist, and he joined the Communist Party of Yugoslavia (CPY). In contrast to many of his counterparts in Russia, however, he was a political moderate. This differentiation between his concept of communism and the more radical and absolutist communism promoted by Vladimir Lenin would mark his increasingly profound differences with the Soviet Union throughout the rest of his life and career. He never lost his independence of thought.

The CPY was outlawed in August 1921, Broz was fired from his job as a metalworker because of his overt communist activities, but he continued to work—illegally—for the party. Installed in the CPY district committee, he was arrested in 1924—but acquitted, because the prosecutor, an anti-Catholic, hated the priest who had turned him in. From this point on, however, he and his family were continually harassed by government authorities. He began working in a shipyard in Croatia but was arrested again in 1925 and sentenced to seven months' probation. The ceaseless government harassment only strengthened his resolve, and he now began a rapid climb up the communist hierarchy, gaining membership in the Zagreb Committee of the CPY in 1927, and in 1928 becoming deputy of the Politburo of the Central Committee of the CPY, as well as secretary general of the Croatian and Slavonian committees. In August 1928, Broz was again arrested. At trial, he defiantly declared that the tribunal had no right to judge him. As if by way of response, he was sentenced to a prison term of five years.

After his release in 1934, Broz traveled throughout Europe on behalf of the party and wrote for communist journals using the pen name Tito, which, for security reasons and in an effort to protect his family, he adopted and used thereafter. He moved to Moscow in 1935 and was assigned to the Balkan section of the Comintern, the organization of international Communism. In August 1936, Tito was named organizational secretary of the CPY Politburo.

The next year, 1937, was the midpoint of the Moscow Trials (1936-1938), the infamous show trials by which a ruthlessly paranoid Joseph Stalin purged the Soviet communist party. Prominent Yugoslav Communists were among those marked for "liquidation," some eight hundred Yugoslavs disappearing in the Soviet Union. Action by the Comintern saved the hard-hit CPY from total dissolution, and Tito, a member of the Comintern staff, not only escaped the purge, but, by the end of 1937, was named secretary general by the Executive Council of the Comintern. He returned to Yugoslavia to reorganize the CPY there and was formally named secretary general of the Communist Party of Yugoslavia in October 1940.

The Molotov-Ribbentrop Pact—a non-aggression alliance between Stalin and Hitler—was signed on August 23, 1939, stunning the international communist movement, which saw it as a betrayal of communism's unshakable opposition to fascism and Nazism. Yugoslavia itself was officially neutral when Hitler's invasion of Poland on September 1, 1939, began World War II, but the religious and ethnic gulf dividing Croat and Serb widened. The Serbs, who made up the majority of the armed forces, were pro-Allied, but the Croats and others, although not opposed to the Allies, were unwilling to challenge the Axis. Ultimately, the issue of Yugoslav neutrality became moot because Germany not only dominated the country's foreign trade, it also owned a controlling share of its important non-ferrous mines. Early in the war, Yugoslavia's head of state, Prince Paul (who served as regent to the underage King Peter) repeatedly gave in to German demands for the cheap export of agricultural produce and raw materials. Paul also yielded to Hitler on the matter of Jewish policy, instituting a government program of anti-Semitic discrimination and persecution.

Yugoslavia was in a poor position for opposing Hitler's juggernaut. Its neighbors, Hungary, Romania, and Bulgaria, had already entered the Axis orbit, and neither Britain nor France could offer military aid for a resistance movement. Yugoslavia was surrounded by Axis powers, continuing to exist at the mercy of Hitler and his fascist ally Benito Mussolini. Indeed, Hitler saw in Yugoslavia an important source of agricultural produce and strategic ores, including copper, chrome, lead, zinc, and bauxite (aluminum ore). Moreover, the nation was geographically positioned to serve as a route of rapid traverse across the entire Balkan region. On March 25, 1941, Prince Paul added his signature to the Tripartite (Axis) Pact, making Yugoslavia an official German ally.

Signing onto the Axis Pact hardly stabilized the country. Serbian nationalists took to the streets and joined various elements of the military to stage a coup on March 27. Prince Paul was overthrown, and a new government was formed under the presidency of General Dušan Simović. The coup, however, failed to end the alliance with Germany, as the Croats, who were part of the new coalition government, demanded that Yugoslavia continue to adhere to the Axis Pact. Fearing a German invasion, the Serb majority agreed—only to be confronted by Hitler, who issued "Directive 25," ordering an end to Yugoslavian sovereignty.

On April 6, 1941, Germany invaded Yugoslavia, starting with the bombing of Belgrade and followed by ground operations. Government-organized resistance rapidly crumbled, and Yugoslavia surrendered on April 17. Hitler appointed General Milan Nedić to head a puppet government, which administered a program to "Germanize" Yugoslavia, beginning with the genocide of Croatia's Serb minority as well as Jews, Gypsies, and others the Nazis deemed "undesirable." Hitler suborned Croats to carry out these programs—an action that instantly and at last galvanized the Serbian will to resist the Axis. A Serb uprising erupted, which was soon organized into a widespread and quite effective Partisan movement.

While the Partisans began their military resistance, King Peter (now free of Prince Paul's regency) arrived in London in June 1941 and proclaimed a government in exile. Winston Churchill, however, recognized that neither Peter nor his government-in-exile had popular support. Someone on the ground was needed, and, guided by Churchill, the Allies threw their support not behind Peter but behind the communist Partisan leadership of Tito. Churchill intervened to create a coalition between Tito and King Peter by broadly hinting to Tito this would put him into position to take control of most of Yugoslavia after the Germans had been ejected. Churchill was anticommunist to the core, but the war made strange bedfellows indeed, and he knew an effective leader when he saw one. He had no compunction about buying Tito's cooperation.

It was a spectacularly good bargain for both the Allies and Tito, who led—personally and from the field—his followers in a well-coordinated campaign of sabotage and resistance against the occupying Germans. Not only charismatic and politically astute, Tito was a well-trained military leader and a natural tactician, well-practiced in working behind enemy lines. His Partisan-conducted sabotage and outright combat missions in a political and military movement was so successful that, in the summer of 1942, Tito was able to organize an offensive into Bosnia and Croatia. This forced Hitler to commit disproportionately large numbers of troops in an effort to disrupt the Partisans. Against this counteroffensive, Tito's Partisans held their own, so that, in December 1943, he was able to credibly announce the formation of a provisional Yugoslav government, with himself as president, secretary of defense, and marshal of the armed forces. By this time, Tito's forces were a substantial army of about 200,000 men, far larger than the military assets of any other anti-German resistance force in any other occupied European country. This army had succeeded in pinning down thirty-five Axis divisions, about three-quarters of a million soldiers, who would otherwise be fighting the Western Allies in Italy or the Soviet Red Army on the Eastern Front.

With the defeat of Nazi Germany in May 1945, Tito went about the business of establishing his government on a permanent basis. He formed a Politburo within the CPY and held Soviet-style elections in November 1945. In the manner of Lenin and Stalin, he promulgated a Five Year Plan for economic recovery and development. In these efforts, he was greatly aided by his nearly universal popularity as a war hero and patriot. It was, however, the very qualities Stalin both envied and feared. Unlike communist leaders in other countries adjacent to the Soviet Union, it became abundantly clear to Stalin that Tito had no intention of governing Yugoslavia as a Soviet satellite. Tito defined himself as, first and foremost, a Yugoslav nationalist. Only secondarily was he committed to communism.

Tito's clear defiance of Stalin further enhanced his popularity, not only in Yugoslavia, but in the democratic West. "Titoism" became a new postwar coinage to describe opposition by Iron Curtain countries to Soviet domination. When he died on May 4, 1980, just short of eighty-eighth birthday, he was a living legend in Yugoslavia and around the world. He guided Yugoslavia to economic and ideological coexistence with capitalist nations, which resulted in a standard of living higher than elsewhere in the communist sphere of influence. Nevertheless, his death brought the rapid dissolution of Yugoslavia, as the former ethnic, religious, and local nationalist drives brought about a series of brutal conflicts—especially the Bosnian War (1992-1995) and the Kosovo War (1998-1999)—which were characterized by "ethnic cleansing" and outright genocide.

SELECT BIBLIOGRAPHY

Chiang Kai-shek

Fenby, Jonathan. *Chiang Kai-shek: China's Generalissimo and the Nation He Lost.* New York: Carroll & Graf, 2003.

Hahn, Emily. *Chiang Kai-shek: An Unauthorized Biography.* New York: Open Road Media, 2015.

Taylor, Jay. *The Generalissimo.* Cambridge, MA: Harvard University Press, 2009.

Winston Churchill

Addison, Paul. *Churchill: The Unexpected Hero.* London and New York: Oxford University Press, 2004.

Gilbert, Martin. *Churchill: A Life.* London: Heinemann, 1991.

Jenkins, Roy. *Churchill: A Biography.* New York: Farrar, Straus and Giroux, 2001.

Keegan, John. *Winston Churchill.* New York: Viking Press, 2002.

Charles de Gaulle

De Gaulle, Charles. *The Complete War Memoirs.* New York: Carroll & Graf Publishers, 1998.

Fenby, Jonathan. *The General: Charles de Gaulle and the France He Saved* New York: Skyhorse Publishing, 2012.

Williams, Charles. *The Last Great Frenchman: A Life of General De Gaulle.* New York: John Wiley and Sons, 1997.

Albert Einstein

Folsin, Albrecht. *Albert Einstein: A Biography.* New York: Viking, 1997.

Isaacson, Walter. *Einstein: His Life and Universe.* New York: Simon & Schuster, 2007.

Rigden, John S. *Einstein 1905: The Standard of Greatness.* Cambridge, MA: Harvard University Press, 2006.

Dwight David Eisenhower

Ambrose, Stephen E. *Eisenhower: Soldier and President.* New York: Simon & Schuster, 1991.

d'Este, Carlo. *Eisenhower: A Soldier's Life.* New York: Henry Holt and Co., 2002.

Eisenhower, Dwight David. *Crusade in Europe.* Baltimore: Johns Hopkins University Press, 1997.

Johnson, Paul. *Eisenhower: A Life.* New York: Penguin Books, 2015.

Joseph Goebbels

Goebbels, Joseph. *The Goebbels Diaries.* New York: Penguin, 1984.

Longerich, Peter. *Goebbels: A Biography.* New York: Random House, 2015.

Manvell, Roger. *Doctor Goebbels: His Life and Death.* New York: Skyhorse Publishing, 2010.

Hermann Göring

Manvell, Roger, and Heinrich Fraenkel. *Goering: The Rise and Fall of the Notorious Nazi Leader.* New York: Skyhorse Publishing, 2011.

Irving, David. *Göring: A Biography.* New York: William Morrow & Co., 1989.

Mosley, Leonard. *The Reich Marshal: A Biography of Hermann Goering.* Garden City, NY: Doubleday, 1974.

Heinz Guderian

Guderian, Heinz. *Achtung—Panzer!* London: Cassell Military Classics, 1999.

Hart, Russell A. *Guderian: Panzer Pioneer or Myth Maker?* Dulles, VA: Potomac Books, 2006.

Manstein, Erich von. *Lost Victories: The War Memoirs of Hitler's Most Brilliant General.* St. Paul, MN: Zenith Press, 2004.

Arthur "Bomber" Harris

Harris, Arthur. *Bomber Offensive.* Barnsley, UK: Frontline Books, 2016.

Probert, Henry. *Bomber Harris: His Life and Times: The Biography of Marshal of the Royal Air Force Sir Arthur Harris, Wartime Chief of Bomber Command.* Barnsley, UK: Greenhill Books, 2006.

Reinhard Heydrich

Dederichs, Mario. *Heydrich: The Face of Evil.* Drexel Hill, PA; Casemate, 2009.

Gerwarth, Robert. *Hitler's Hangman: The Life of Heydrich.* New Haven, CT: Yale University Press, 2011.

Williams, Max. *Heydrich: Dark Shadow of the SS.* Stroud, UK: Fonthill Media, 2018.

Heinrich Himmler

Longerich, Peter. *Heinrich Himmler.* London and New York: Oxford University Press, 2013.

Manvell, Roger, and Heinrich Fraenkel. *Heinrich Himmler: The Sinister Life of the Head of the SS and Gestapo.* New York: Skyhorse Publishing, 2007.

Padfield, Peter. *Himmler.* London: Thistle Publishing, 2013.

Hirohito

Behr, Edward. *Hirohito: Behind the Myth.* New York: Villard, 1989.

Bix, Herbert P. *Hirohito and the Making of Modern Japan.* New York: HarperCollins, 2000.

Kawamura, Noriko. *Emperor Hirohito and the Pacific War.* Seattle: University of Washington Press, 2015.

Adolf Hitler

Fest, Joachim. *Hitler.* New York: Harcourt, 1974.

Hitler, Adolf. *Mein Kampf.* Boston: Houghton Mifflin Company, 1998.

Kershaw, Ian. *Hitler: A Biography.* New York: W. W. Norton & Company, 2010.

Toland, John. *Adolf Hitler: The Definitive Biography.* New York: Random House, 1976.

Curtis E. LeMay

Coffey, Thomas M. Iron Eagle: The Turbulent Life of General Curtis LeMay. New York: Random House, 1987.

Kozak, Warren. Curtis LeMay: Strategist and Tactician. Washington, DC: Regnery, 2009.

Tillman, Barrett. LeMay: A Biography. New York: Palgrave Macmillan, 2007.

Douglas MacArthur

Manchester, William. *American Caesar: Douglas MacArthur 1880–1964.* Boston: Little, Brown: 1976.

MacArthur, Douglas. *Reminiscences.* Annapolis, MD: Naval Institute Press, 1964.

Perret, Geoffrey. *Old Soldiers Never Die: The Life and Legend of Douglas MacArthur.* New York: Random House, 1996.

George C. Marshall

Cray, Ed. *General of the Army: George C. Marshall, Soldier and Statesman.* New York: Cooper Square Press, 2000.

Jeffers, H. Paul, and Alan Axelrod. *Marshall: A Biography.* New York: Palgrave Macmillan, 2010.

Stoler, Mark A. *George C. Marshall: Soldier-Statesman of the American Century.* Boston: Twayne Publishers, 1989.

Bernard Law Montgomery

Brighton, Terry. *Patton, Montgomery, Rommel: Masters of War.* New York: Broadway Books, 2010.

Hamilton, Nigel. *Monty: The Making of a General: 1887-1942.* New York: McGraw-Hill, 1981.

Hamilton, Nigel. *Master of the Battlefield: Monty's War Years 1942-1944.* New York: McGraw-Hill, 1984.

Hamilton, Nigel. *Monty: The Field-Marshal 1944-1976.* Exeter, UK: David & Charles, 1986.

Royle, Trevor. *Montgomery: Lessons in Leadership from the Soldier's General.* New York: Palgrave Macmillan, 2010.

Benito Mussolini

Axelrod, Alan. *Benito Mussolini.* New York: Alpha Books, 2001.

Hibbert, Christopher. *Mussolini: The Rise and Fall of Il Duce.* New York: St. Martin's Press. 2008.

Mussolini, Benito. *My Rise and Fall.* New York: Da Capo, 1998.

Chester W. Nimitz

Borneman, Walter R. *The Admirals: Nimitz, Halsey, Leahy, and King—The Five-Star Admirals Who Won the War at Sea.* New York: Little, Brown, 2013.

Hoyt, Edwin. *How They Won the War in the Pacific: Nimitz and His Admirals.* Guilford, CT: Lyons Press, 2011.

Potter, E. B. *Nimitz.* Annapolis, MD; Naval Institute Press, 1976.

J. Robert Oppenheimer

Bird, Kai, and Martin J. Sherwin. *American Prometheus: The Triumph and Tragedy of J. Robert Oppenheimer.* New York: Random House, 2005.

Pais, Abraham. *J. Robert Oppenheimer: A Life.* New York: Oxford University Press, 2006.

George S. Patton, Jr.

Axelrod, Alan. *Patton: A Biography.* New York: Palgrave Macmillan, 2006.

Axelrod, Alan. *Patton's Drive: The Making of America's Greatest General.* Guilford, CT: Lyons Press, 2009.

d'Este, Carlo. *Patton: A Genius for War.* New York: HarperCollins, 1995.

Philippe Pétain

Williams, Charles. *Pétain: How the Hero of France Became a Convicted Traitor and Changed the Course of History.* New York: Palgrave Macmillan, 2005.

Webster, Paul. *Pétain's Crime: The Complete Story of French Collaboration in the Holocaust.* Chicago: Ivan R. Dee, 1991.

Franklin Delano Roosevelt

Brinkley, Alan. *Franklin Delano Roosevelt.* New York: Oxford University Press, 2010.

Dallek, Robert. *Franklin D. Roosevelt: A Political Life.* New York: Viking, 2017.

Larrabee. Eric. *Commander in Chief: Franklin Delano Roosevelt, His Lieutenants, and Their War.* New York: HarperCollins. 1987.

Haile Selassie

Gorham, Charles. *The Lion of Judah: A life of Haile Selassie I, Emperor of Ethiopia.* New York: Ariel Books, 1966.

Selassie, Bereket Habte. *Emperor Haile Selassie.* Athens: Ohio University Press, 2014.

Joseph Stalin

Khlevniuk, Oleg V., and Nora Seligman Favorov. *Stalin: New Biography of a Dictator.* New Haven, CT: Yale University Press, 2017.

Radzinsky, Edvard. *Stalin: The First In-depth Biography Based on Explosive New Documents from Russia's Secret Archives.* New York: Anchor Books, 1997.

Snyder, Timothy. *Bloodlands: Europe Between Hitler and Stalin.* New York: Basic Books, 2010.

Josip Broz Tito

Beloff, Nora. *Tito's Flawed Legacy: Yugoslavia and the West Since 1939.* London: Routledge, 1986.

West, Richard. *Tito and the Rise and Fall of Yugoslavia.* New York: Carroll & Graf, 1994.

Vuksic, Velimir. *Tito's Partisans 1941–45.* Oxford, UK: Osprey, 2003.

Hideki Tojo

Browne, Courtney. *Tojo.* New York: Da Capo Press, 1998.

Butow, Robert J. C. *Tojo and the Coming of the War.* Palo Alto, CA: Stanford University Press, 1969.

Hoyt, Edwin P. *Warlord: Tojo Against the World.* New York: Cooper Square Press, 2001.

Harry S. Truman

Ferrell, Robert H. *Harry S. Truman: A Life.* Columbia and London: University of Missouri Press, 1994.

McCullough, David. *Truman.* New York: Simon & Schuster, 2003.

Truman, Harry S. *1945: Year of Decision.* Garden City, NY: Doubleday, 1955.

Isoroku Yamamoto

Agawa, Hiroyuki. *The Reluctant Admiral.* New York: Kodansha USA, 1982.

Hoyt, Edwin P. *Yamamoto: The Man Who Planned the Attack on Pearl Harbor.* Guilford, CT: The Lyons Press, 2001.

Stille, Mark. *Yamamoto Isoroku.* Oxford, UK: Osprey Publishing, 2012.

Georgi Konstantinovich Zhukov

Roberts, Geoffrey. *Stalin's General: The Life of Georgy Zhukov.* New York: Random House, 2012.

Zhukov, Georgy. *Marshal of Victory: The Autobiography of General Georgy Zhukov.* Barnsley, UK: Pen and Sword, 2014.

Acknowledgments

My thanks to my editor, Mike Lewis, and to the millions of Allied soldiers, sailors, marines, and airmen, not named in this book, who staked their lives on defending freedom, regaining freedom, and liberating the oppressed in World War II.

About the Author

Alan Axelrod is the author of numerous books on military history, including *How America Won the Great War* (2018), *Lost Destiny: Joe Kennedy Jr. and the Doomed Mission to Save London* (2015), *Patton's Drive: The Making of America's Greatest General* (2009), *Patton: A Biography* (2006), *Bradley: A Biography* (2006), *Encyclopedia of World War II* (2006), and *Benito Mussolini* (2001). The president of Ian Samuel Group, Inc., a creative services firm, he lives in Atlanta.

PERMUTED PRESS
needs **you** to help

SPREAD (THE) INFECTION

FOLLOW US!

ⓕ | Facebook.com/PermutedPress
𝕏 | Twitter.com/PermutedPress

REVIEW US!

Wherever you buy our book, they can be reviewed! We want to know what you like!

GET INFECTED!

Sign up for our mailing list at
PermutedPress.com

PERMUTED
PRESS

KING ARTHUR AND THE KNIGHTS OF THE ROUND TABLE HAVE BEEN REBORN TO SAVE THE WORLD FROM THE CLUTCHES OF MORGANA WHILE SHE PROPELS OUR MODERN WORLD INTO THE MIDDLE AGES.

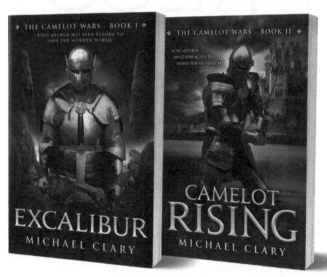

EAN 9781618685018 $15.99   **EAN** 9781682611562 $15.99

Morgana's first attack came in a red fog that wiped out all modern technology. The entire planet was pushed back into the middle ages. The world descended into chaos.

But hope is not yet lost— King Arthur, Merlin, and the Knights of the Round Table have been reborn.

PERMUTED
PRESS

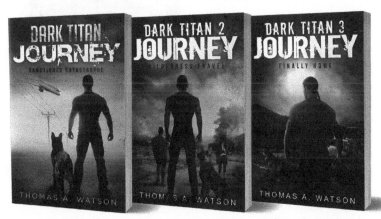

THE MORNINGSTAR STRAIN HAS BEEN LET LOOSE—IS THERE ANY WAY TO STOP IT?

EAN 9781618686497 $16.00

An industrial accident unleashes some of the Morningstar Strain. The doctor who discovered the strain and her assistant will have to fight their way through Sprinters and Shamblers to save themselves, the vaccine, and the base. Then they discover that it wasn't an accident at all—somebody inside the facility did it on purpose. The war with the RSA and the infected is far from over.

This is the fourth book in Z.A. Recht's The Morningstar Strain series, written by Brad Munson.

PERMUTED
PRESS

GATHERED TOGETHER AT LAST, THREE TALES OF FANTASY CENTERING AROUND THE MYSTERIOUS CITY OF SHADOWS...ALSO KNOWN AS CHICAGO.

EAN 9781682612286 $9.99   **EAN** 9781618684639 $5.99   **EAN** 9781618684899 $5.99

From *The New York Times* and *USA Today* bestselling author Richard A. Knaak comes three tales from Chicago, the City of Shadows. Enter the world of the Grey–the creatures that live at the edge of our imagination and seek to be real. Follow the quest of a wizard seeking escape from the centuries-long haunting of a gargoyle. Behold the coming of the end of the world as the Dutchman arrives.

Enter the City of Shadows.